CLIVE BARKER'S
NEXT TESTAMENT

VOLUME TWO

PRAISE FOR
CLIVE BARKER'S NEXT TESTAMENT

"With creative minds like Clive Barker and Mark Miller joining forces, the capacity for invention is boundless... Their graphic novel Next Testament is a refined example of their hellish genius."
— **John Nicol,** *Fangoria*

"An absolute gem of a title."
— **Fanboy Gaming**

"Fans of Barker will not be disappointed."
— **Horror Fix**

"Terrifying"
— **Proactive Continuity**

"5 out of 5"
— **Comic Bastards**

"You read it, then you realize after putting it down that you barely scratched the surface."
— **Comic Spectrum**

"A deep philosophical twist on the horror genre."
— **Geeks of Doom**

"This is a great series — though you may want to be careful about reading just before you go to sleep..."
— **TM Stash**

"A great 'What If' tale laced with pitch-black humor...a must-read."
— **Brian Collins,** *Badass Digest*

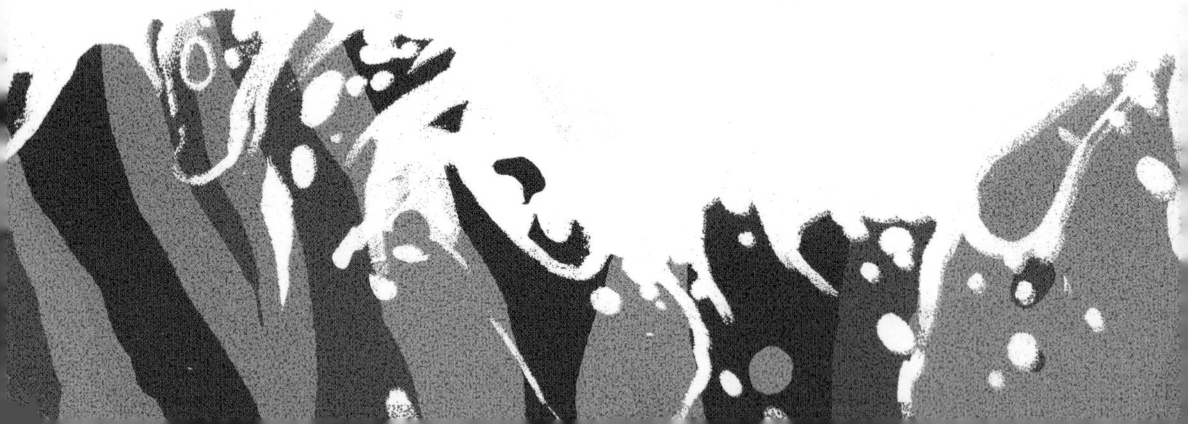

"A brutal, blasphemous, brilliant look at what happens when history's greatest serial killer (God) comes back for seconds."
— **Jason Louv, *VICE***

"A testament to unique story telling."
— **ReadComicBooks**

"Superb. Keeps you on your toes."
— **Legends Comics and Games**

"Brave"
— **PopCultureGalaxy**

"Top notch."
— **Newsarama**

"When we look back at the recent history of horror no other writer has shook the pillars of fear more than Clive Barker. He rewrote the book on how we scare each other."
— **Steve Niles**

"Oddly beautiful."
— **iFanboy**

"Twisted fun."
— **Trusty Henchmen**

"Clive Barker at his best."
— **Drews Views**

"Cinematic. I loved this book!"
— **Inveterate Media Junkies**

"The most entertaining and exciting horror comic I've read. Ever!"
— **Adventures in Poor Taste**

BOOM! STUDIOS

ROSS RICHIE CEO & Founder • **MARK SMYLIE** Founder of Archaia • **MATT GAGNON** Editor-in-Chief • **FILIP SABLIK** President of Publishing & Marketing • **STEPHEN CHRISTY** President of Development
LANCE KREITER VP of Licensing & Merchandising • **PHIL BARBARO** VP of Finance • **BRYCE CARLSON** Managing Editor • **MEL CAYLO** Marketing Manager • **SCOTT NEWMAN** Production Design Manager
IRENE BRADISH Operations Manager • **CHRISTINE DINH** Brand Communications Manager • **DAFNA PLEBAN** Editor • **SHANNON WATTERS** Editor • **ERIC HARBURN** Editor • **REBECCA TAYLOR** Editor
IAN BRILL Editor • **CHRIS ROSA** Assistant Editor • **ALEX GALER** Assistant Editor • **WHITNEY LEOPARD** Assistant Editor • **JASMINE AMIRI** Assistant Editor • **CAMERON CHITTOCK** Assistant Editor
KELSEY DIETERICH Production Designer • **JILLIAN CRAB** Production Designer • **DEVIN FUNCHES** E-Commerce & Inventory Coordinator • **ANDY LIEGL** Event Coordinator • **BRIANNA HART** Administrative Coordinator
AARON FERRARA Operations Assistant • **JOSÉ MEZA** Sales Assistant • **MICHELLE ANKLEY** Sales Assistant • **ELIZABETH LOUGHRIDGE** Accounting Assistant • **STEPHANIE HOCUTT** PR Assistant

BOOM! Studios, 5670 Wilshire Boulevard, Suite 450, Los Angeles, CA 90036-5679. Printed in China. First Printing.
ISBN: 978-1-60886-489-8, eISBN: 978-1-61398-343-0

WRITTEN BY
CLIVE BARKER
& MARK MILLER

ILLUSTRATED BY
HAEMI JANG

COLORS BY
VLADIMIR POPOV

LETTERS BY
STEVE WANDS

COVER BY
GOÑI MONTES

DESIGNER
KARA LEOPARD

ASSISTANT EDITOR
CHRIS ROSA

EDITOR
IAN BRILL

SPECIAL THANKS TO CHRISTIAN FRANCIS,
BEN MEARES, AND STEFANIE MILLER

INTRODUCTION BY LIAM SHARP

Ah, now—THIS kind of book is in my sweet spot!

I'm on a quest, you see, like many of us. I'm riding a large ball of magma with a thin rock crust through a near-empty void, tethered by invisible cords, elastic laws, to a star.

And, like many of us, I want to know why.

Carl Sagan suggests we are the Universe witnessing itself. Others have suggested we are the children of monsters—and all gods are monstrous, let's be clear on that one! Whether in conception, scale, love or cruelty, they are not us. They are other. They are bigger. They are more.

Clive Barker creations always have you facing into a mirror that you somehow know will shatter in a burst of silvery shards, tearing your flesh into strips. Slivers like diamond pins will puncture your eyes, and you'll see yourself reflected in jagged distortions before darkness steals that reality. That's just what he does. And he takes his sweet time about it — slows time in fact — so that he can make sure it's beautiful; that it matters. His metaphors are brutal, but they impact. They change you. They leave you open, more able to question the nature of things.

The myths we build are magnificent and obscure, futile and selfish. They tell the tale of our art; of our psychology; of our grand many-thousand (or more) year delusions; and—most keenly—of our longings (And aren't all longings filled with a little dread?). Next Testament, co-created by Mark Miller, riffs on one of the biggest of our myths, reintroducing us to a god we have forgotten—one unfathomable in his compassion. Jealous, remorseless, and utterly, utterly alien. Theirs is the god of "Numbers," who appears as a column of smoke to Moses and complains about the eating habits of his worshippers. A god whose whims you can never fully appease, who will damn three generations of your guiltless offspring and hold your love to ransom.

There are no celestial choirs here, no promise of any kind of placid, subjugated afterlife, nor of a sulphur-choked hell. The Earth herself wants us gone—and good riddance! But, y'know, she'll keep a few of us around— to play with. To show us what it's like to be fucked with, maybe.

Then again—that might just be too logical.

Effortless and enthralling, Next Testament draws you in. It's charming, disarming (literally in places) and casually brutal. All the best gods are like that. Our protagonist of many colours is beguiling—beautiful even. Eyes light up with wonder on seeing him, but once witnessed the viewer is left on a precipice, subject to whim. To fully understand the Grand Canyon you must, it could be argued, feel the might of it; dread its vastness. You must stand at its very edge, arms wide. Know that the blind and mindless wind might choose a devastating future for you at any moment—but that it would be worth it, to momentarily bask in such majesty!

And yet we, the children, remain no more than brief witnesses. And why should gods care, rather than be fleetingly fascinated? Lives passing before them like wind-blown sand—only less hardy, less substantial?

We: so full of our own self-importance, strong only in that we can dream ourselves eternal.

Gods: outliving the deaths of universes and perhaps birthing new ones.

(We would be wiser to pray that they don't exist!)

Barker and Miller work seamlessly together. There's definitely a companionable trust, no clash of egos. Miller's voice is clear in the mix. In his novels Barker writes with poetic authority. He gnaws at the words, delights in puns and the paraphernalia of the hand-written (and it is all handwritten) tome, the chance-written future clichés of lesser writers. Here, though, is the language of comics. Miller lets the medium breathe, without losing the impetus of the story. He knows how to get the best of Barker, and the best of a fused medium—words and pictures sharing the same space. And he gives everyone space, and lets the dread build page to page.

Barker fans will delight in this book, but they will find here also a new, bright talent in Mark Miller. And I can tell you—as I know the man—he's not unlike the god of this book! He's a tall, handsome fella with a disarming smile and no small amount of warmth, but anybody as steeped in the dark vaults and catacombs of Barker's mind as he is…well. You've read the books. You bear the scars!

CHAPTER FIVE

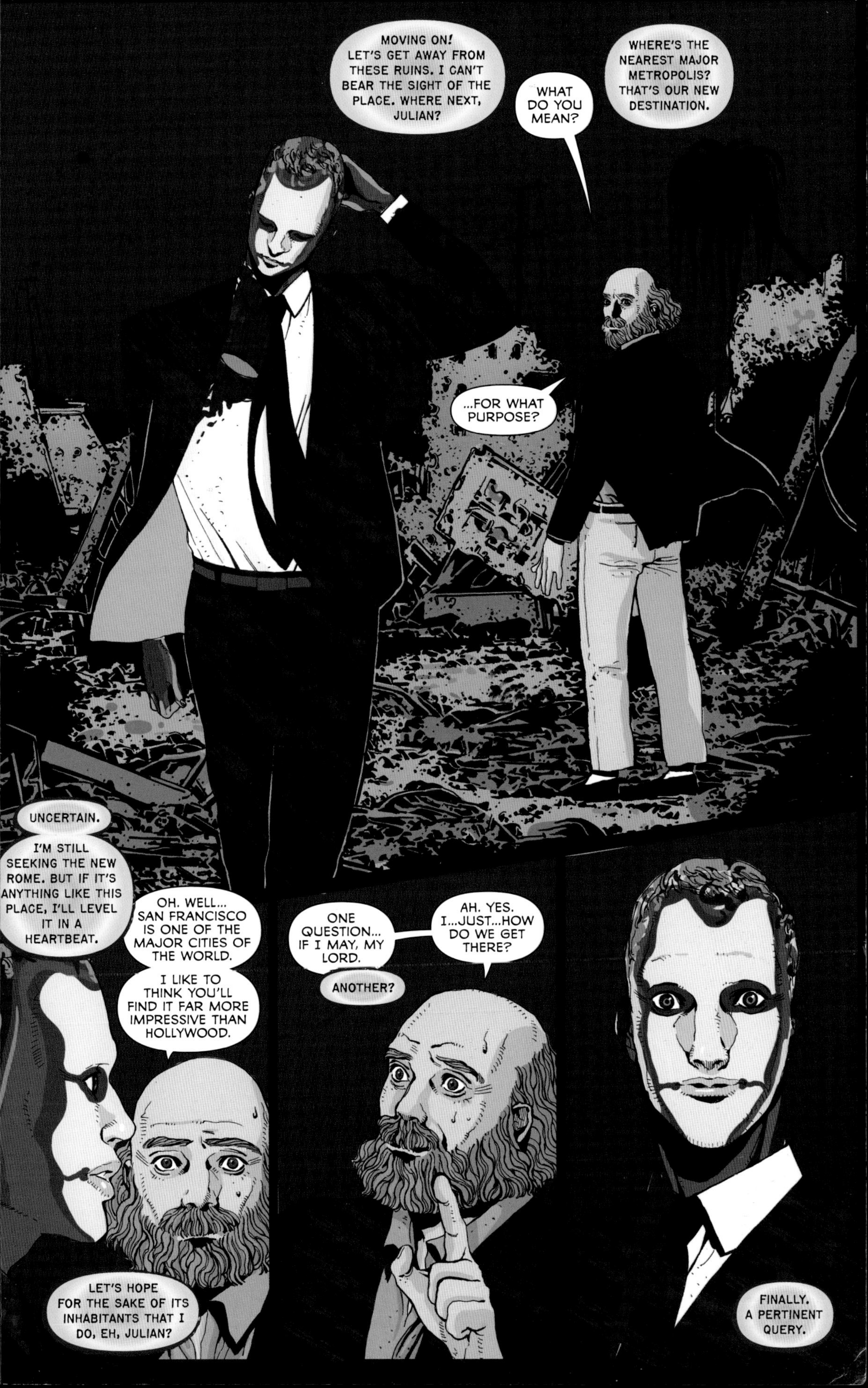
MOVING ON! LET'S GET AWAY FROM THESE RUINS. I CAN'T BEAR THE SIGHT OF THE PLACE. WHERE NEXT, JULIAN?
WHAT DO YOU MEAN?
WHERE'S THE NEAREST MAJOR METROPOLIS? THAT'S OUR NEW DESTINATION.
...FOR WHAT PURPOSE?
UNCERTAIN.
I'M STILL SEEKING THE NEW ROME. BUT IF IT'S ANYTHING LIKE THIS PLACE, I'LL LEVEL IT IN A HEARTBEAT.
OH. WELL... SAN FRANCISCO IS ONE OF THE MAJOR CITIES OF THE WORLD.
I LIKE TO THINK YOU'LL FIND IT FAR MORE IMPRESSIVE THAN HOLLYWOOD.
LET'S HOPE FOR THE SAKE OF ITS INHABITANTS THAT I DO, EH, JULIAN?
ONE QUESTION... IF I MAY, MY LORD.
ANOTHER?
AH. YES. I...JUST...HOW DO WE GET THERE?
FINALLY. A PERTINENT QUERY.

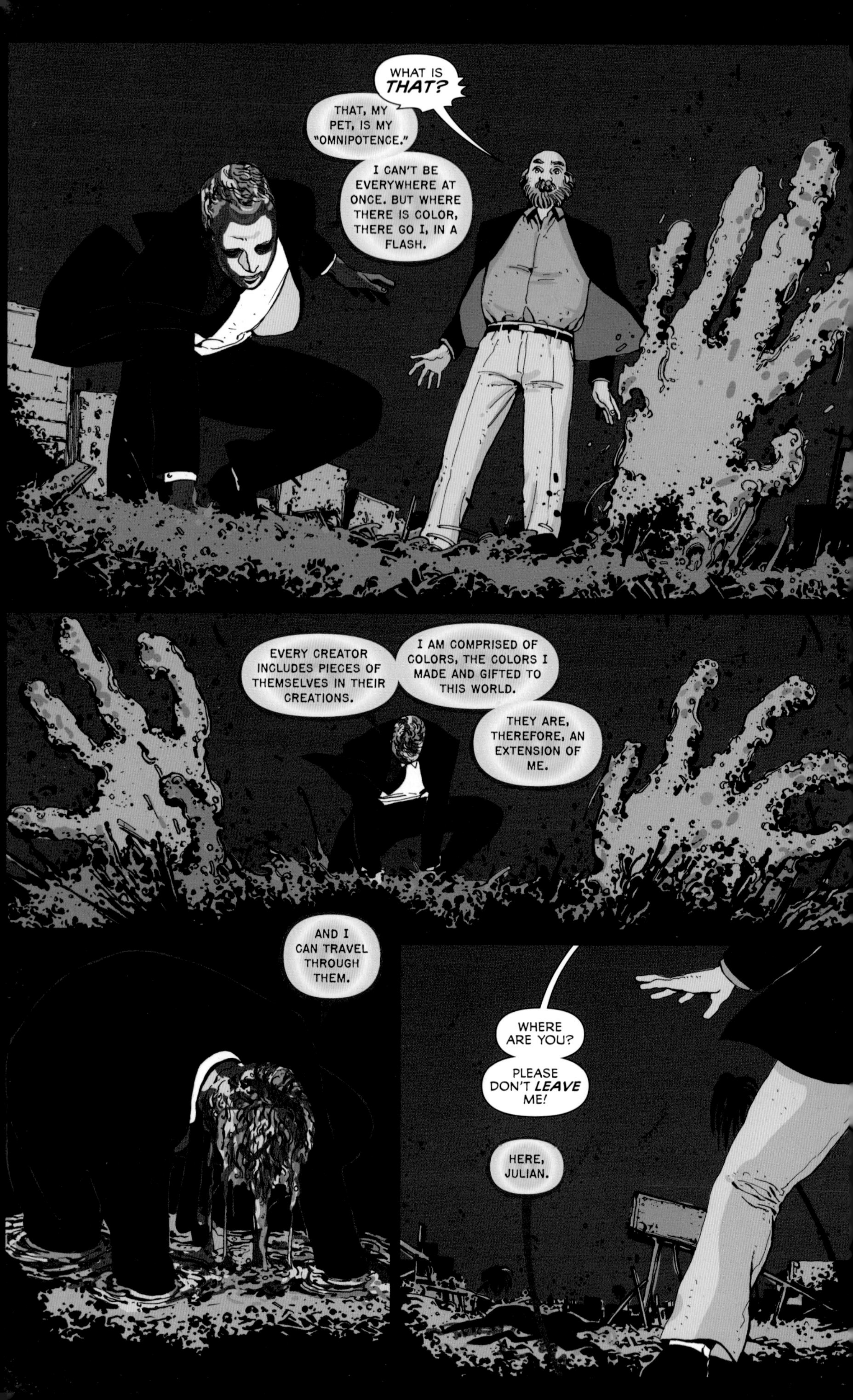
WHAT IS *THAT?*
THAT, MY PET, IS MY "OMNIPOTENCE."
I CAN'T BE EVERYWHERE AT ONCE. BUT WHERE THERE IS COLOR, THERE GO I, IN A FLASH.
EVERY CREATOR INCLUDES PIECES OF THEMSELVES IN THEIR CREATIONS.
I AM COMPRISED OF COLORS, THE COLORS I MADE AND GIFTED TO THIS WORLD.
THEY ARE, THEREFORE, AN EXTENSION OF ME.
AND I CAN TRAVEL THROUGH THEM.
WHERE ARE YOU?
PLEASE DON'T *LEAVE* ME!
HERE, JULIAN.

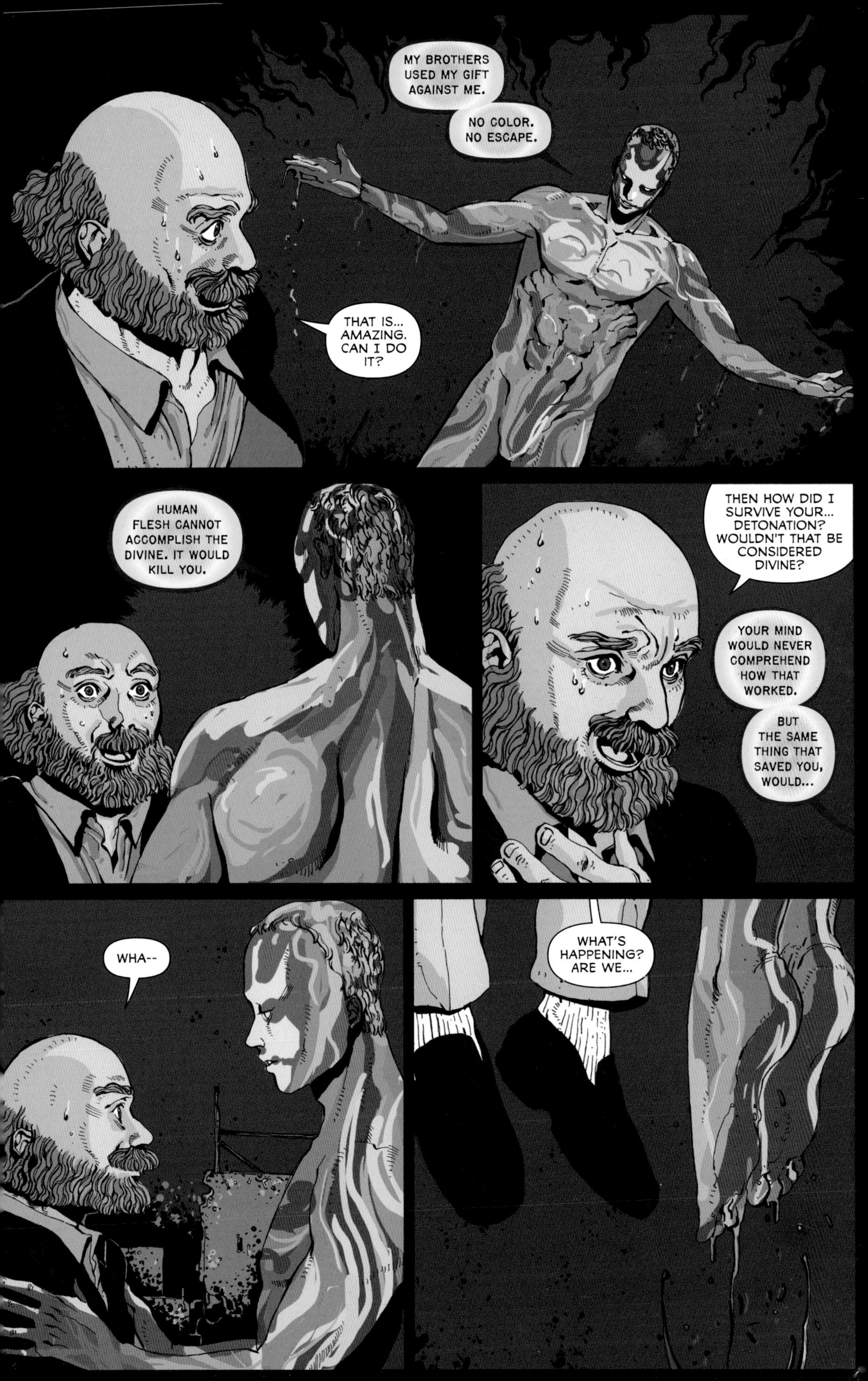
MY BROTHERS USED MY GIFT AGAINST ME.
NO COLOR. NO ESCAPE.
THAT IS... AMAZING. CAN I DO IT?
HUMAN FLESH CANNOT ACCOMPLISH THE DIVINE. IT WOULD KILL YOU.
THEN HOW DID I SURVIVE YOUR... DETONATION? WOULDN'T THAT BE CONSIDERED DIVINE?
YOUR MIND WOULD NEVER COMPREHEND HOW THAT WORKED.
BUT THE SAME THING THAT SAVED YOU, WOULD...
WHA--
WHAT'S HAPPENING? ARE WE...

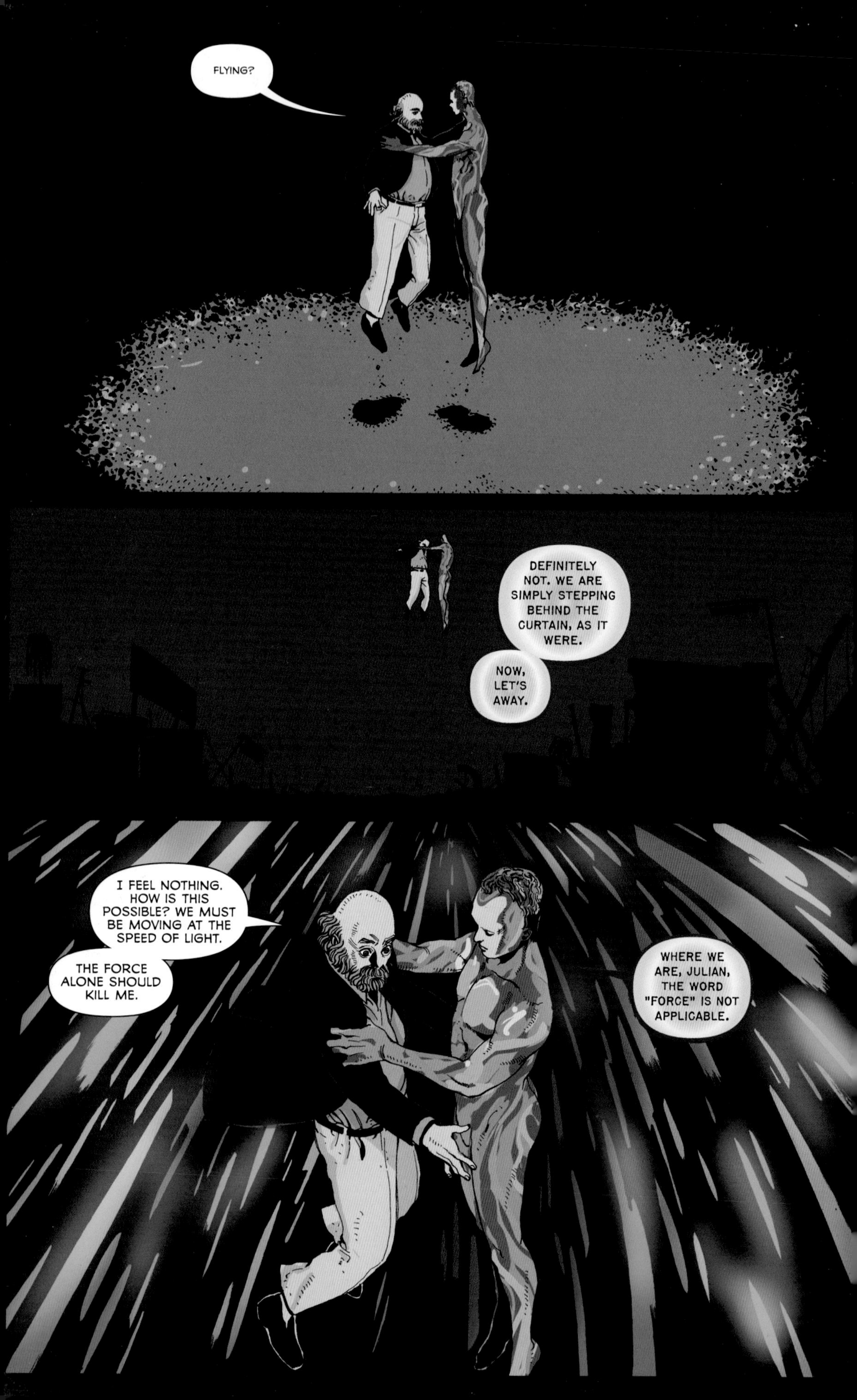
FLYING?
DEFINITELY NOT. WE ARE SIMPLY STEPPING BEHIND THE CURTAIN, AS IT WERE.
NOW, LET'S AWAY.
I FEEL NOTHING. HOW IS THIS POSSIBLE? WE MUST BE MOVING AT THE SPEED OF LIGHT.
THE FORCE ALONE SHOULD KILL ME.
WHERE WE ARE, JULIAN, THE WORD "FORCE" IS NOT APPLICABLE.

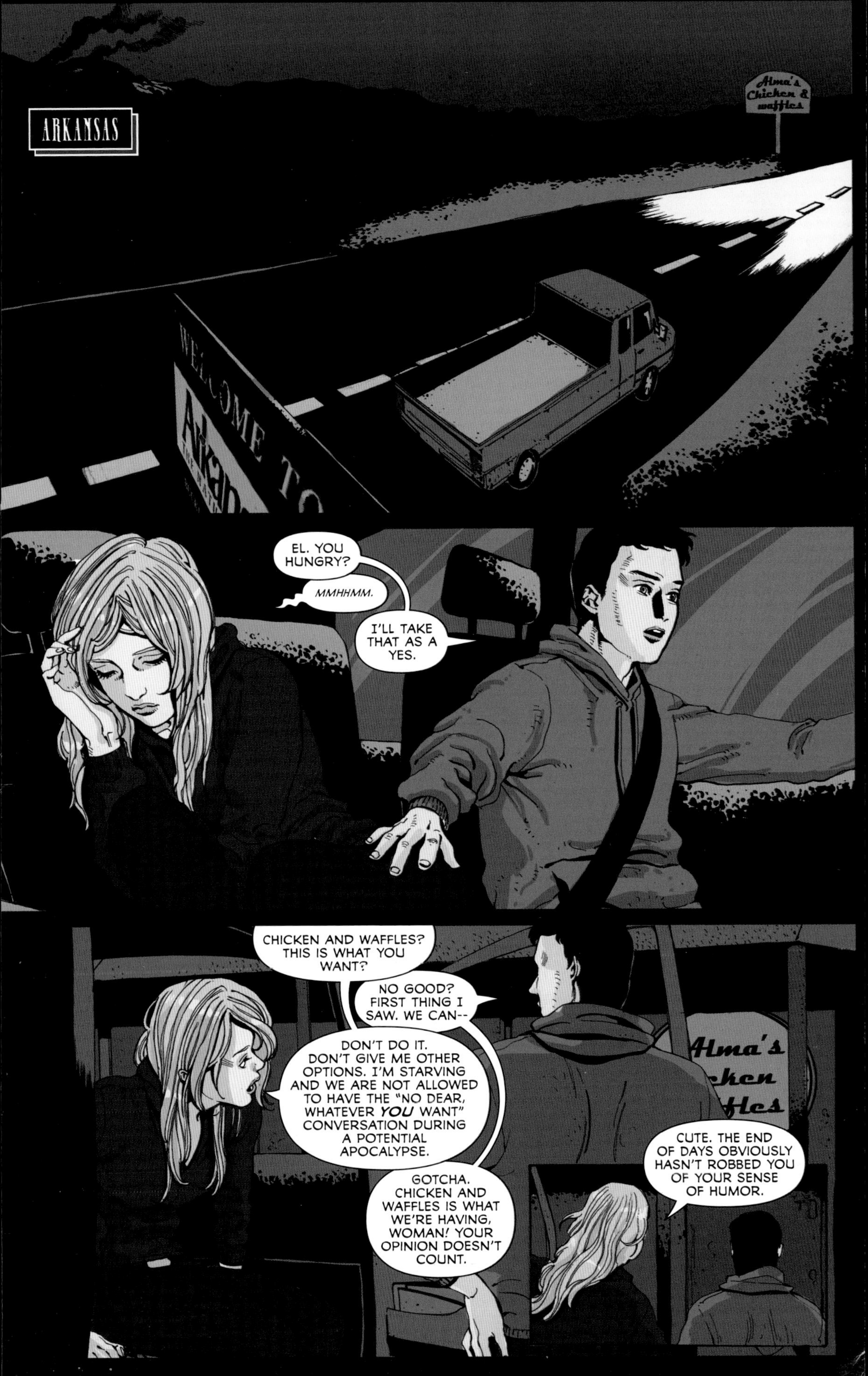
ARKANSAS
Alma's Chicken & waffles
WELCOME TO
EL. YOU HUNGRY?
MMHHMM.
I'LL TAKE THAT AS A YES.
CHICKEN AND WAFFLES? THIS IS WHAT YOU WANT?
NO GOOD? FIRST THING I SAW. WE CAN--
DON'T DO IT. DON'T GIVE ME OTHER OPTIONS. I'M STARVING AND WE ARE NOT ALLOWED TO HAVE THE "NO DEAR, WHATEVER *YOU* WANT" CONVERSATION DURING A POTENTIAL APOCALYPSE.
GOTCHA. CHICKEN AND WAFFLES IS WHAT WE'RE HAVING, WOMAN! YOUR OPINION DOESN'T COUNT.
CUTE. THE END OF DAYS OBVIOUSLY HASN'T ROBBED YOU OF YOUR SENSE OF HUMOR.

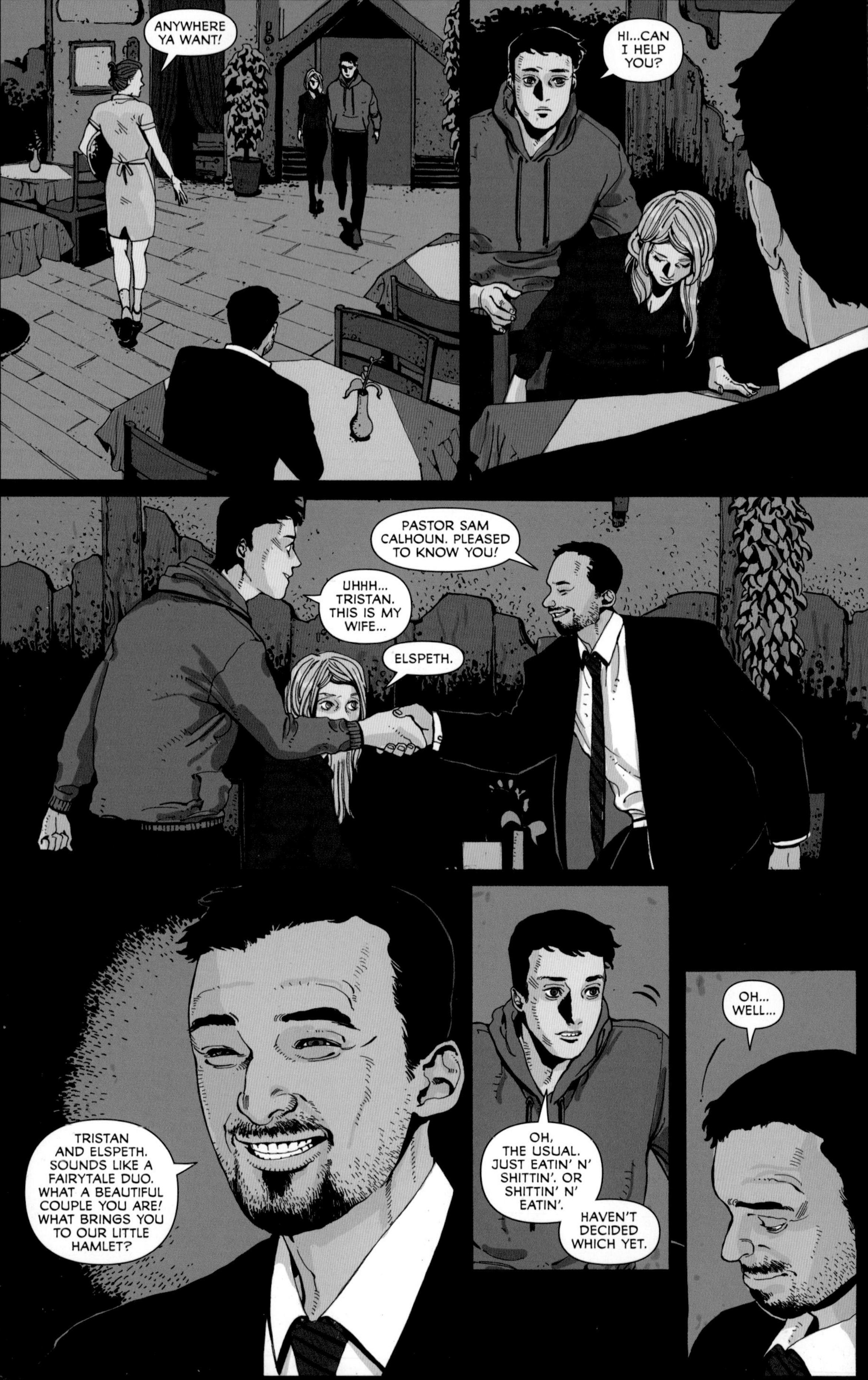
ANYWHERE YA WANT!
HI...CAN I HELP YOU?
PASTOR SAM CALHOUN. PLEASED TO KNOW YOU!
UHHH... TRISTAN. THIS IS MY WIFE...
ELSPETH.
TRISTAN AND ELSPETH. SOUNDS LIKE A FAIRYTALE DUO. WHAT A BEAUTIFUL COUPLE YOU ARE! WHAT BRINGS YOU TO OUR LITTLE HAMLET?
OH, THE USUAL. JUST EATIN' N' SHITTIN'. OR SHITTIN' N' EATIN'.
HAVEN'T DECIDED WHICH YET.
OH... WELL...

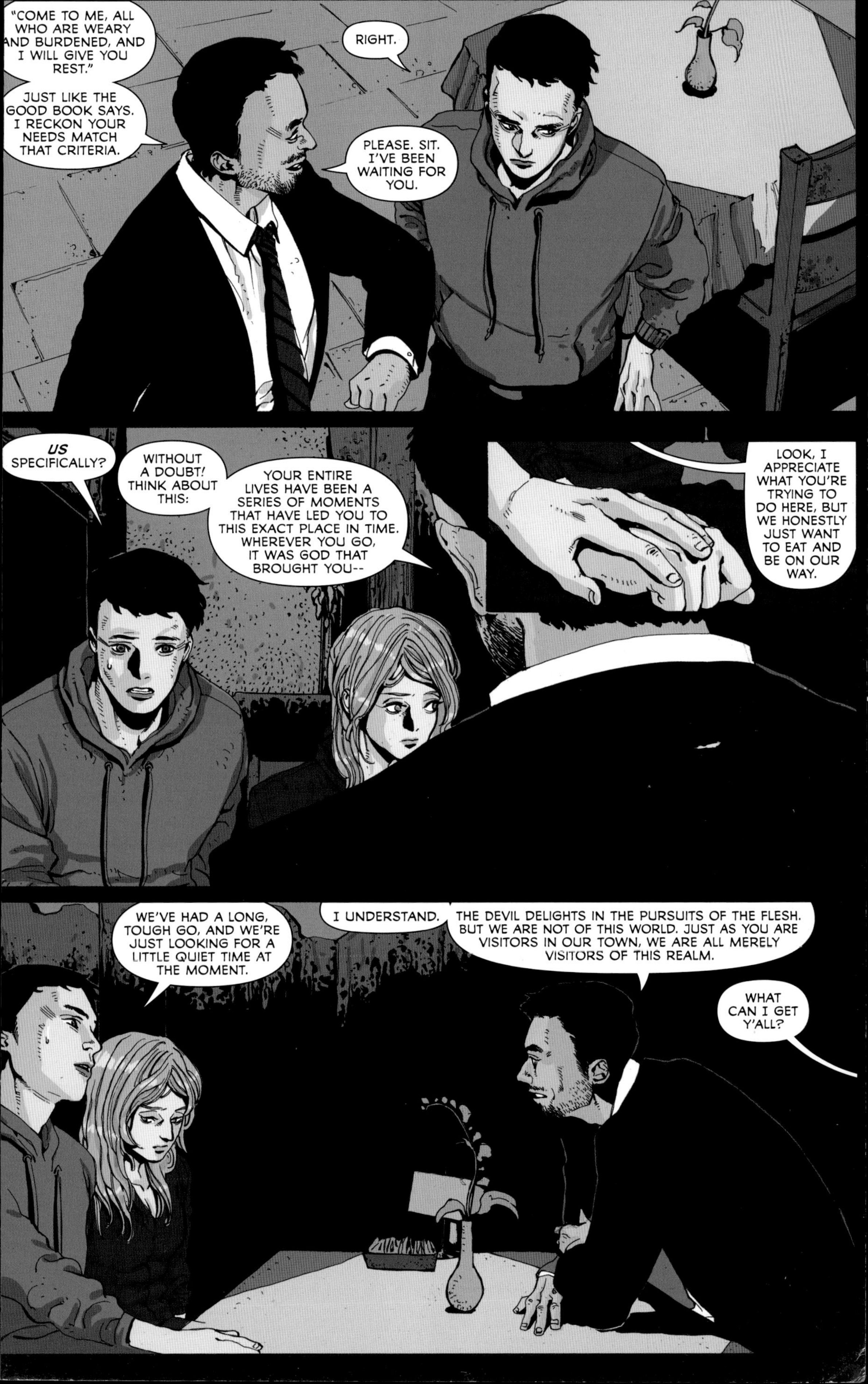
"COME TO ME, ALL WHO ARE WEARY AND BURDENED, AND I WILL GIVE YOU REST."
JUST LIKE THE GOOD BOOK SAYS. I RECKON YOUR NEEDS MATCH THAT CRITERIA.
RIGHT.
PLEASE. SIT. I'VE BEEN WAITING FOR YOU.
US SPECIFICALLY?
WITHOUT A DOUBT! THINK ABOUT THIS:
YOUR ENTIRE LIVES HAVE BEEN A SERIES OF MOMENTS THAT HAVE LED YOU TO THIS EXACT PLACE IN TIME. WHEREVER YOU GO, IT WAS GOD THAT BROUGHT YOU--
LOOK, I APPRECIATE WHAT YOU'RE TRYING TO DO HERE, BUT WE HONESTLY JUST WANT TO EAT AND BE ON OUR WAY.
WE'VE HAD A LONG, TOUGH GO, AND WE'RE JUST LOOKING FOR A LITTLE QUIET TIME AT THE MOMENT.
I UNDERSTAND.
THE DEVIL DELIGHTS IN THE PURSUITS OF THE FLESH. BUT WE ARE NOT OF THIS WORLD. JUST AS YOU ARE VISITORS IN OUR TOWN, WE ARE ALL MERELY VISITORS OF THIS REALM.
WHAT CAN I GET Y'ALL?

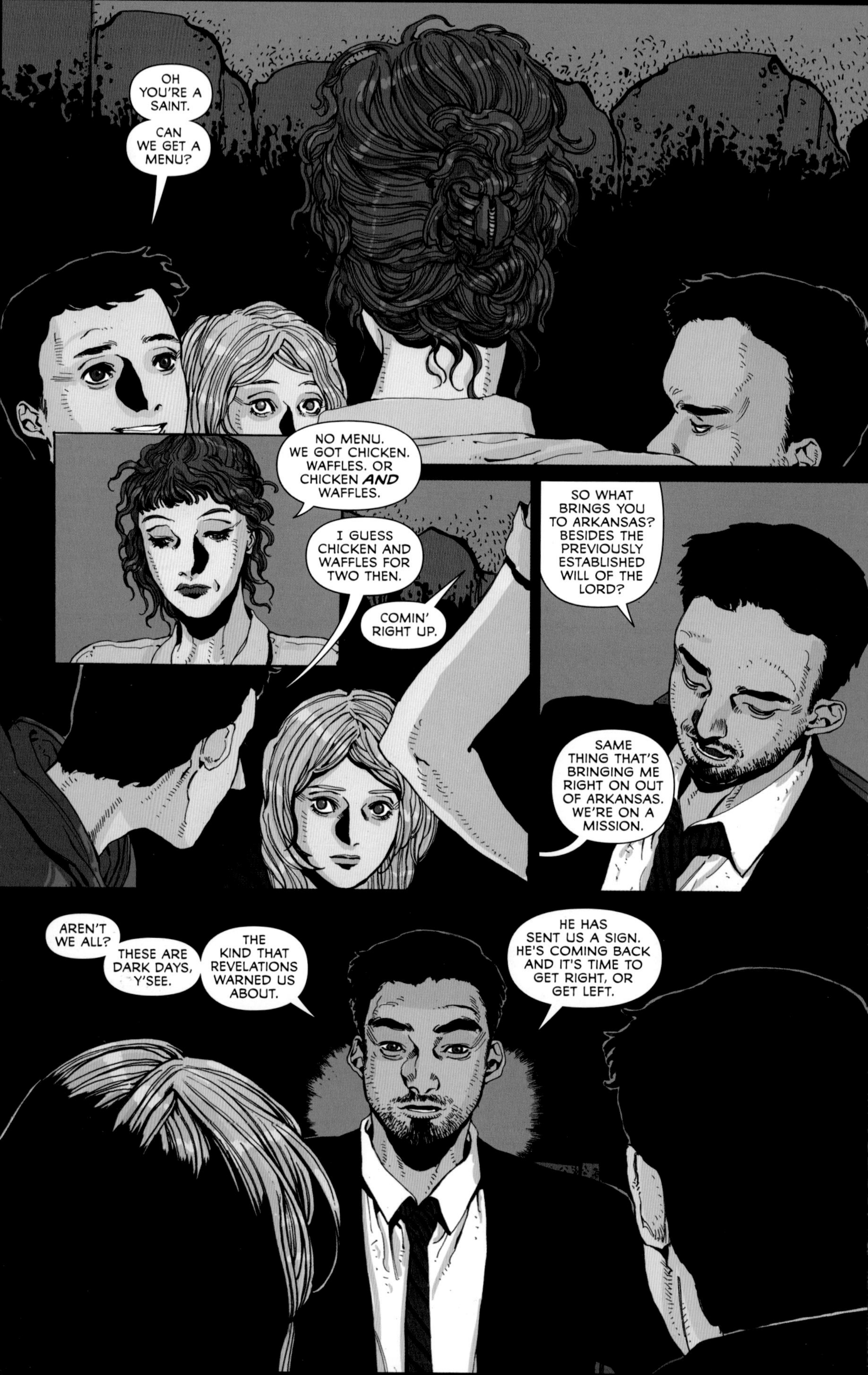
OH YOU'RE A SAINT.
CAN WE GET A MENU?
NO MENU. WE GOT CHICKEN. WAFFLES. OR CHICKEN *AND* WAFFLES.
I GUESS CHICKEN AND WAFFLES FOR TWO THEN.
COMIN' RIGHT UP.
SO WHAT BRINGS YOU TO ARKANSAS? BESIDES THE PREVIOUSLY ESTABLISHED WILL OF THE LORD?
SAME THING THAT'S BRINGING ME RIGHT ON OUT OF ARKANSAS. WE'RE ON A MISSION.
AREN'T WE ALL?
THESE ARE DARK DAYS, Y'SEE.
THE KIND THAT REVELATIONS WARNED US ABOUT.
HE HAS SENT US A SIGN. HE'S COMING BACK AND IT'S TIME TO GET RIGHT, OR GET LEFT.

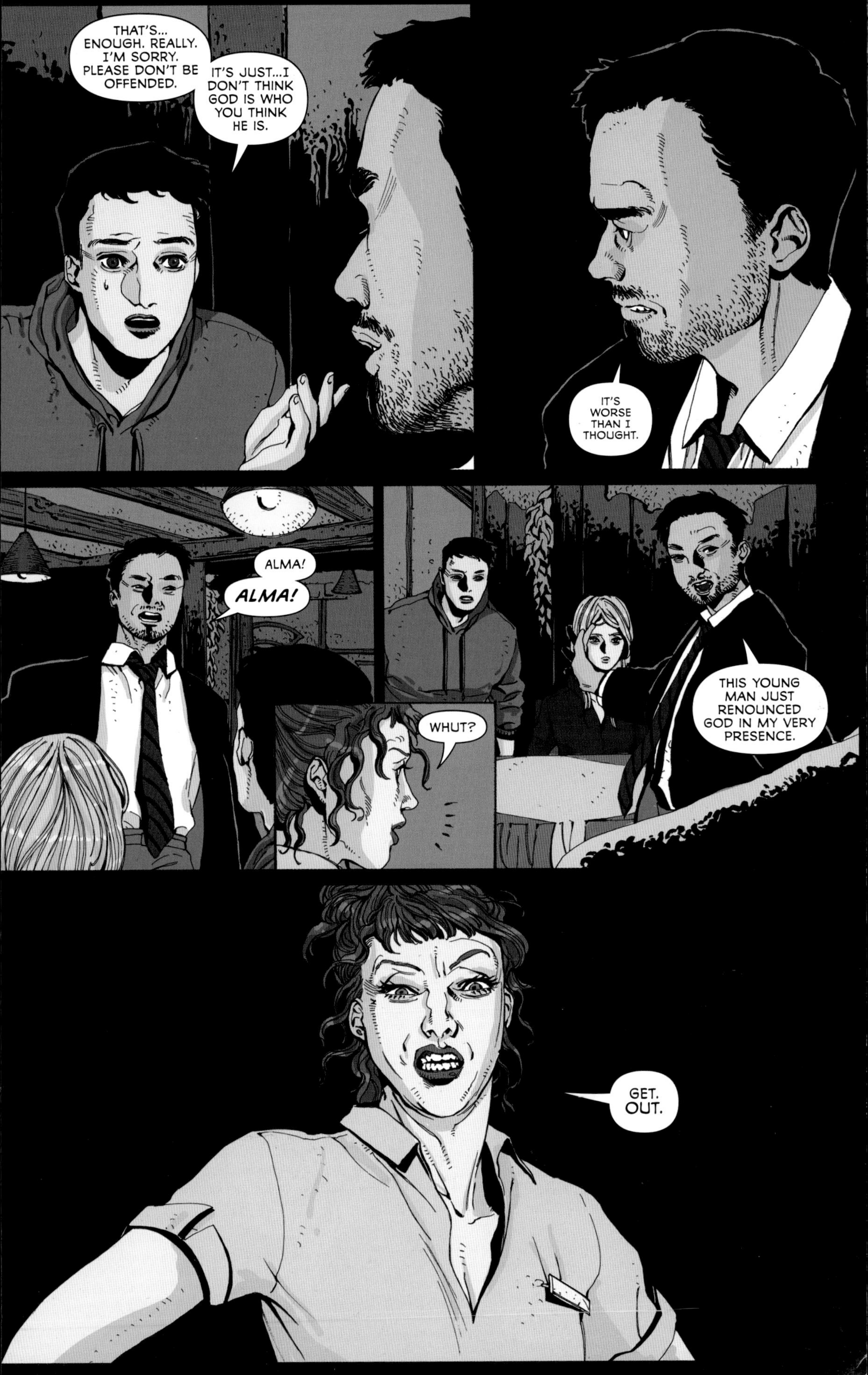
THAT'S... ENOUGH. REALLY. I'M SORRY. PLEASE DON'T BE OFFENDED.
IT'S JUST...I DON'T THINK GOD IS WHO YOU THINK HE IS.
IT'S WORSE THAN I THOUGHT.
ALMA!
ALMA!
WHUT?
THIS YOUNG MAN JUST RENOUNCED GOD IN MY VERY PRESENCE.
GET. OUT.

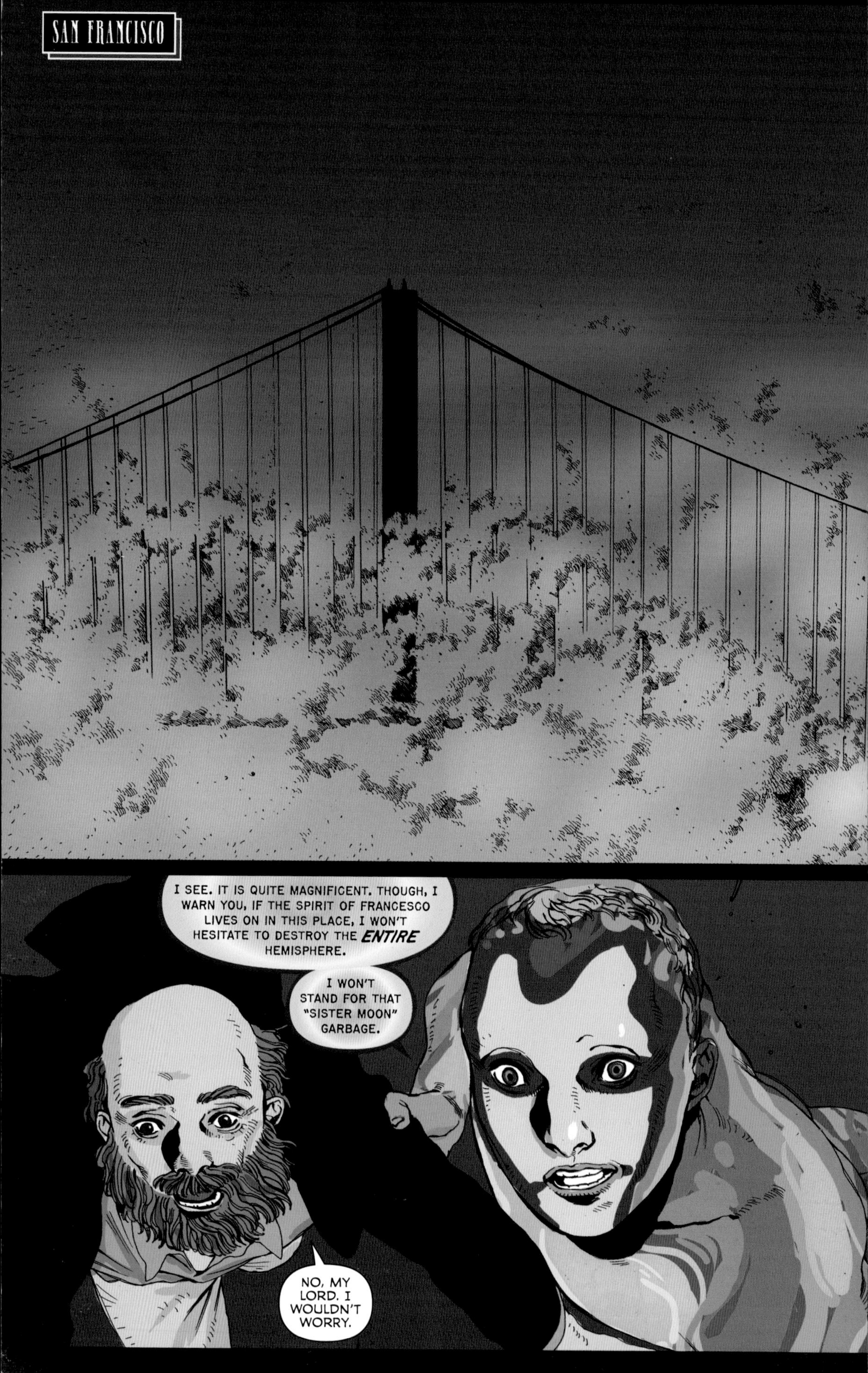
SAN FRANCISCO
I SEE. IT IS QUITE MAGNIFICENT. THOUGH, I WARN YOU, IF THE SPIRIT OF FRANCESCO LIVES ON IN THIS PLACE, I WON'T HESITATE TO DESTROY THE *ENTIRE* HEMISPHERE.
I WON'T STAND FOR THAT "SISTER MOON" GARBAGE.
NO, MY LORD. I WOULDN'T WORRY.

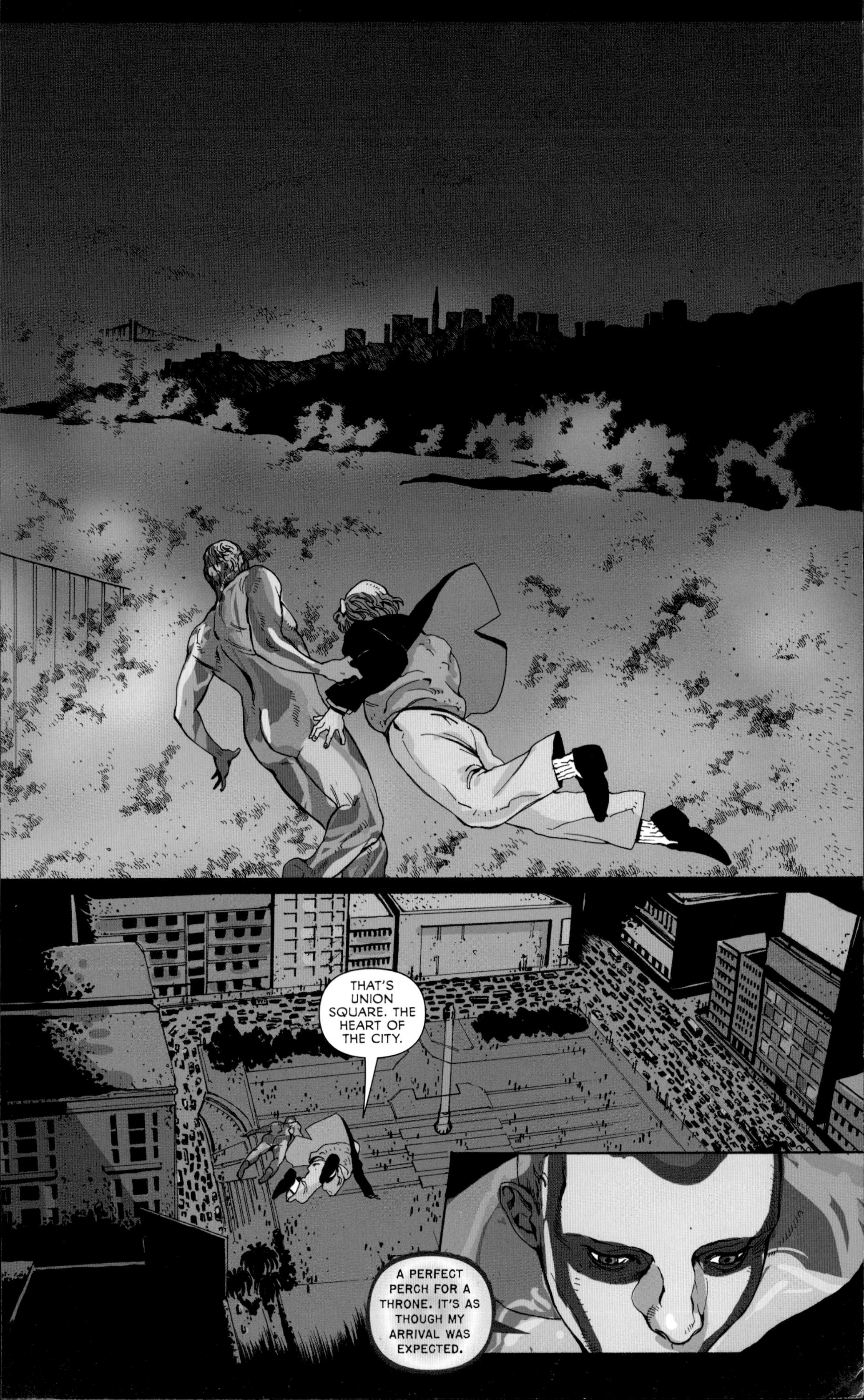
THAT'S UNION SQUARE. THE HEART OF THE CITY.
A PERFECT PERCH FOR A THRONE. IT'S AS THOUGH MY ARRIVAL WAS EXPECTED.

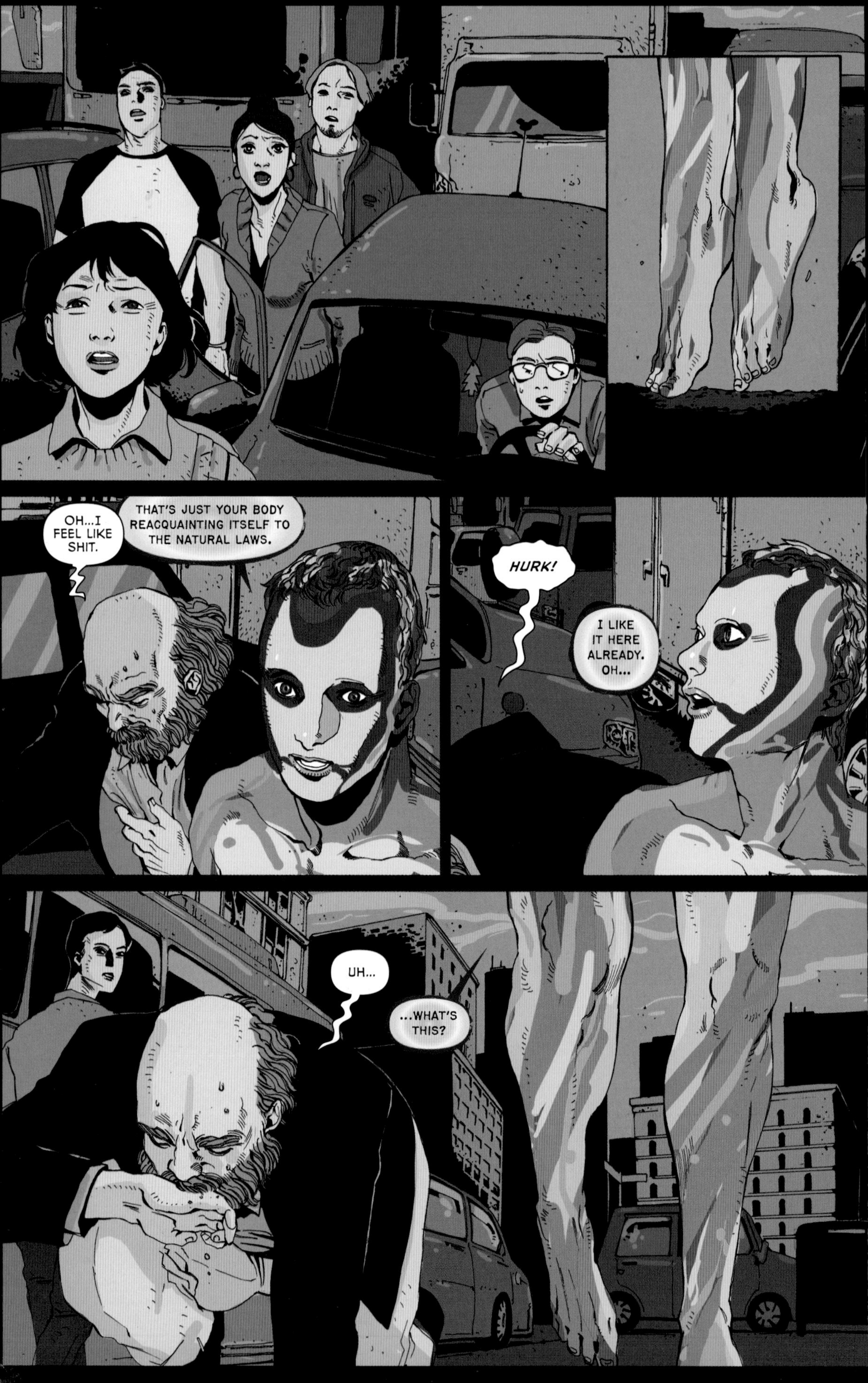
OH...I FEEL LIKE SHIT.
THAT'S JUST YOUR BODY REACQUAINTING ITSELF TO THE NATURAL LAWS.
HURK!
I LIKE IT HERE ALREADY. OH...
UH...
...WHAT'S THIS?

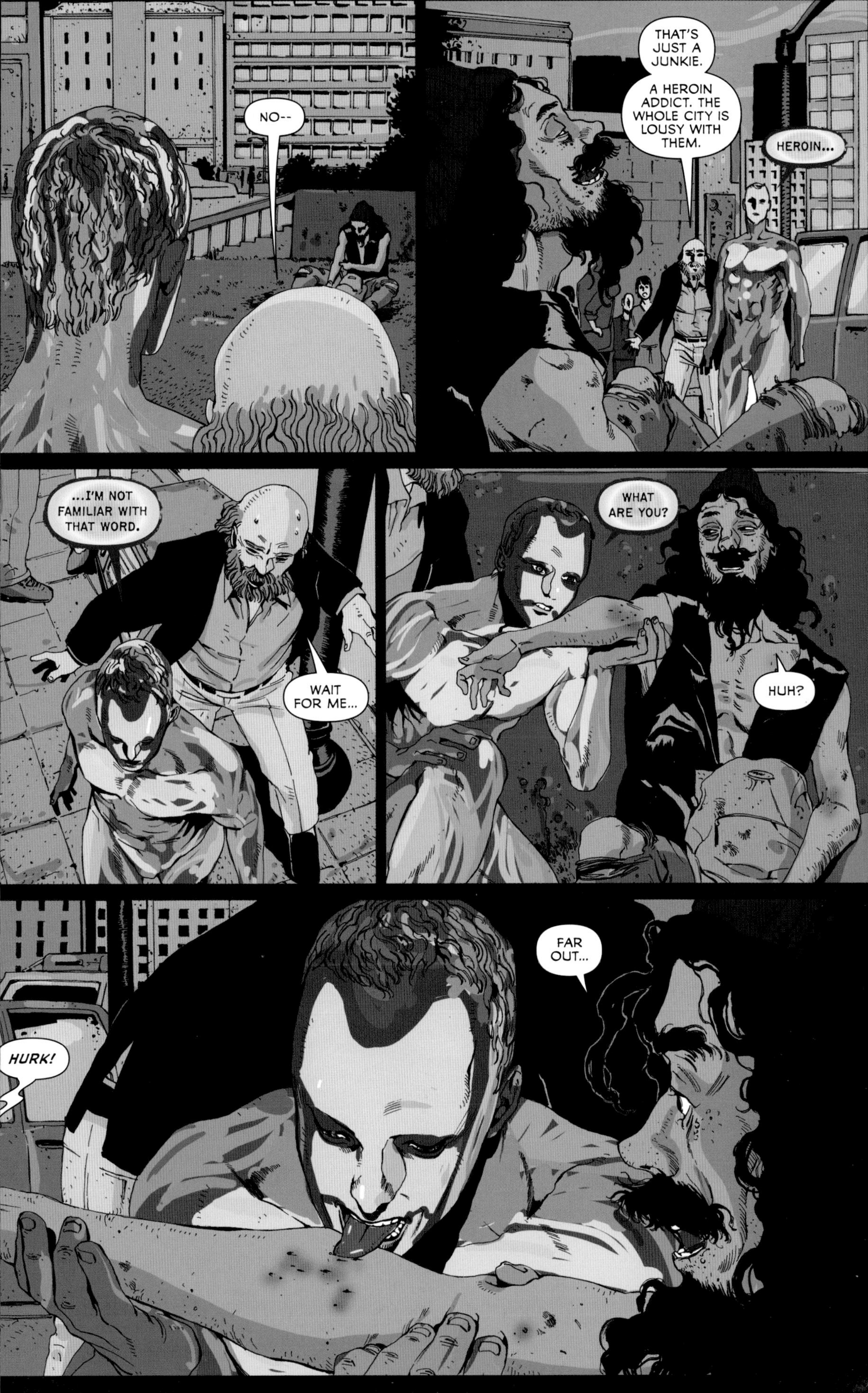
NO--
THAT'S JUST A JUNKIE.
A HEROIN ADDICT. THE WHOLE CITY IS LOUSY WITH THEM.
HEROIN...
...I'M NOT FAMILIAR WITH THAT WORD.
WAIT FOR ME...
WHAT ARE YOU?
HUH?
FAR OUT...
HURK!

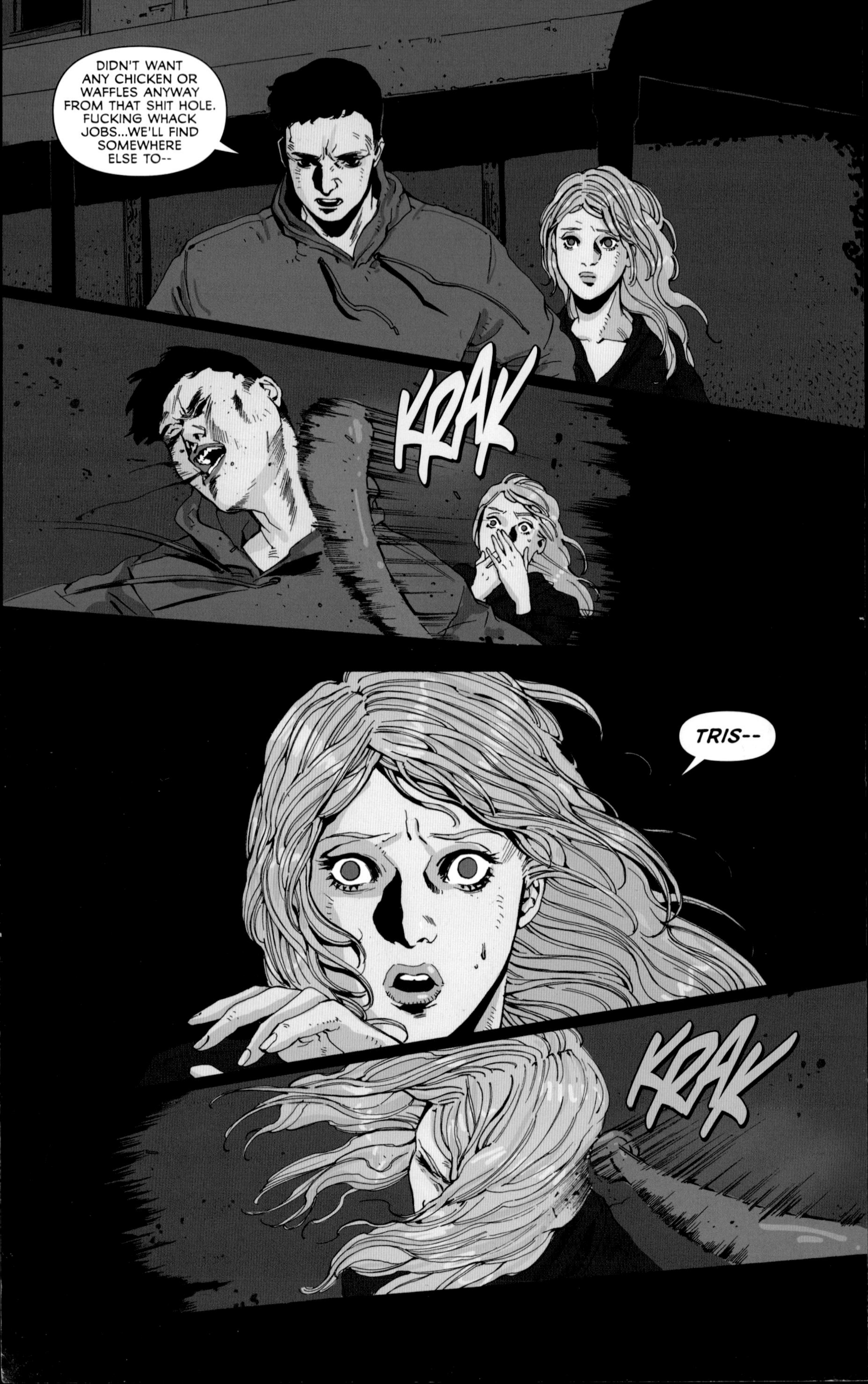
DIDN'T WANT ANY CHICKEN OR WAFFLES ANYWAY FROM THAT SHIT HOLE. FUCKING WHACK JOBS...WE'LL FIND SOMEWHERE ELSE TO--
KRAK
TRIS--
KRAK

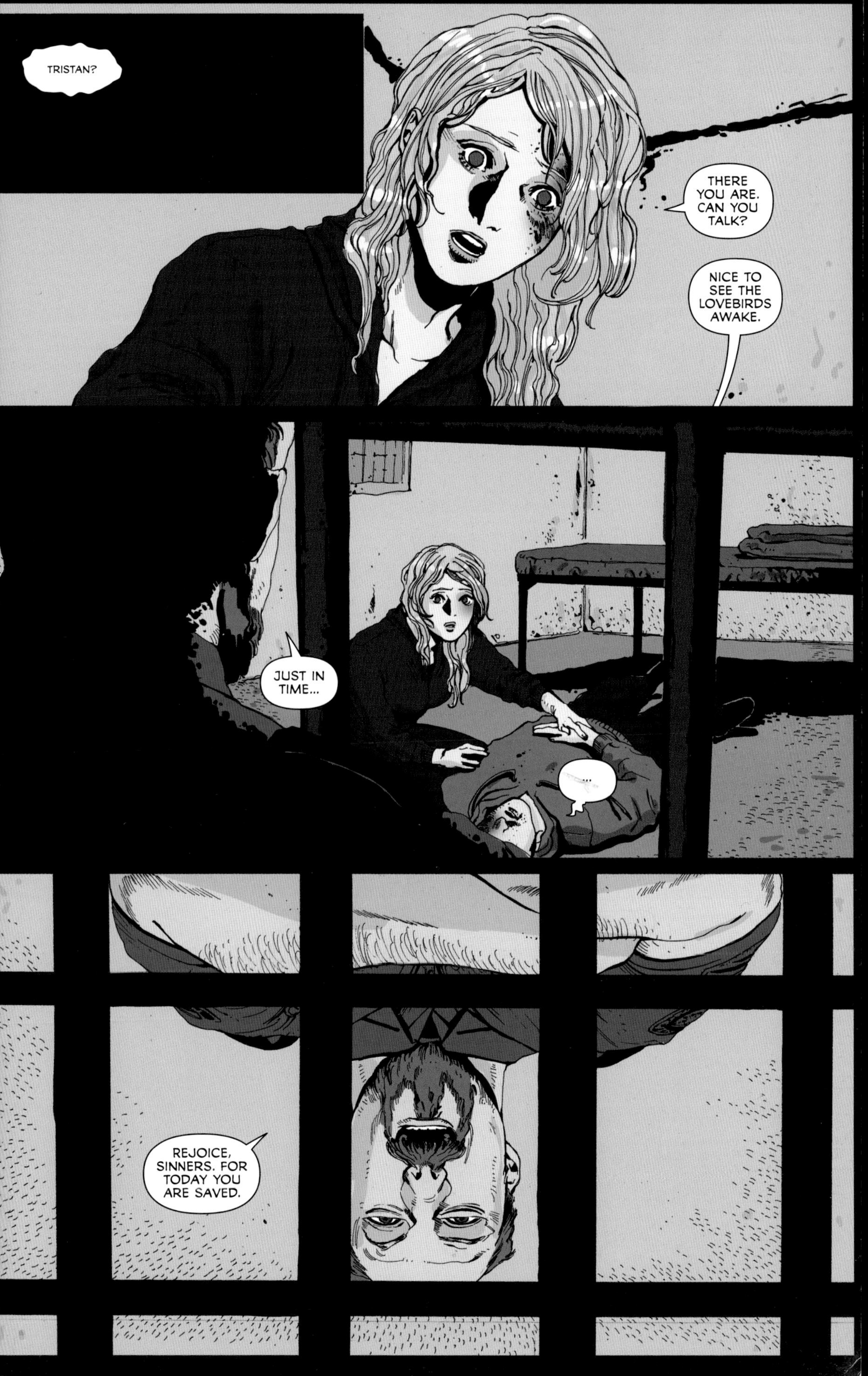
TRISTAN?
THERE YOU ARE. CAN YOU TALK?
NICE TO SEE THE LOVEBIRDS AWAKE.
JUST IN TIME...
REJOICE, SINNERS. FOR TODAY YOU ARE SAVED.

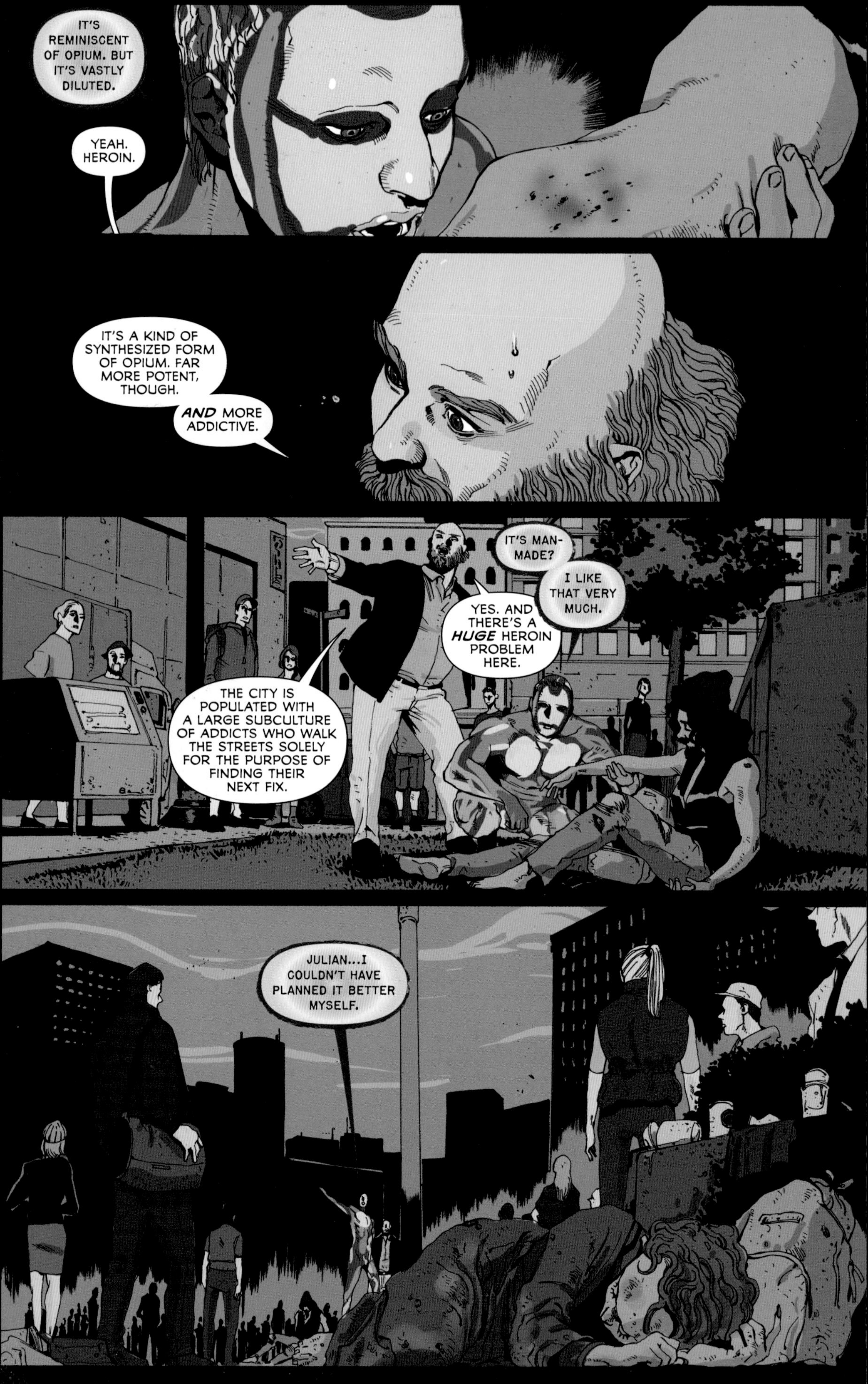
IT'S REMINISCENT OF OPIUM. BUT IT'S VASTLY DILUTED.
YEAH. HEROIN.
IT'S A KIND OF SYNTHESIZED FORM OF OPIUM. FAR MORE POTENT, THOUGH.
AND MORE ADDICTIVE.
IT'S MAN-MADE?
I LIKE THAT VERY MUCH.
YES. AND THERE'S A HUGE HEROIN PROBLEM HERE.
THE CITY IS POPULATED WITH A LARGE SUBCULTURE OF ADDICTS WHO WALK THE STREETS SOLELY FOR THE PURPOSE OF FINDING THEIR NEXT FIX.
JULIAN...I COULDN'T HAVE PLANNED IT BETTER MYSELF.

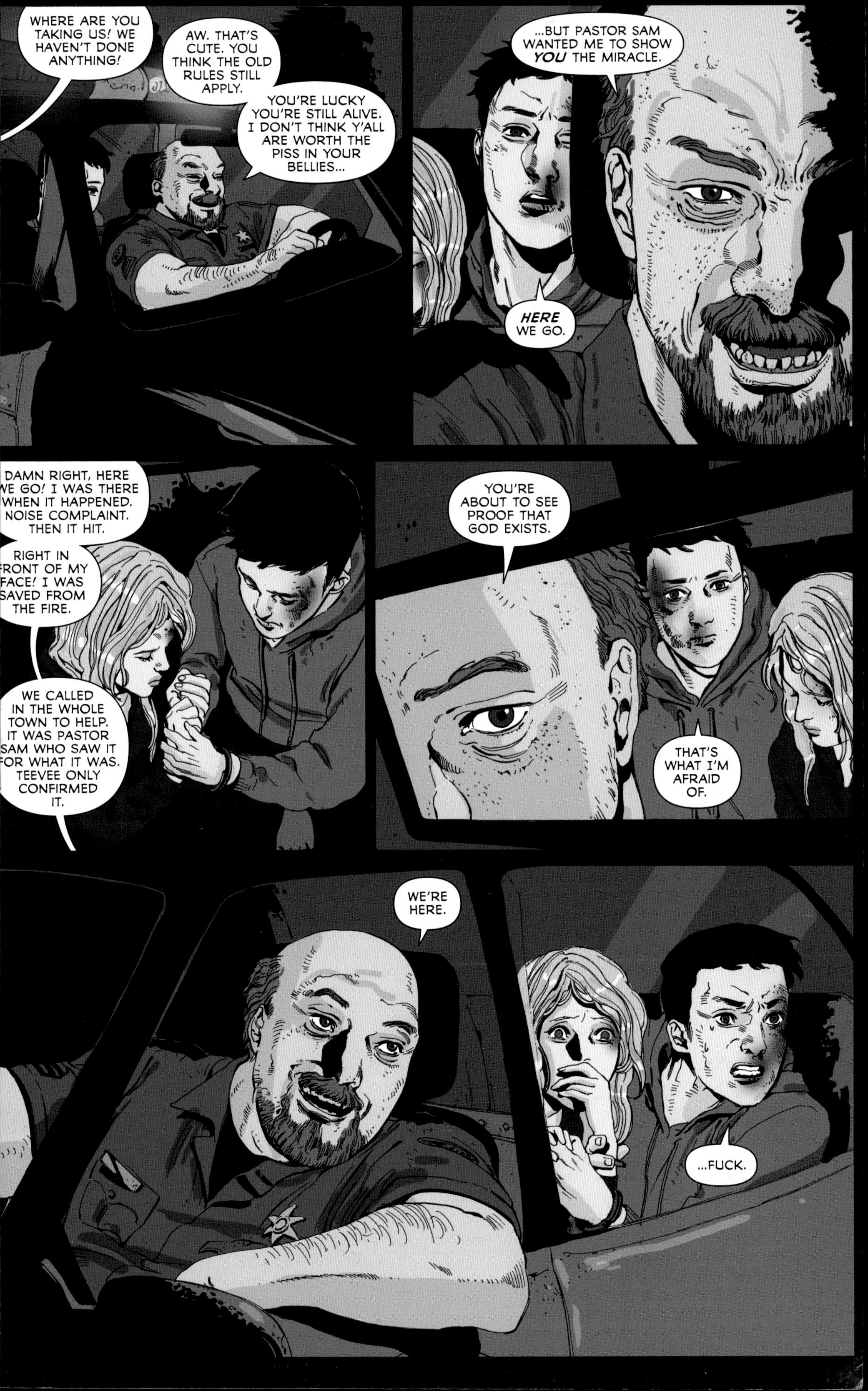
WHERE ARE YOU TAKING US! WE HAVEN'T DONE ANYTHING!
AW. THAT'S CUTE. YOU THINK THE OLD RULES STILL APPLY.
YOU'RE LUCKY YOU'RE STILL ALIVE. I DON'T THINK Y'ALL ARE WORTH THE PISS IN YOUR BELLIES...
...BUT PASTOR SAM WANTED ME TO SHOW *YOU* THE MIRACLE.
HERE WE GO.
DAMN RIGHT, HERE WE GO! I WAS THERE WHEN IT HAPPENED. NOISE COMPLAINT. THEN IT HIT.
RIGHT IN FRONT OF MY FACE! I WAS SAVED FROM THE FIRE.
WE CALLED IN THE WHOLE TOWN TO HELP. IT WAS PASTOR SAM WHO SAW IT FOR WHAT IT WAS. TEEVEE ONLY CONFIRMED IT.
YOU'RE ABOUT TO SEE PROOF THAT GOD EXISTS.
THAT'S WHAT I'M AFRAID OF.
WE'RE HERE.
...FUCK.

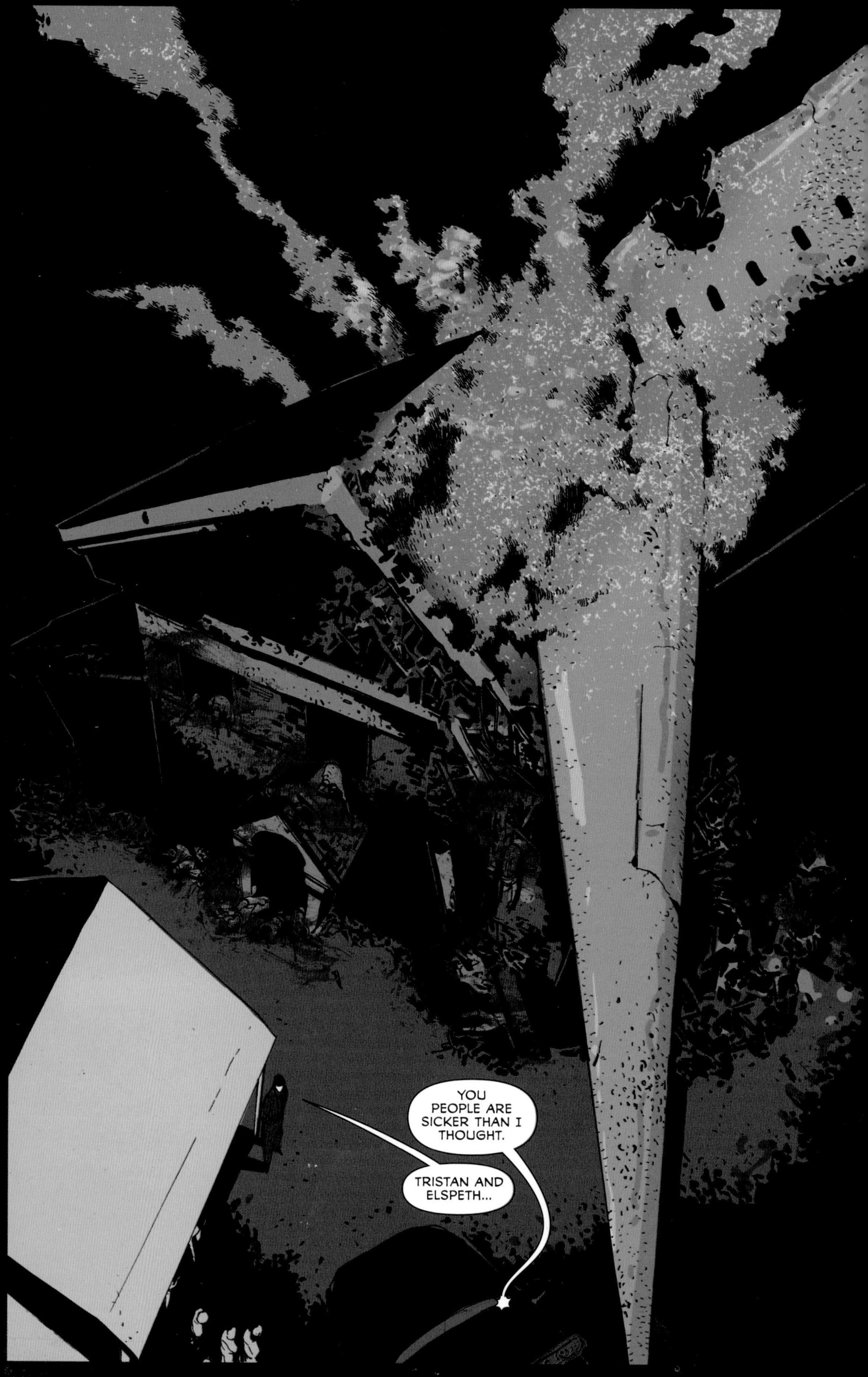

TRISTAN AND ELSPETH...
YOU PEOPLE ARE SICKER THAN I THOUGHT.

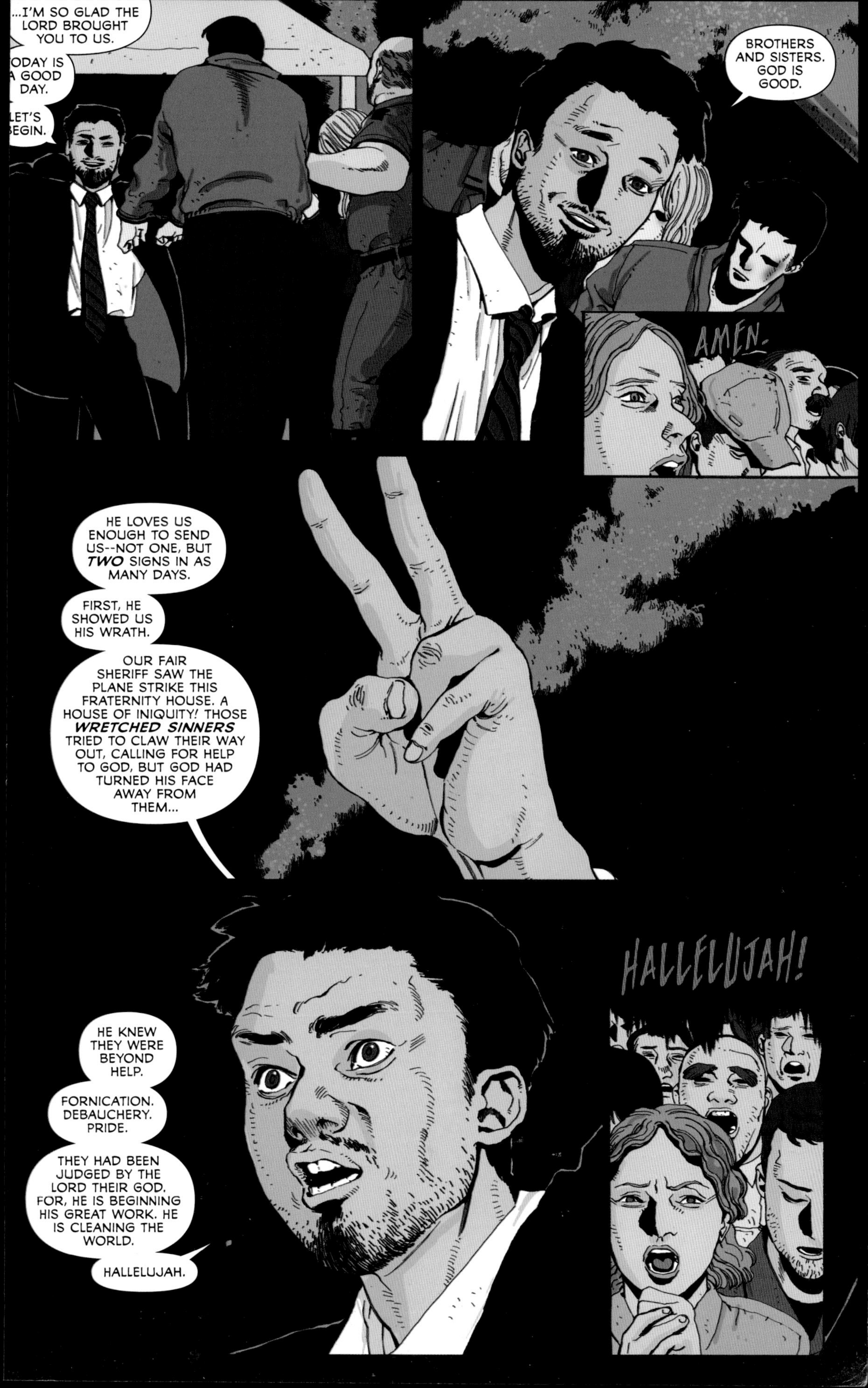

...I'M SO GLAD THE LORD BROUGHT YOU TO US.
ODAY IS A GOOD DAY.
LET'S BEGIN.
BROTHERS AND SISTERS. GOD IS GOOD.
AMEN.
HE LOVES US ENOUGH TO SEND US--NOT ONE, BUT TWO SIGNS IN AS MANY DAYS.
FIRST, HE SHOWED US HIS WRATH.
OUR FAIR SHERIFF SAW THE PLANE STRIKE THIS FRATERNITY HOUSE. A HOUSE OF INIQUITY! THOSE WRETCHED SINNERS TRIED TO CLAW THEIR WAY OUT, CALLING FOR HELP TO GOD, BUT GOD HAD TURNED HIS FACE AWAY FROM THEM...
HE KNEW THEY WERE BEYOND HELP.
FORNICATION. DEBAUCHERY. PRIDE.
THEY HAD BEEN JUDGED BY THE LORD THEIR GOD. FOR, HE IS BEGINNING HIS GREAT WORK. HE IS CLEANING THE WORLD.
HALLELUJAH.
HALLELUJAH!

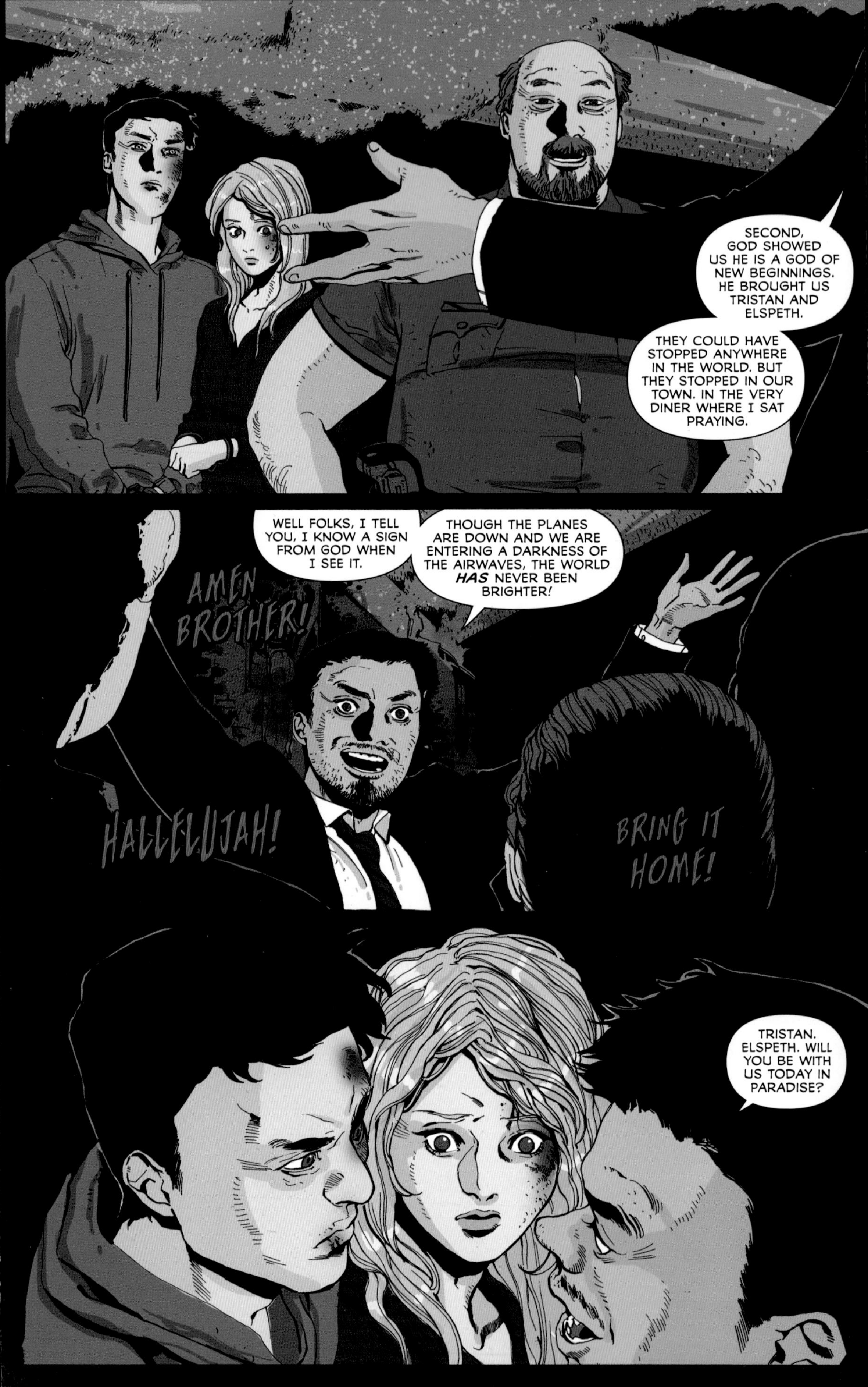
SECOND, GOD SHOWED US HE IS A GOD OF NEW BEGINNINGS. HE BROUGHT US TRISTAN AND ELSPETH.
THEY COULD HAVE STOPPED ANYWHERE IN THE WORLD. BUT THEY STOPPED IN OUR TOWN. IN THE VERY DINER WHERE I SAT PRAYING.
WELL FOLKS, I TELL YOU, I KNOW A SIGN FROM GOD WHEN I SEE IT.
THOUGH THE PLANES ARE DOWN AND WE ARE ENTERING A DARKNESS OF THE AIRWAVES, THE WORLD *HAS* NEVER BEEN BRIGHTER!
AMEN BROTHER!
HALLELUJAH!
BRING IT HOME!
TRISTAN. ELSPETH. WILL YOU BE WITH US TODAY IN PARADISE?

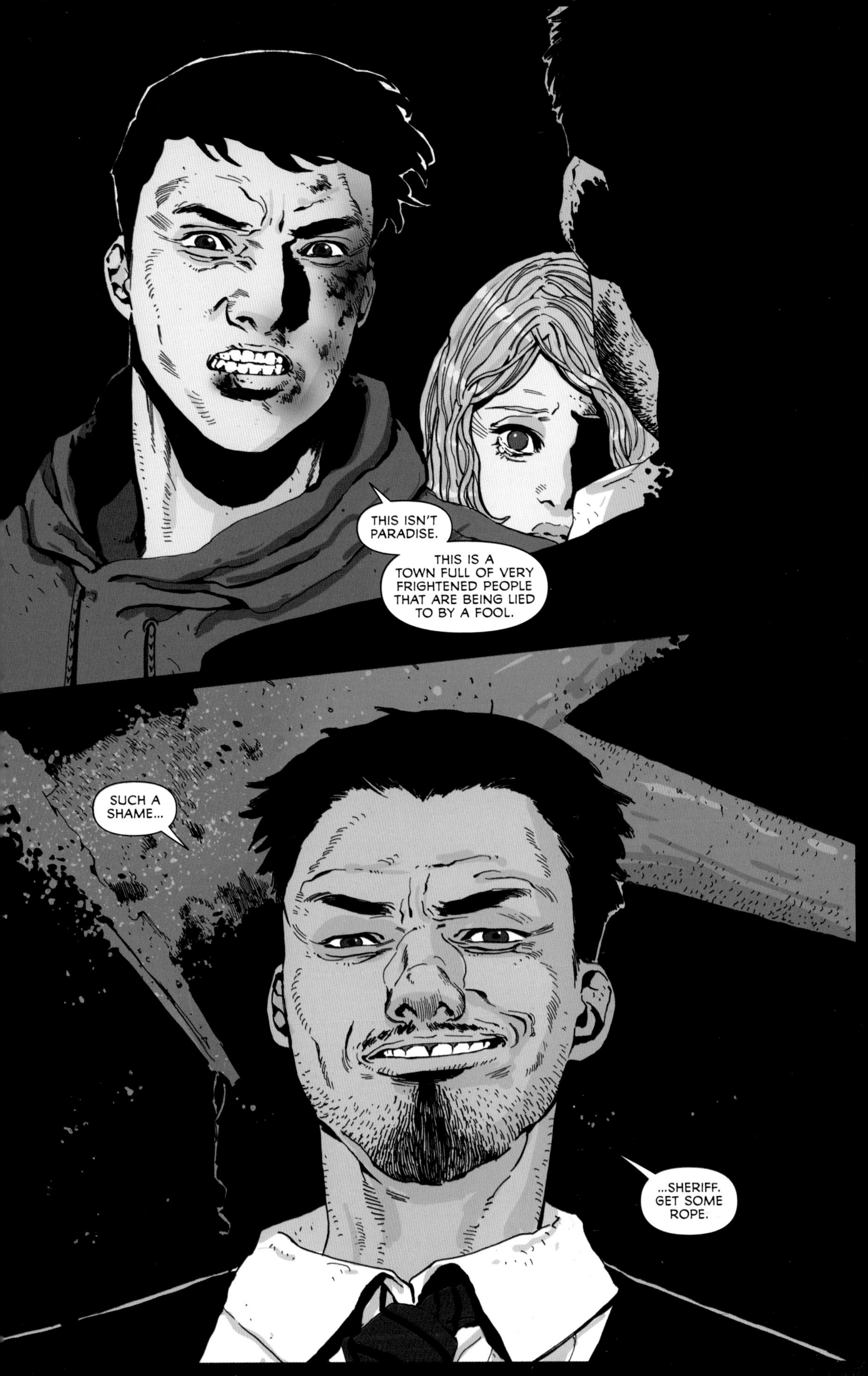
THIS ISN'T PARADISE.
THIS IS A TOWN FULL OF VERY FRIGHTENED PEOPLE THAT ARE BEING LIED TO BY A FOOL.
SUCH A SHAME...
...SHERIFF. GET SOME ROPE.

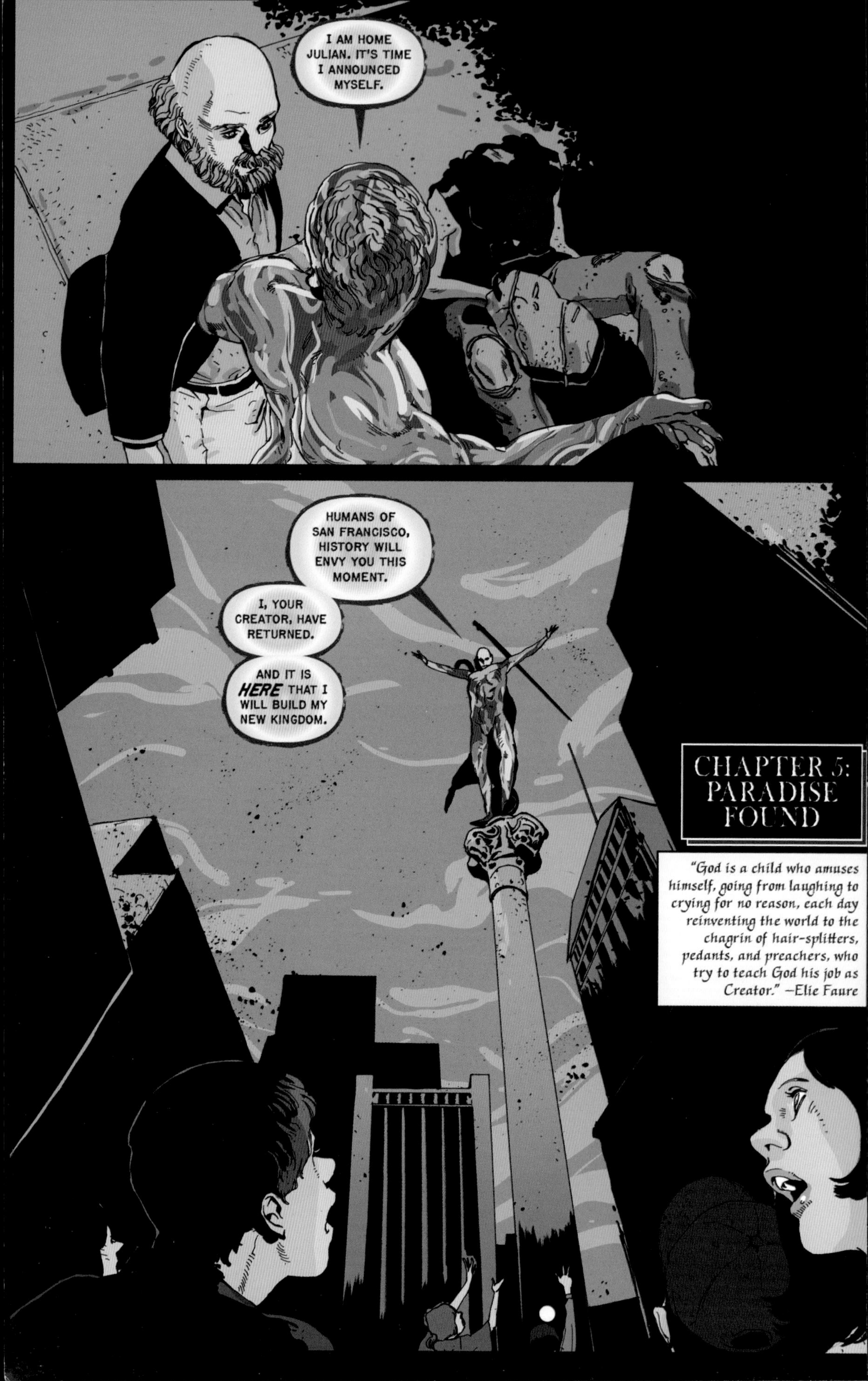
I AM HOME JULIAN. IT'S TIME I ANNOUNCED MYSELF.
HUMANS OF SAN FRANCISCO, HISTORY WILL ENVY YOU THIS MOMENT.
I, YOUR CREATOR, HAVE RETURNED.
AND IT IS *HERE* THAT I WILL BUILD MY NEW KINGDOM.
CHAPTER 5: PARADISE FOUND
"God is a child who amuses himself, going from laughing to crying for no reason, each day reinventing the world to the chagrin of hair-splitters, pedants, and preachers, who try to teach God his job as Creator." —Elie Faure

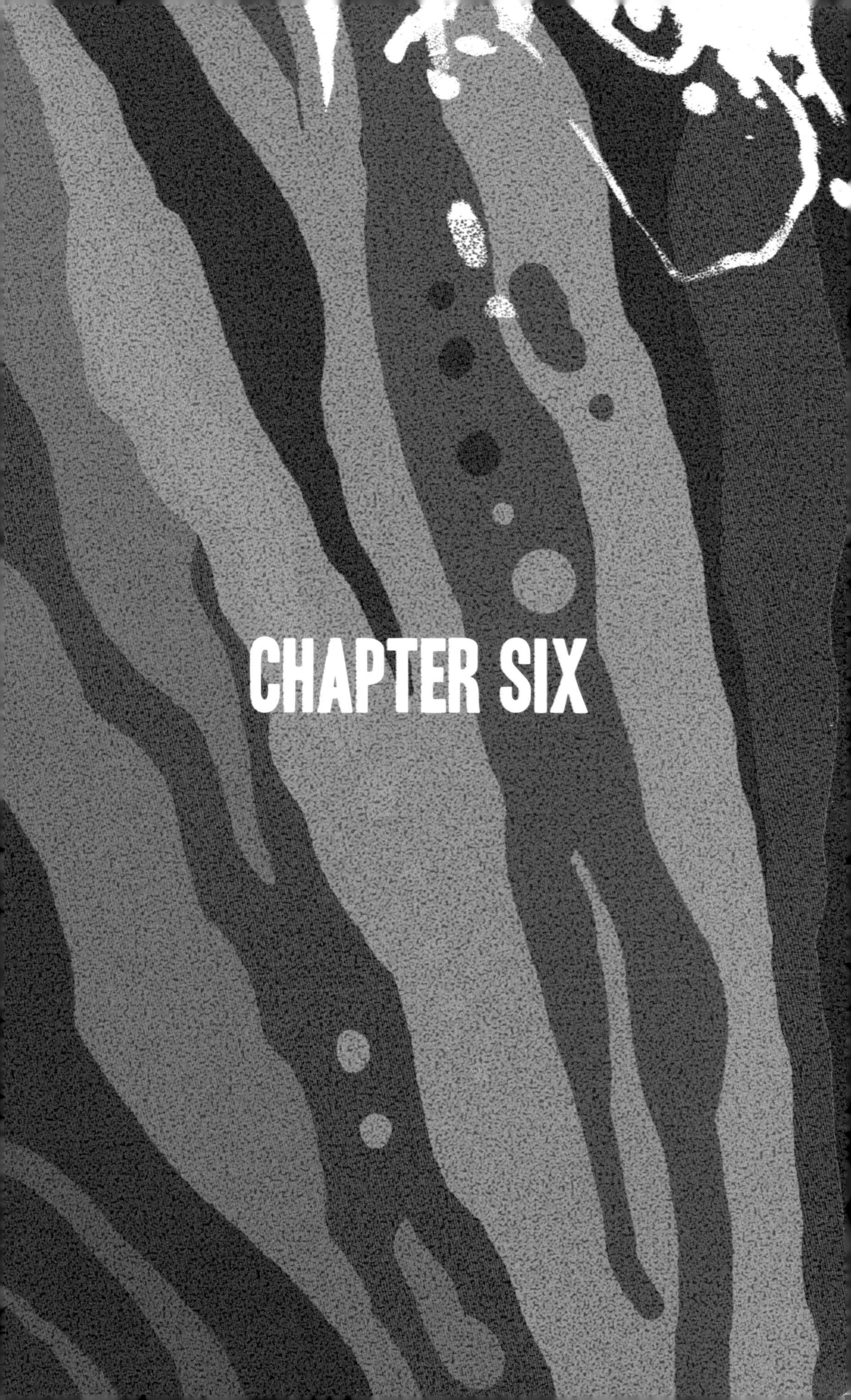
CHAPTER SIX

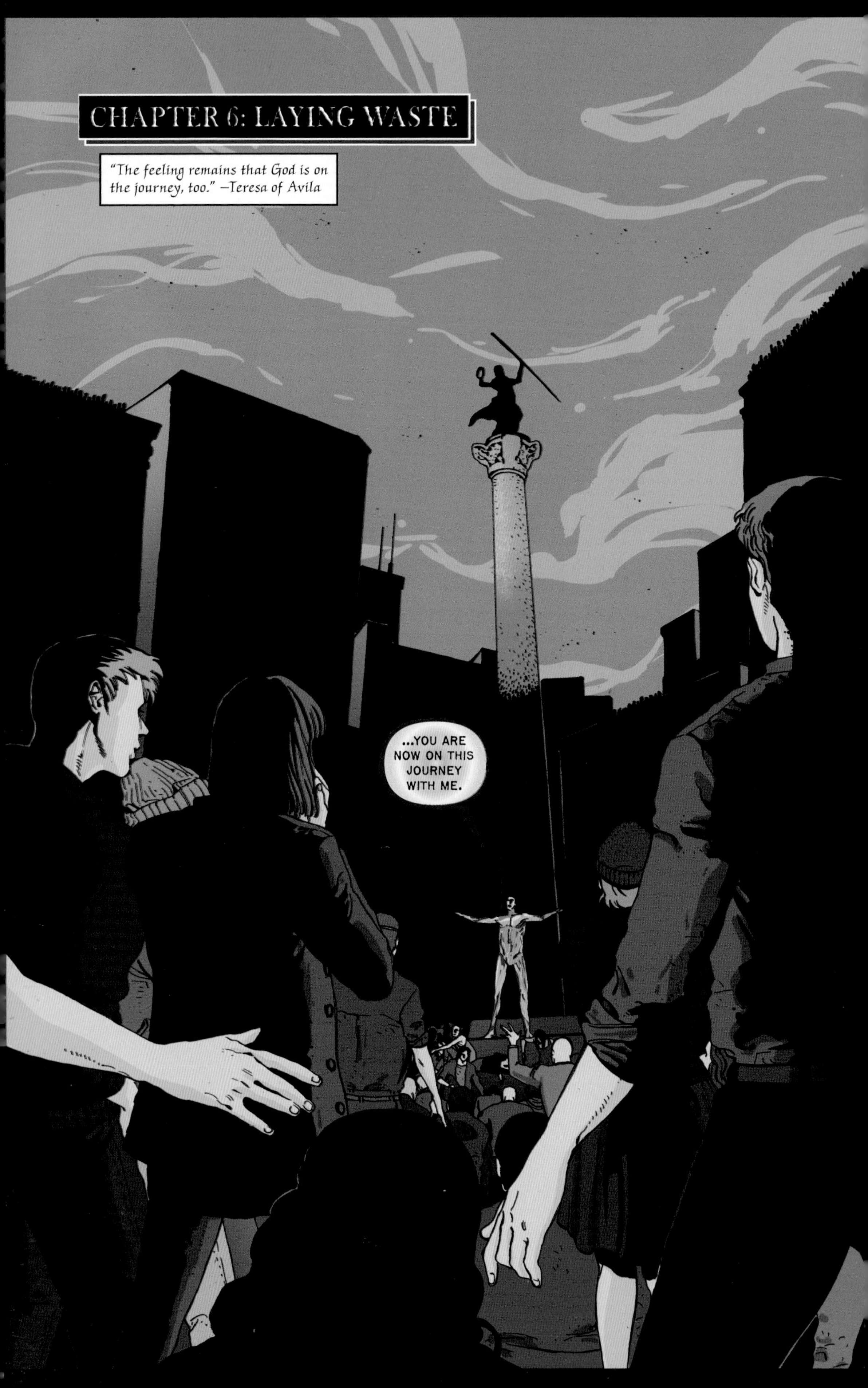
CHAPTER 6: LAYING WASTE
"The feeling remains that God is on the journey, too." —Teresa of Avila
...YOU ARE NOW ON THIS JOURNEY WITH ME.

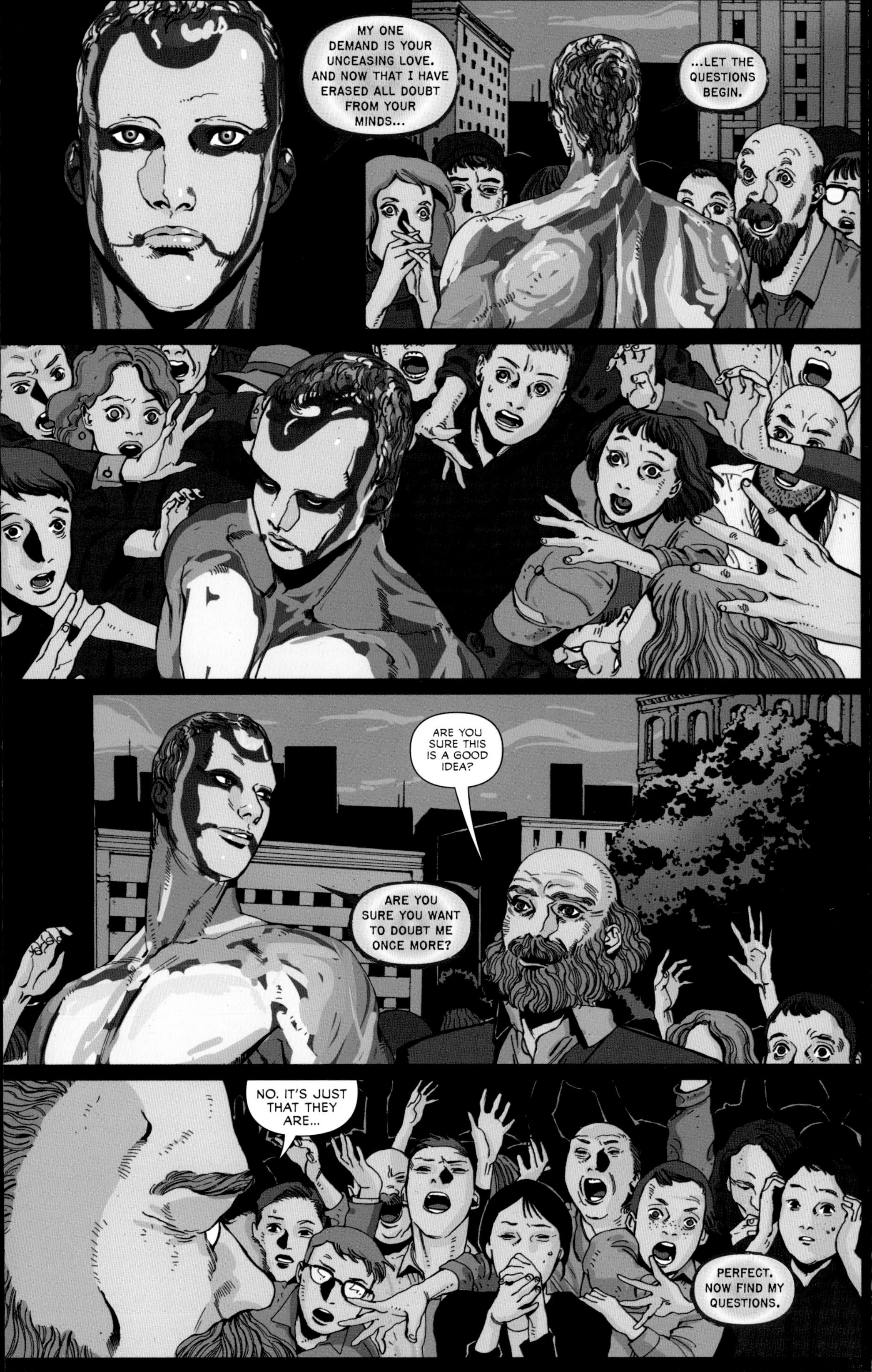
MY ONE DEMAND IS YOUR UNCEASING LOVE. AND NOW THAT I HAVE ERASED ALL DOUBT FROM YOUR MINDS...
...LET THE QUESTIONS BEGIN.
ARE YOU SURE THIS IS A GOOD IDEA?
ARE YOU SURE YOU WANT TO DOUBT ME ONCE MORE?
NO. IT'S JUST THAT THEY ARE...
PERFECT. NOW FIND MY QUESTIONS.

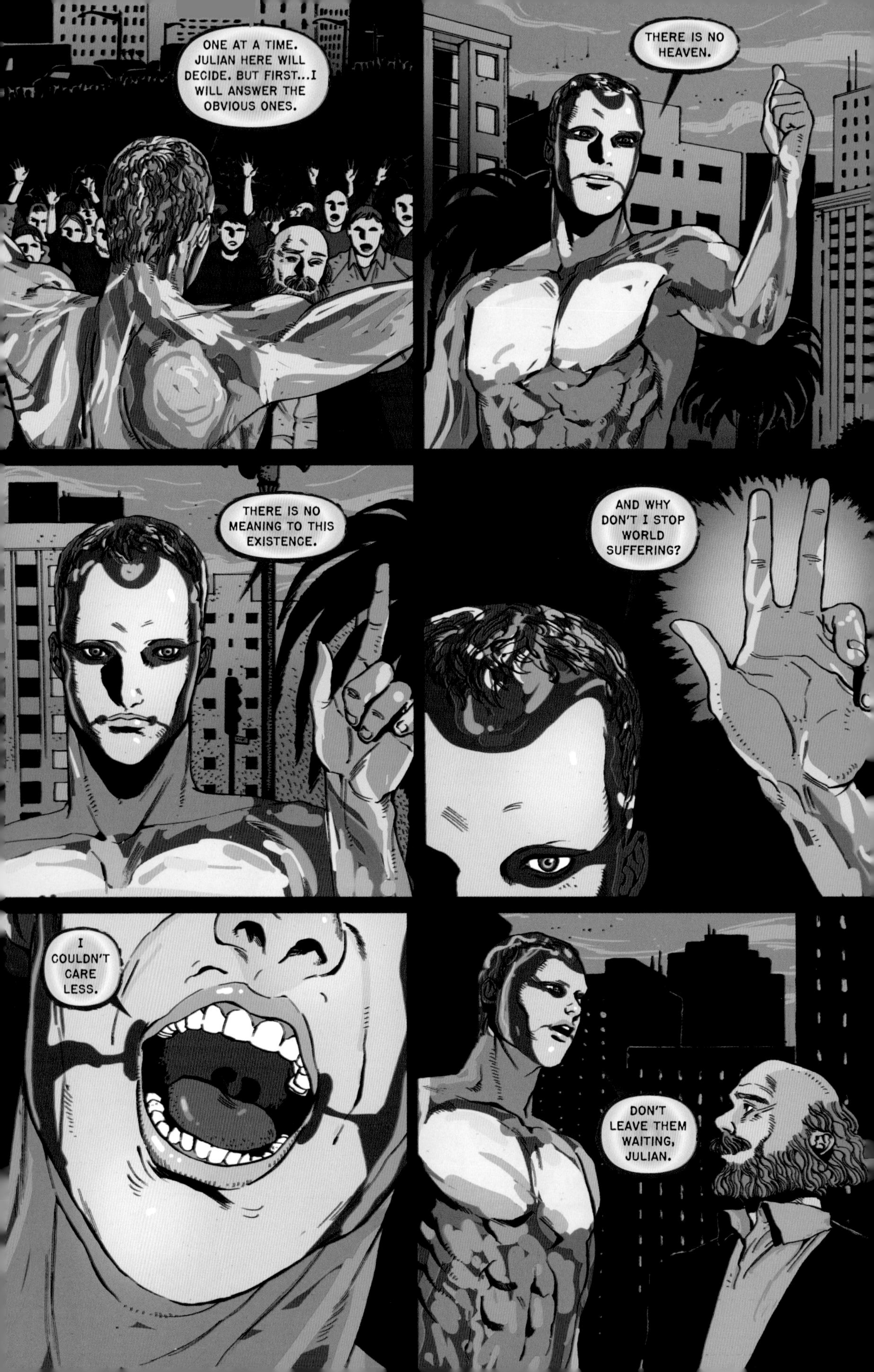
ONE AT A TIME. JULIAN HERE WILL DECIDE. BUT FIRST...I WILL ANSWER THE OBVIOUS ONES.
THERE IS NO HEAVEN.
THERE IS NO MEANING TO THIS EXISTENCE.
AND WHY DON'T I STOP WORLD SUFFERING?
I COULDN'T CARE LESS.
DON'T LEAVE THEM WAITING, JULIAN.

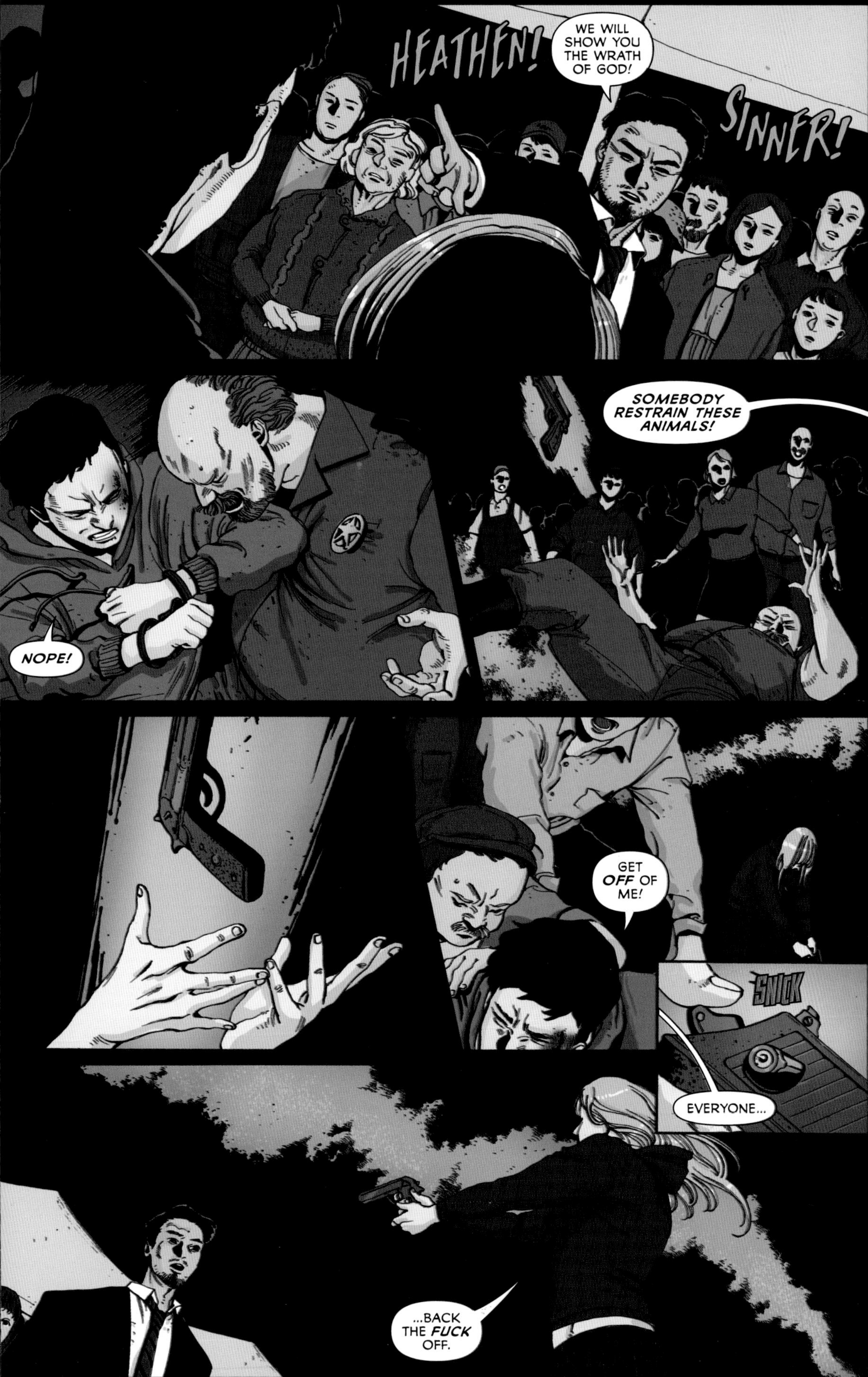
HEATHEN!
WE WILL SHOW YOU THE WRATH OF GOD!
SINNER!
NOPE!
SOMEBODY RESTRAIN THESE ANIMALS!
GET OFF OF ME!
SNICK
EVERYONE...
...BACK THE FUCK OFF.

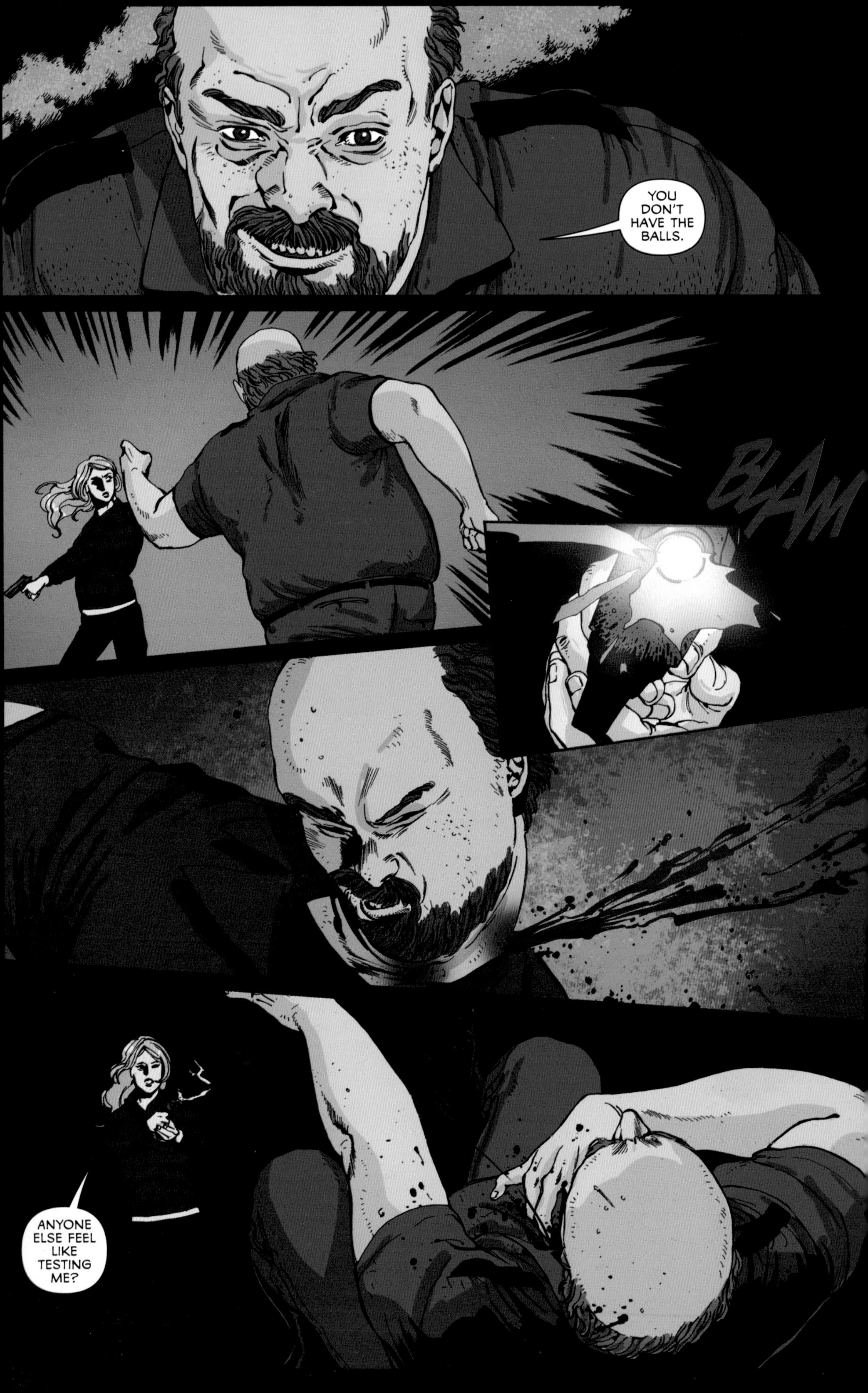
YOU DON'T HAVE THE BALLS.
BLAM
ANYONE ELSE FEEL LIKE TESTING ME?

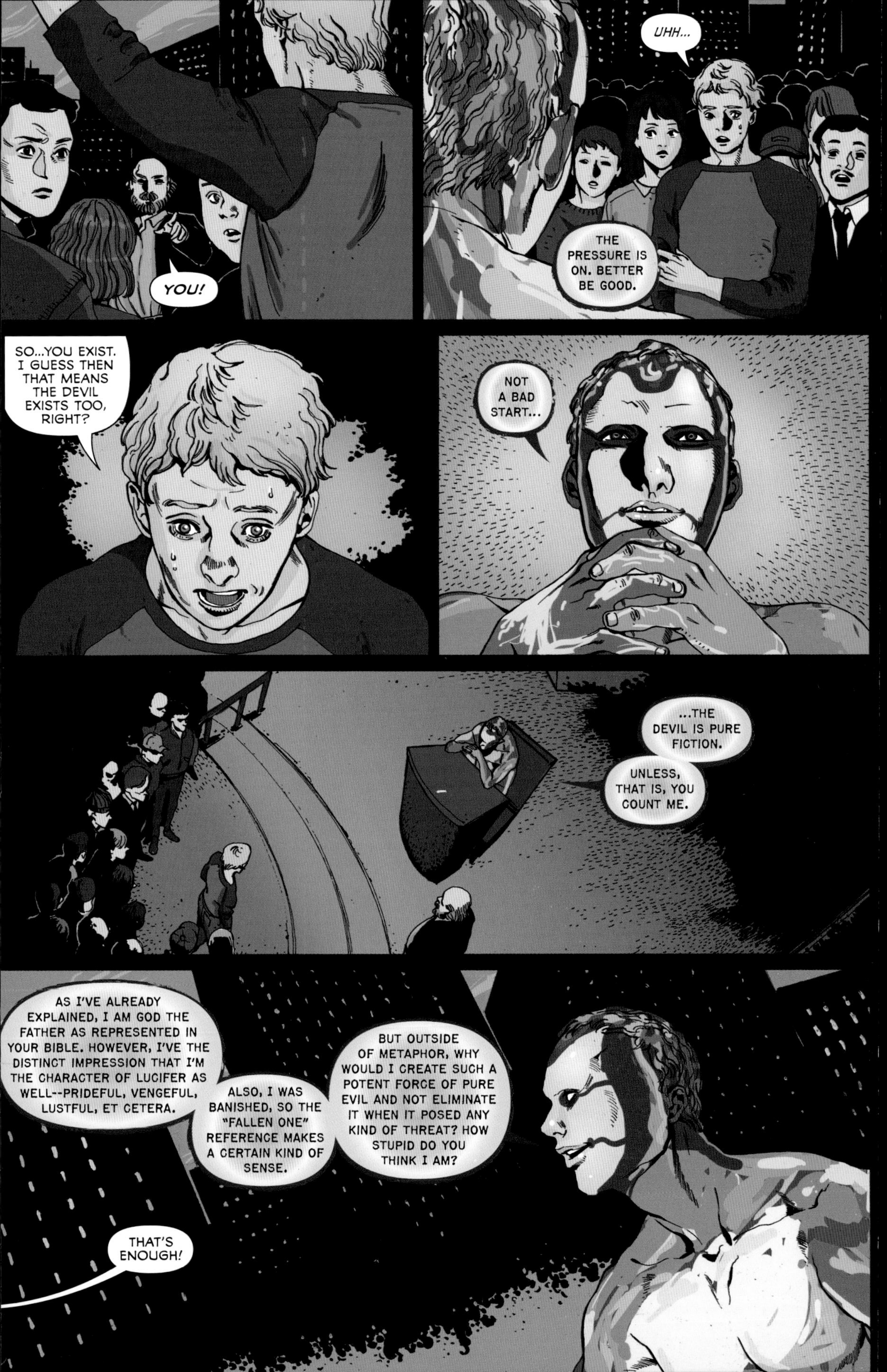
YOU!
UHH...
THE PRESSURE IS ON. BETTER BE GOOD.
SO...YOU EXIST. I GUESS THEN THAT MEANS THE DEVIL EXISTS TOO, RIGHT?
NOT A BAD START...
...THE DEVIL IS PURE FICTION.
UNLESS, THAT IS, YOU COUNT ME.
AS I'VE ALREADY EXPLAINED, I AM GOD THE FATHER AS REPRESENTED IN YOUR BIBLE. HOWEVER, I'VE THE DISTINCT IMPRESSION THAT I'M THE CHARACTER OF LUCIFER AS WELL--PRIDEFUL, VENGEFUL, LUSTFUL, ET CETERA.
ALSO, I WAS BANISHED, SO THE "FALLEN ONE" REFERENCE MAKES A CERTAIN KIND OF SENSE.
BUT OUTSIDE OF METAPHOR, WHY WOULD I CREATE SUCH A POTENT FORCE OF PURE EVIL AND NOT ELIMINATE IT WHEN IT POSED ANY KIND OF THREAT? HOW STUPID DO YOU THINK I AM?
THAT'S ENOUGH!

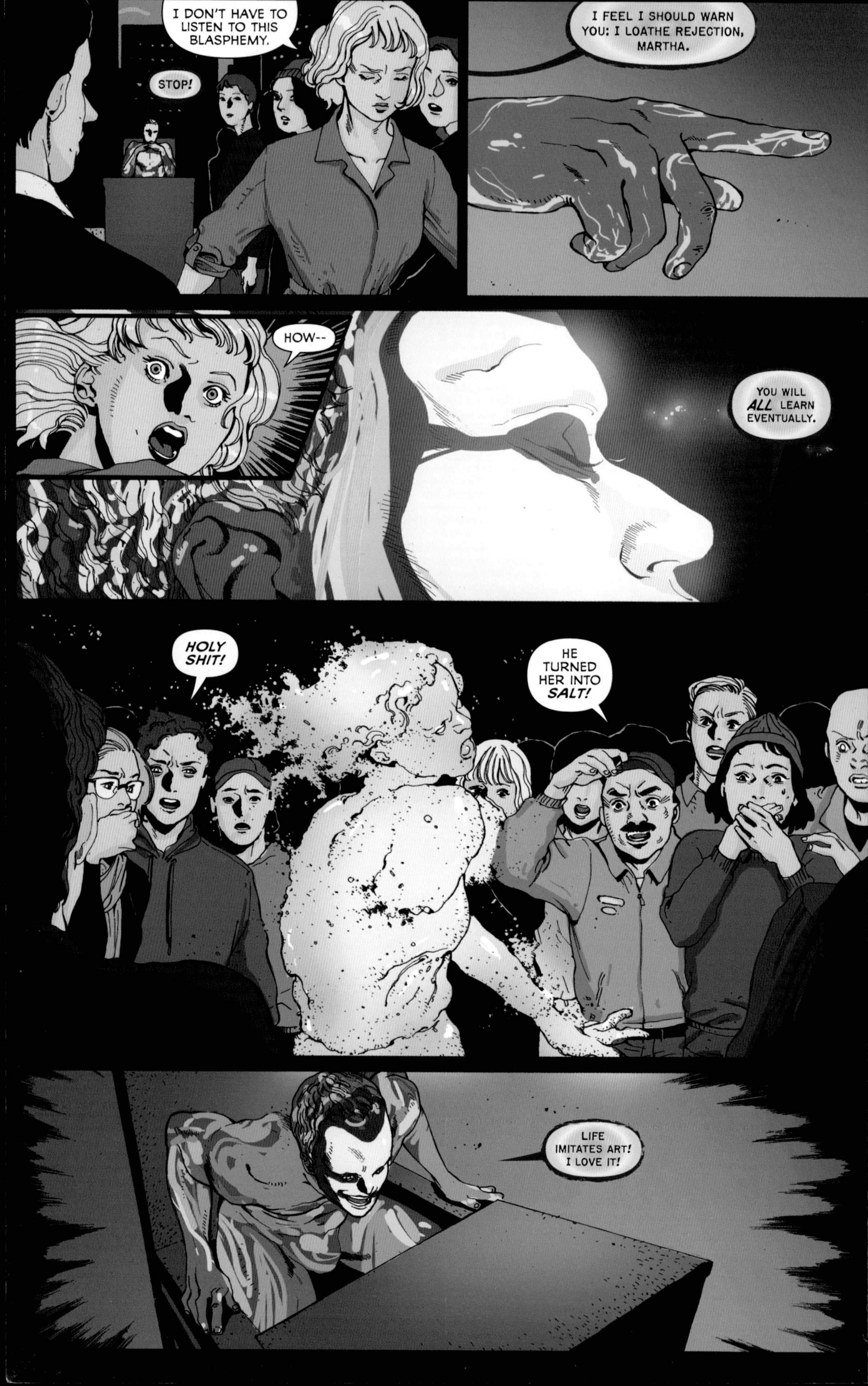
I DON'T HAVE TO LISTEN TO THIS BLASPHEMY.
STOP!
I FEEL I SHOULD WARN YOU: I LOATHE REJECTION, MARTHA.
HOW--
YOU WILL ALL LEARN EVENTUALLY.
HOLY SHIT!
HE TURNED HER INTO SALT!
LIFE IMITATES ART! I LOVE IT!

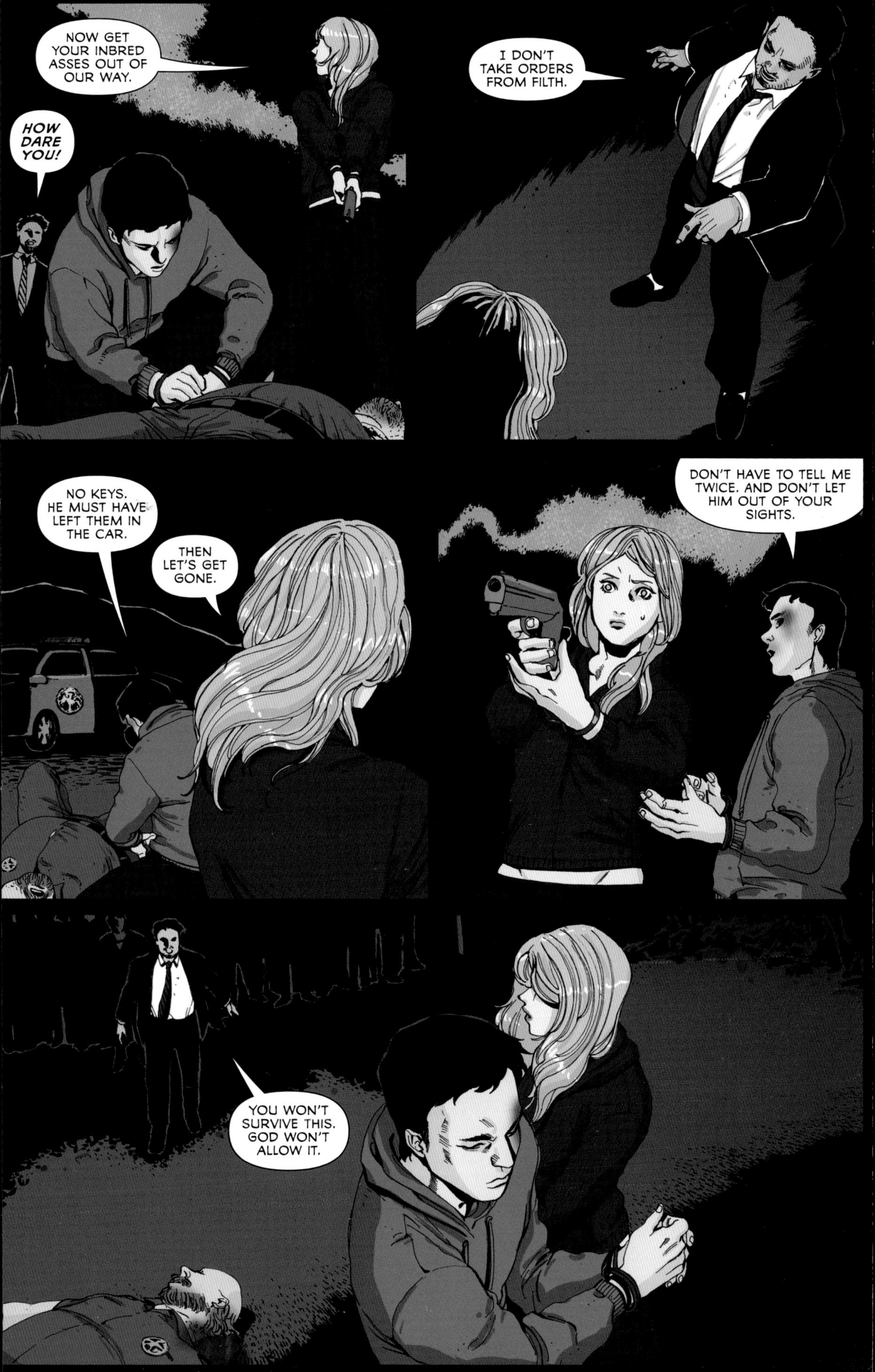
NOW GET YOUR INBRED ASSES OUT OF OUR WAY.
HOW DARE YOU!
I DON'T TAKE ORDERS FROM FILTH.
NO KEYS. HE MUST HAVE LEFT THEM IN THE CAR.
THEN LET'S GET GONE.
DON'T HAVE TO TELL ME TWICE. AND DON'T LET HIM OUT OF YOUR SIGHTS.
YOU WON'T SURVIVE THIS. GOD WON'T ALLOW IT.

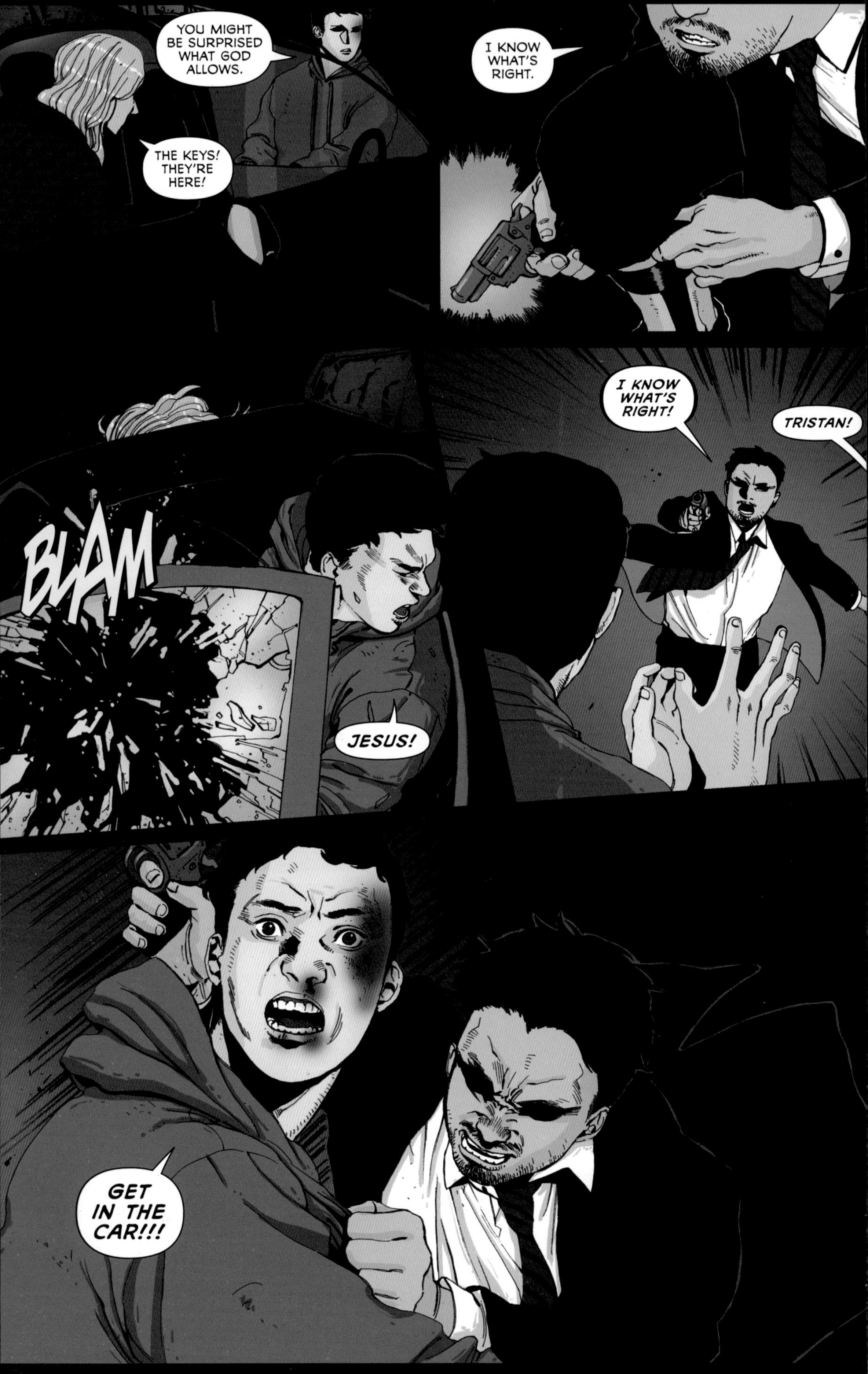
YOU MIGHT BE SURPRISED WHAT GOD ALLOWS.
THE KEYS! THEY'RE HERE!
I KNOW WHAT'S RIGHT.
BLAM
JESUS!
I KNOW WHAT'S RIGHT!
TRISTAN!
GET IN THE CAR!!!

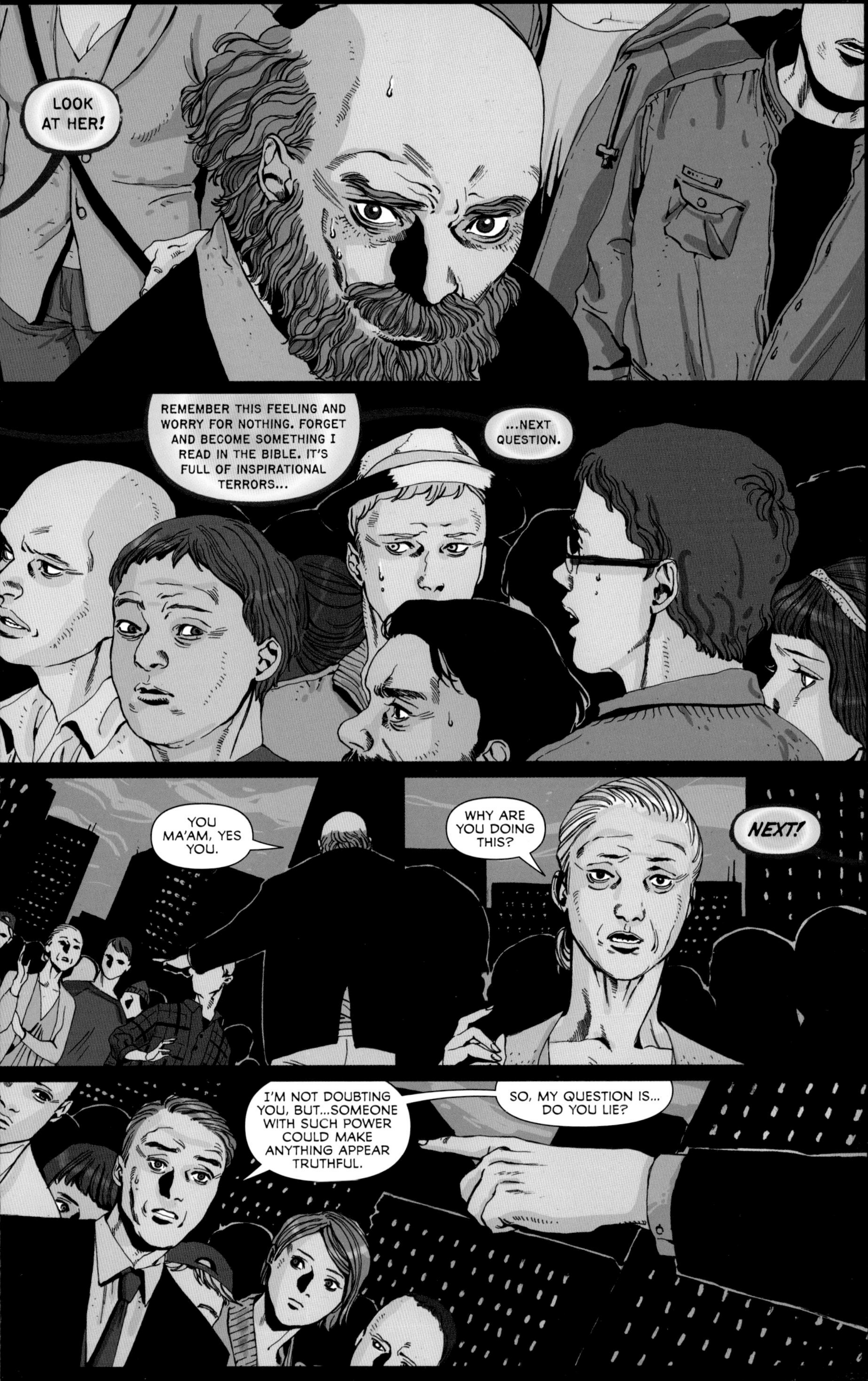
LOOK AT HER!
REMEMBER THIS FEELING AND WORRY FOR NOTHING. FORGET AND BECOME SOMETHING I READ IN THE BIBLE. IT'S FULL OF INSPIRATIONAL TERRORS...
...NEXT QUESTION.
YOU MA'AM, YES YOU.
WHY ARE YOU DOING THIS?
NEXT!
I'M NOT DOUBTING YOU, BUT...SOMEONE WITH SUCH POWER COULD MAKE ANYTHING APPEAR TRUTHFUL.
SO, MY QUESTION IS... DO YOU LIE?

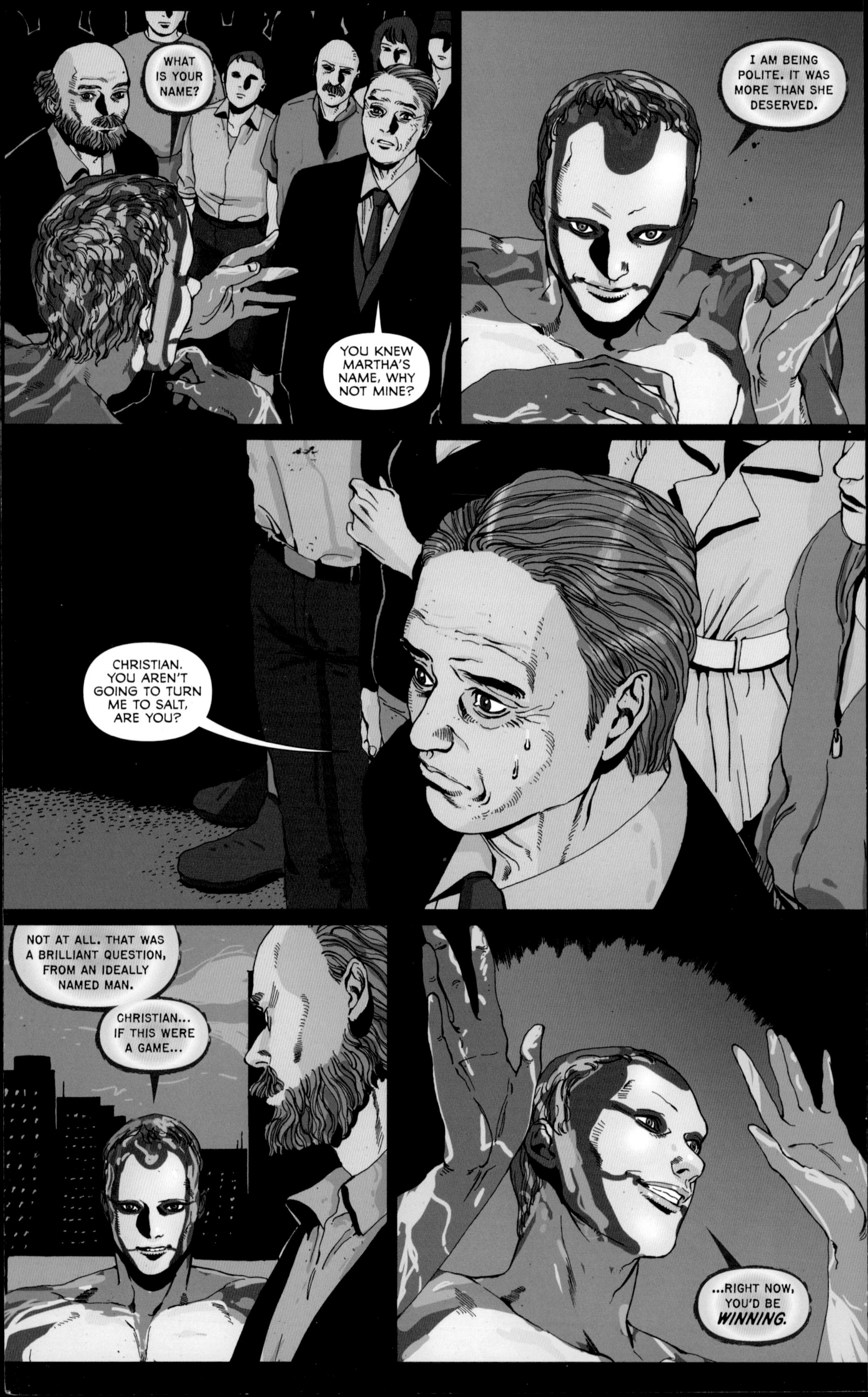
WHAT IS YOUR NAME?
YOU KNEW MARTHA'S NAME, WHY NOT MINE?
I AM BEING POLITE. IT WAS MORE THAN SHE DESERVED.
CHRISTIAN. YOU AREN'T GOING TO TURN ME TO SALT, ARE YOU?
NOT AT ALL. THAT WAS A BRILLIANT QUESTION, FROM AN IDEALLY NAMED MAN.
CHRISTIAN... IF THIS WERE A GAME...
...RIGHT NOW, YOU'D BE *WINNING.*

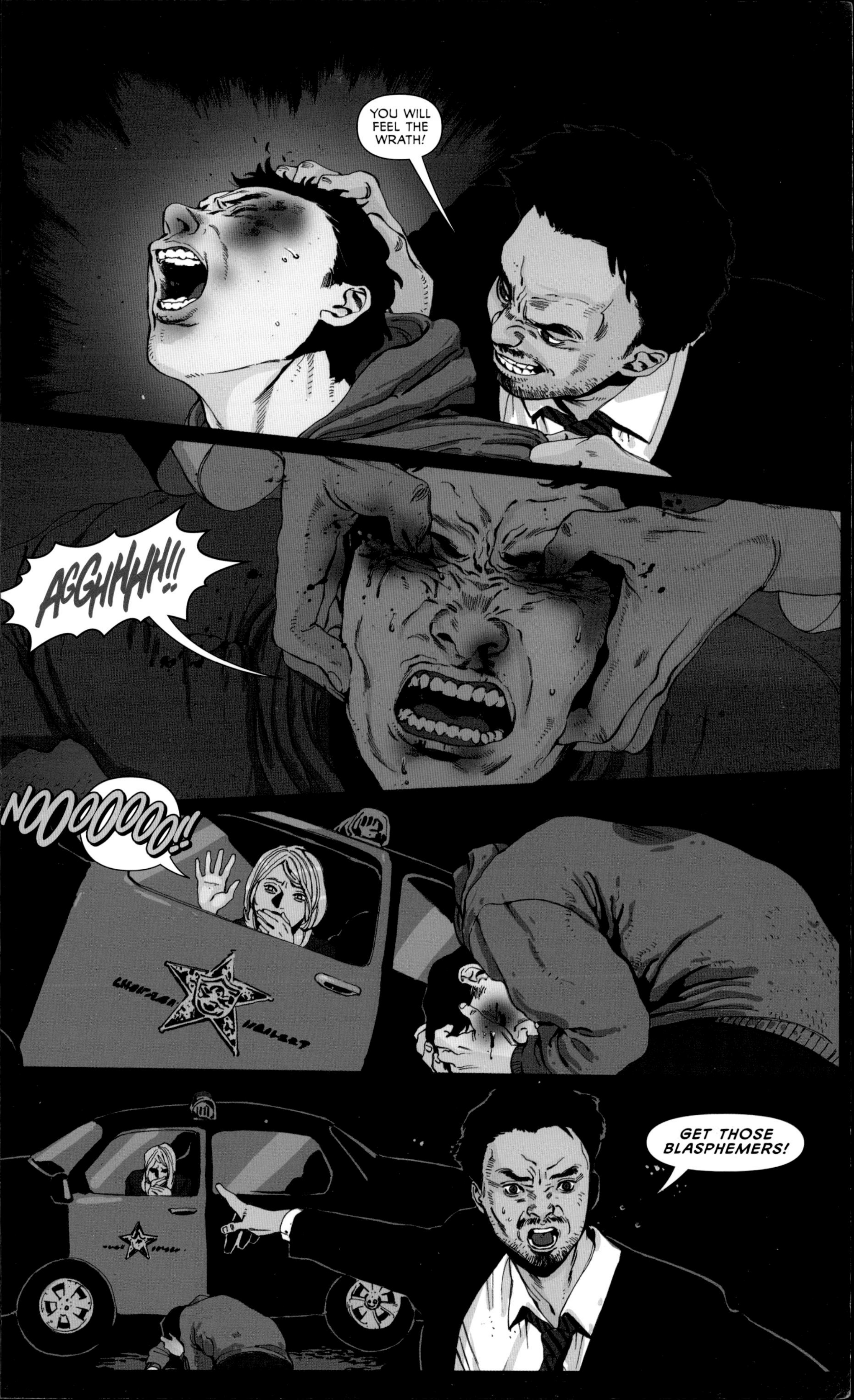
YOU WILL FEEL THE WRATH!
AGGHHHH!!
NOOOOOOO!!
GET THOSE BLASPHEMERS!

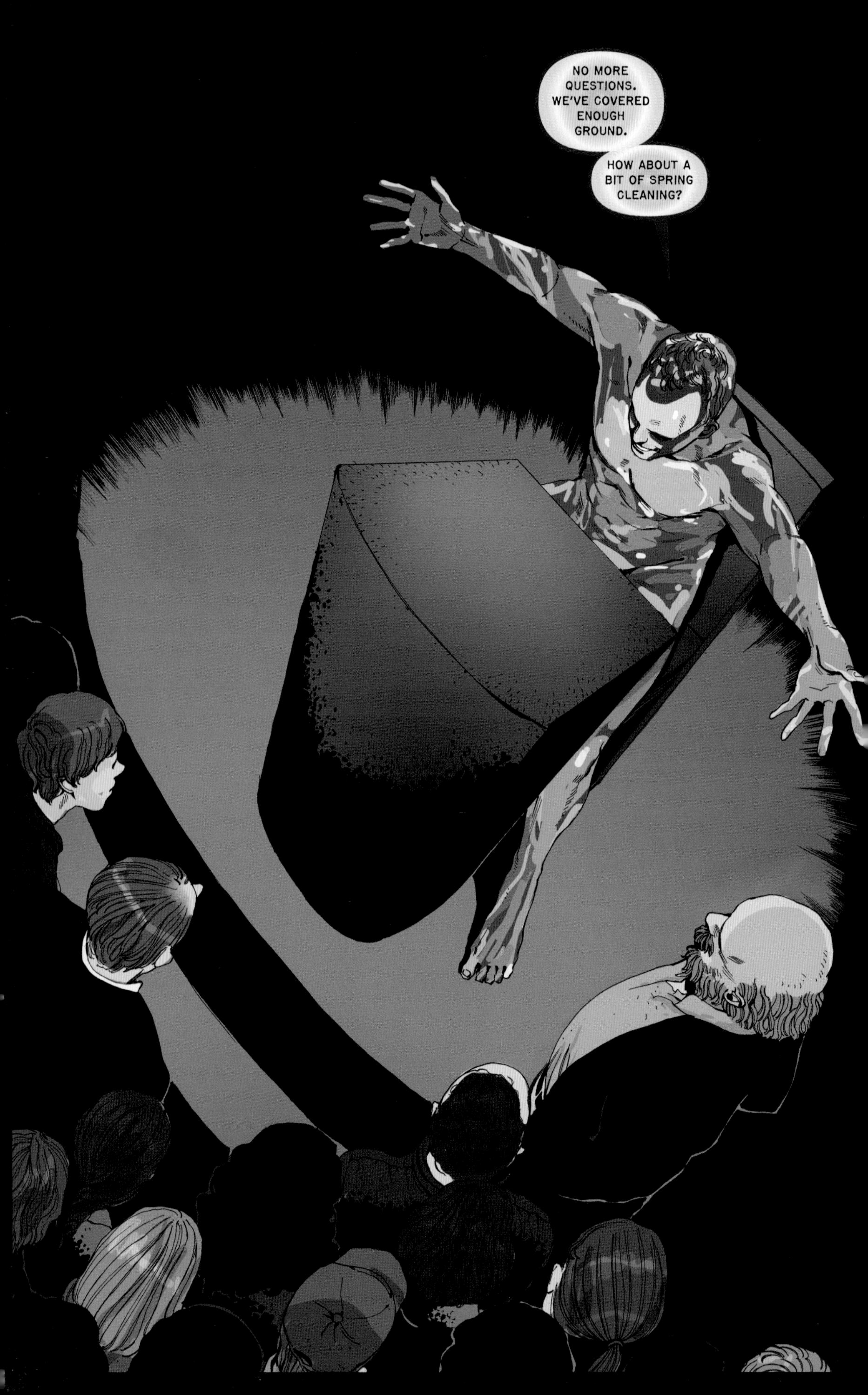
NO MORE QUESTIONS. WE'VE COVERED ENOUGH GROUND.
HOW ABOUT A BIT OF SPRING CLEANING?

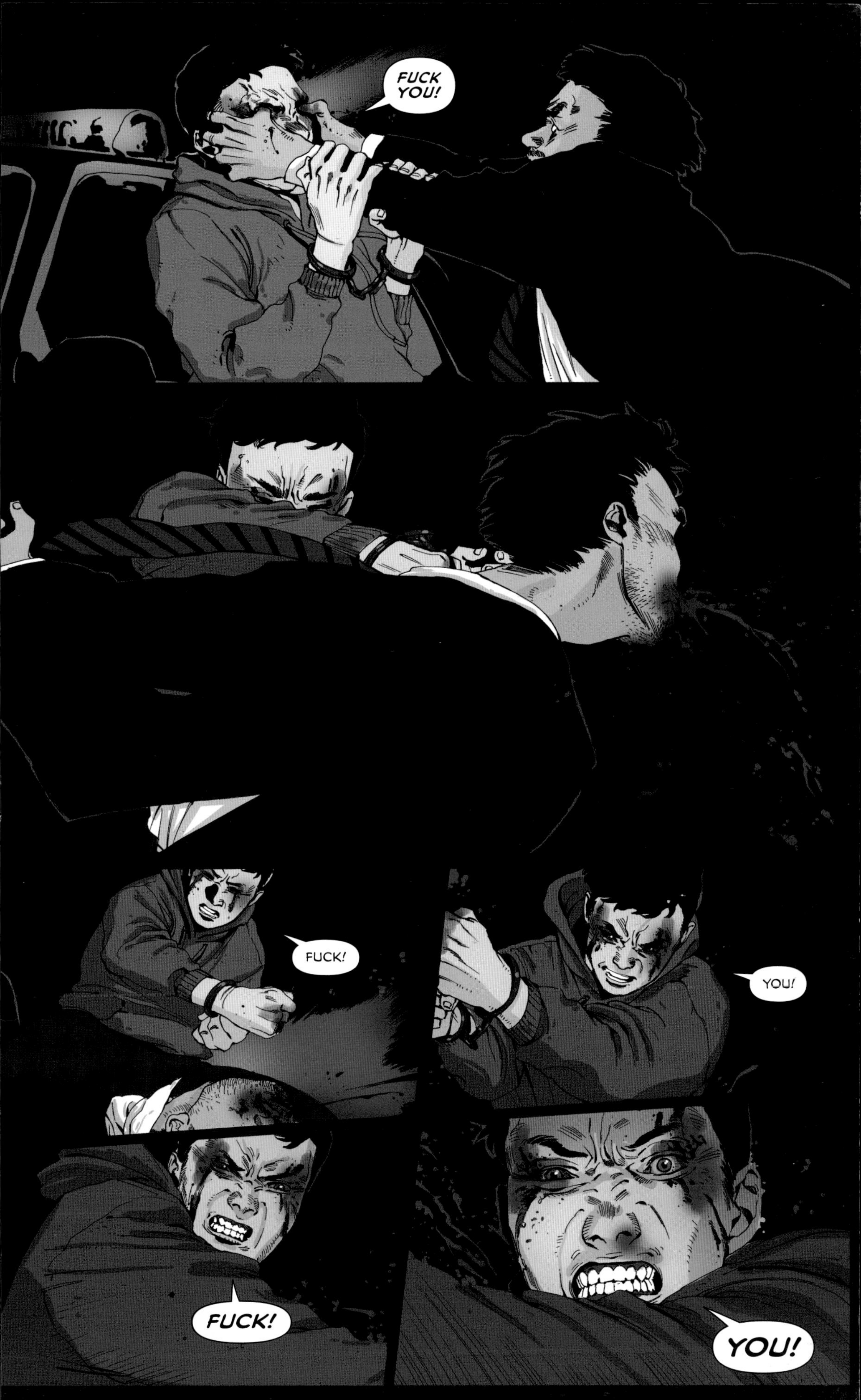
FUCK YOU!
FUCK!
YOU!
FUCK!
YOU!

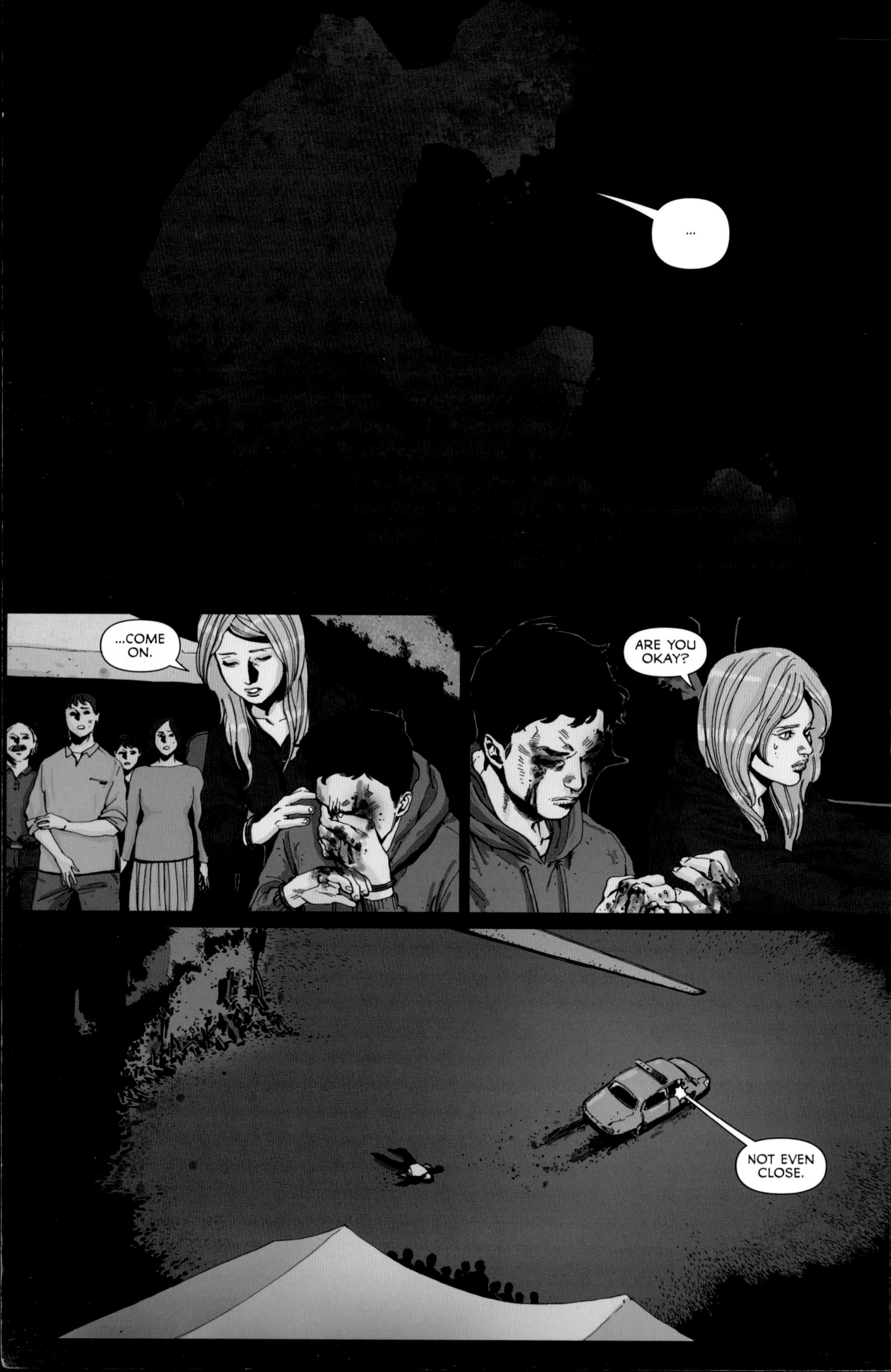
...
...COME ON.
ARE YOU OKAY?
NOT EVEN CLOSE.

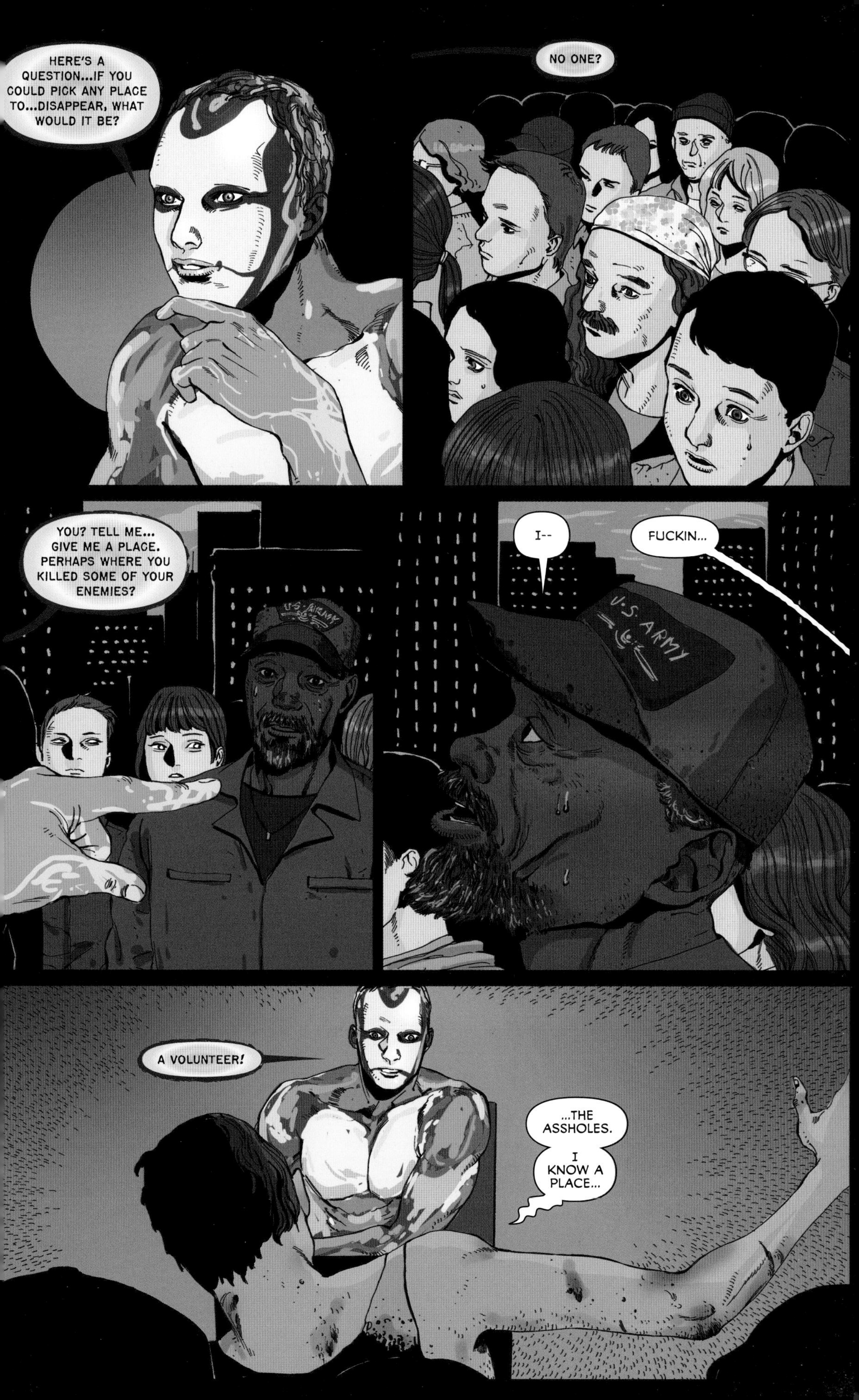
HERE'S A QUESTION...IF YOU COULD PICK ANY PLACE TO...DISAPPEAR, WHAT WOULD IT BE?
NO ONE?
YOU? TELL ME... GIVE ME A PLACE. PERHAPS WHERE YOU KILLED SOME OF YOUR ENEMIES?
U.S. ARMY
I--
FUCKIN...
U.S. ARMY
A VOLUNTEER!
...THE ASSHOLES.
I KNOW A PLACE...

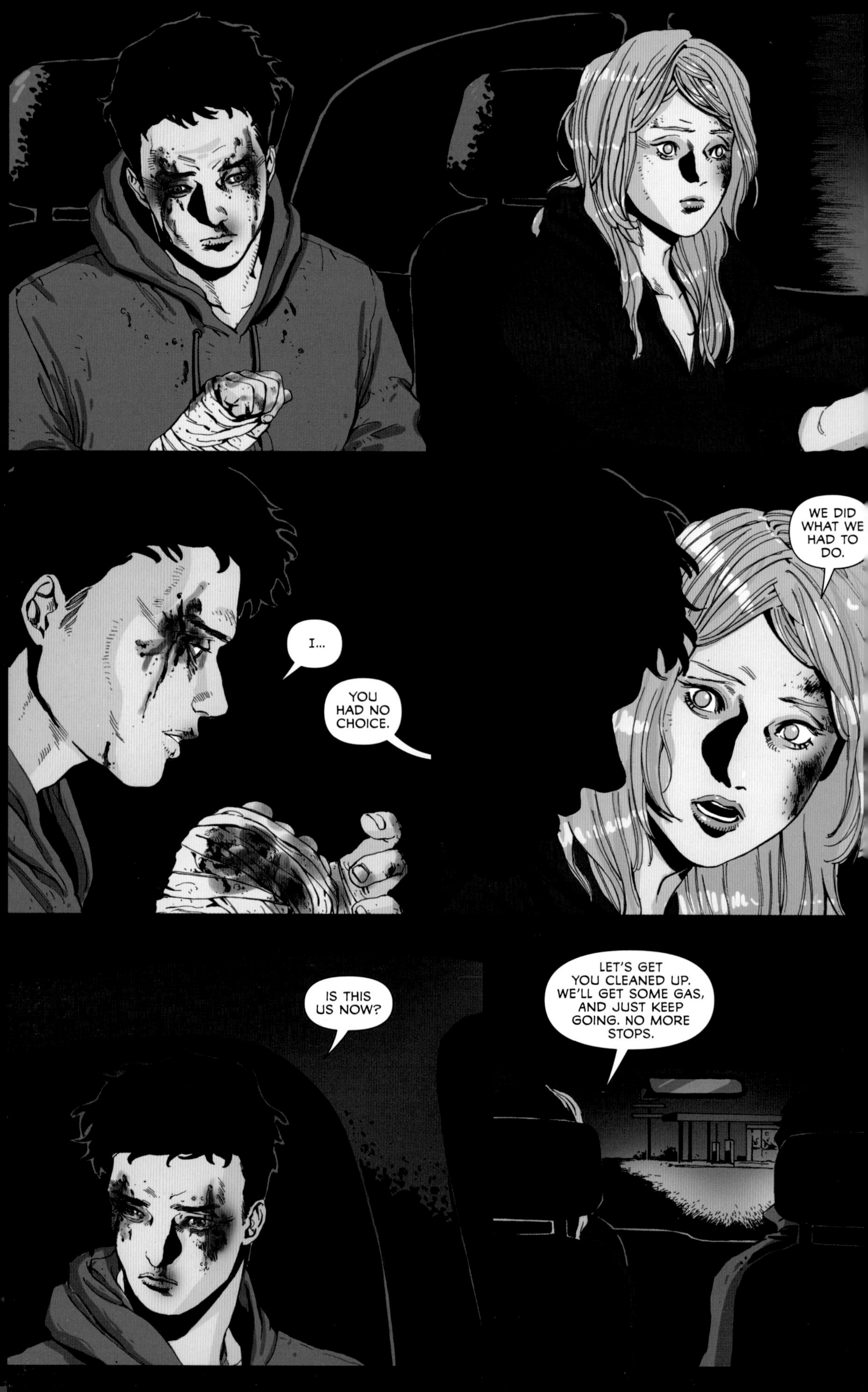
I...
YOU HAD NO CHOICE.
WE DID WHAT WE HAD TO DO.
IS THIS US NOW?
LET'S GET YOU CLEANED UP. WE'LL GET SOME GAS, AND JUST KEEP GOING. NO MORE STOPS.

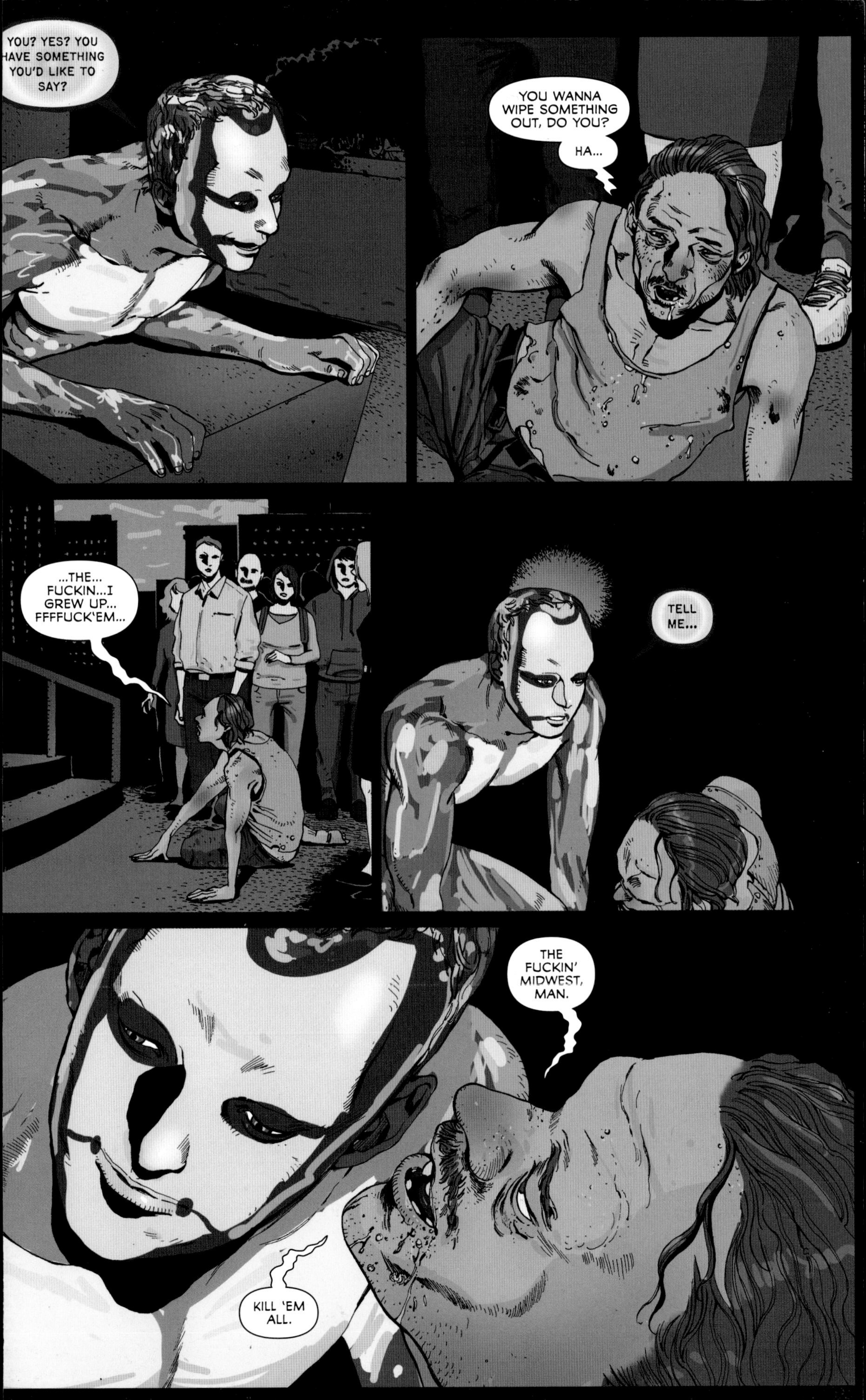
YOU? YES? YOU HAVE SOMETHING YOU'D LIKE TO SAY?
YOU WANNA WIPE SOMETHING OUT, DO YOU?
HA...
...THE... FUCKIN...I GREW UP... FFFFUCK'EM...
TELL ME...
THE FUCKIN' MIDWEST, MAN.
KILL 'EM ALL.

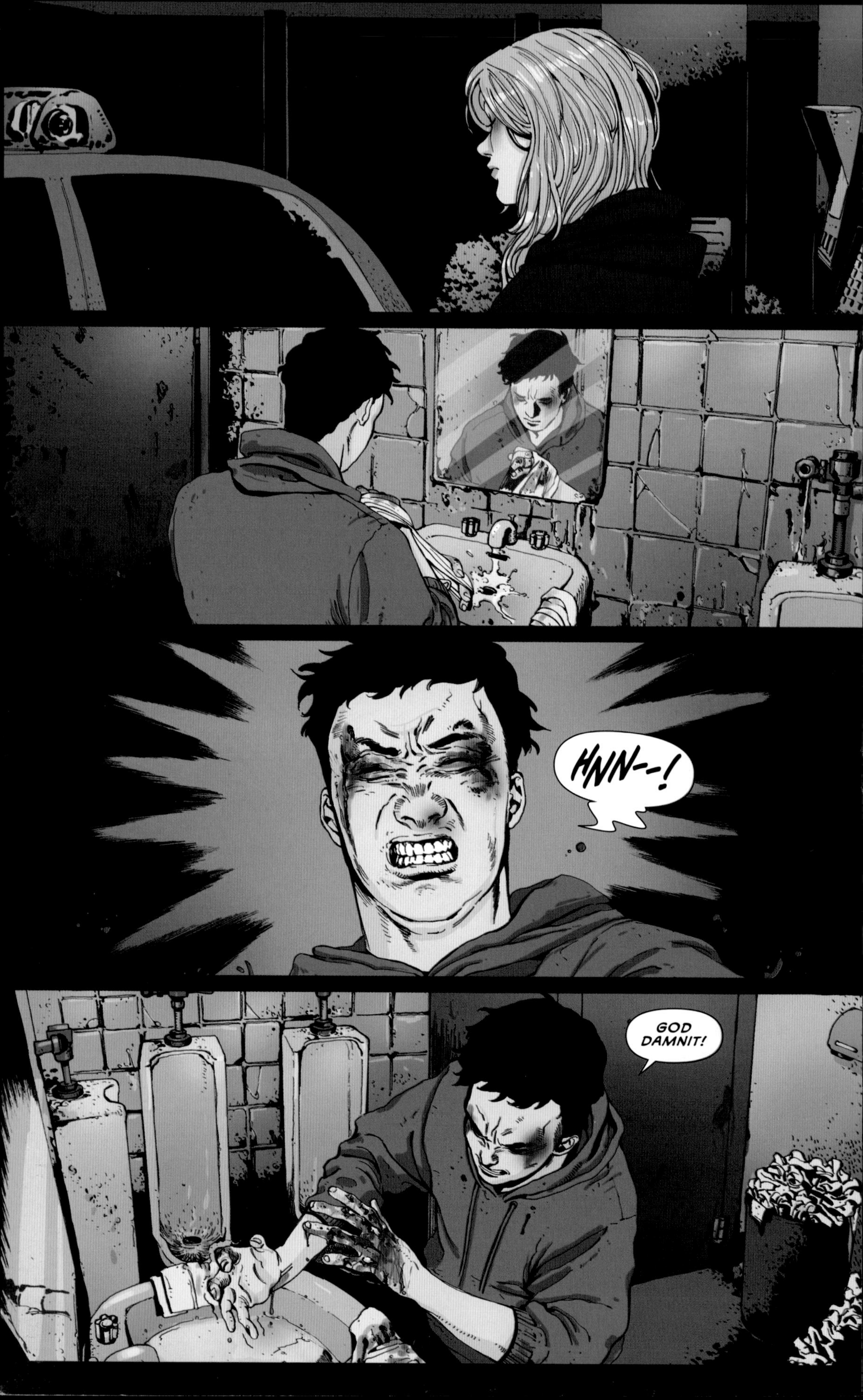
HNN--!
GOD DAMNIT!

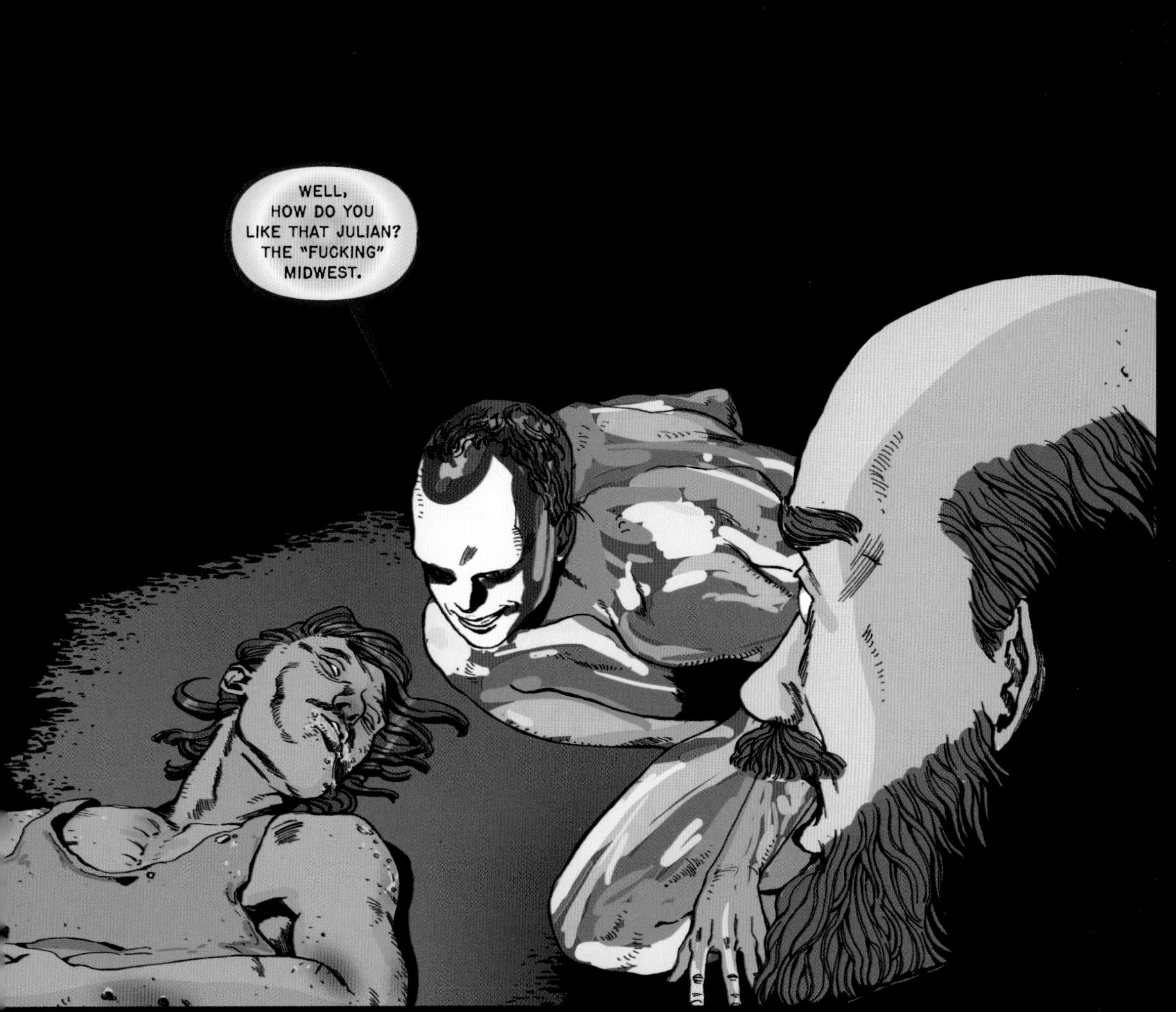
WELL, HOW DO YOU LIKE THAT JULIAN? THE "FUCKING" MIDWEST.

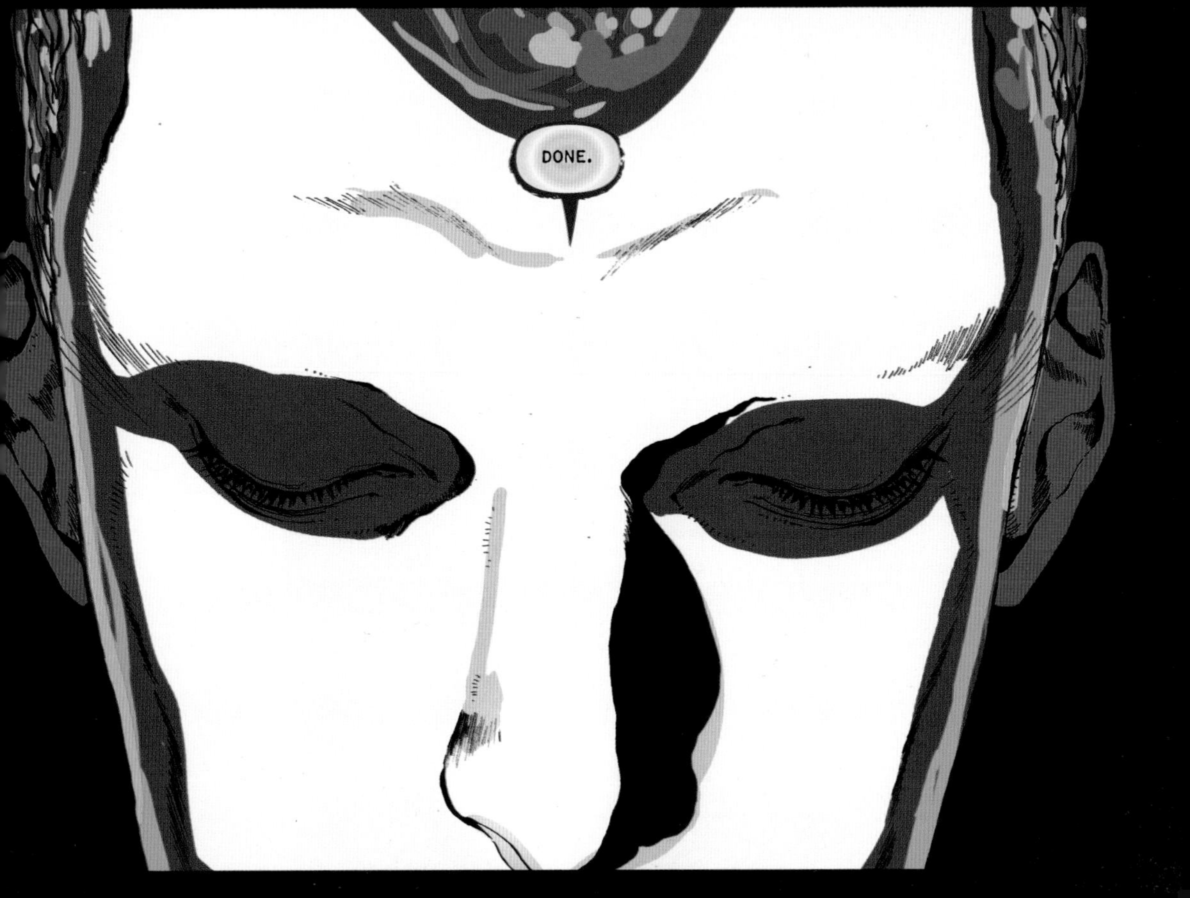
DONE.

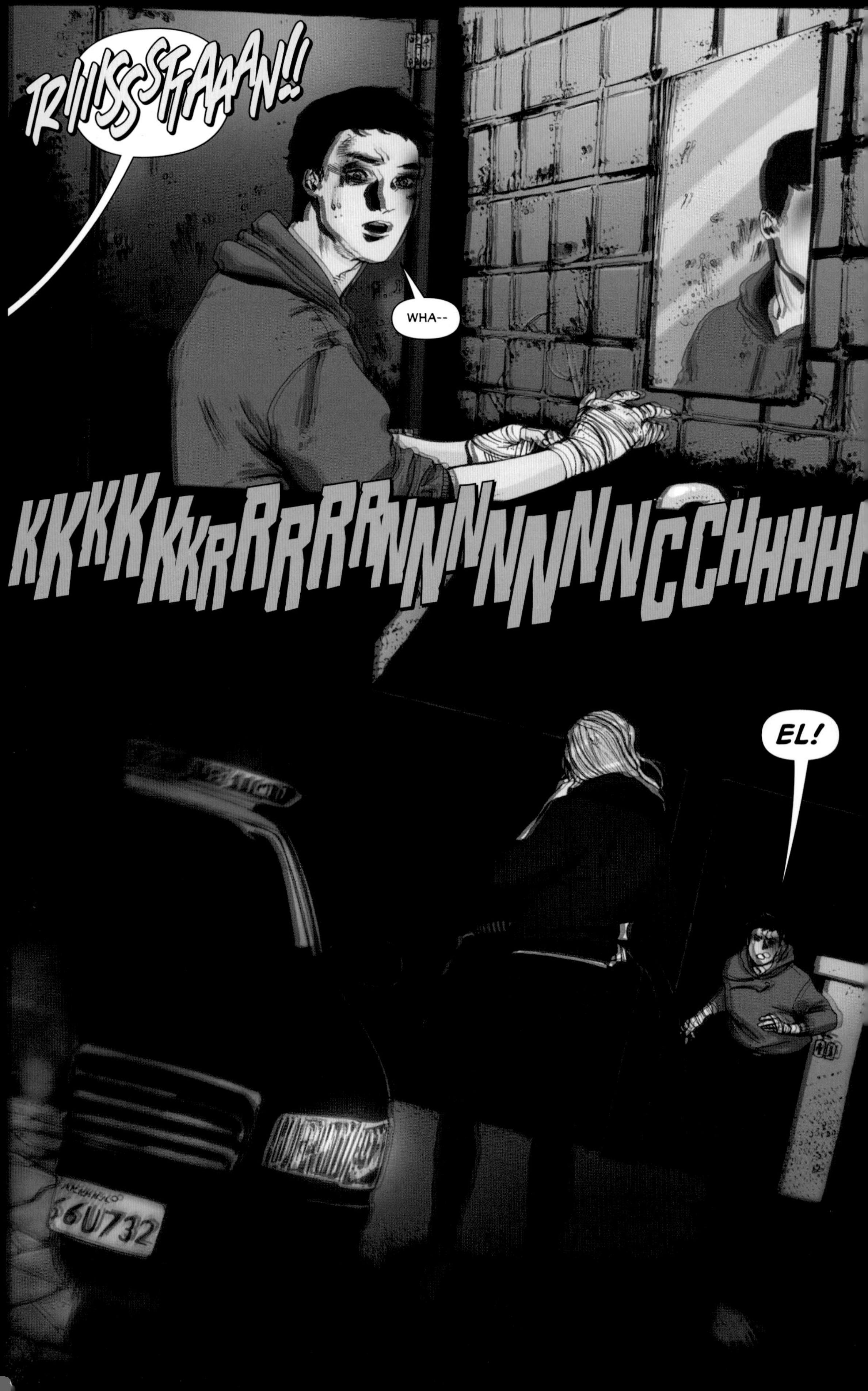
TRIIISSSHAAAN!!
WHA--
KKKKKKRRRRRNNNNNNNNCCHHHH
EL!

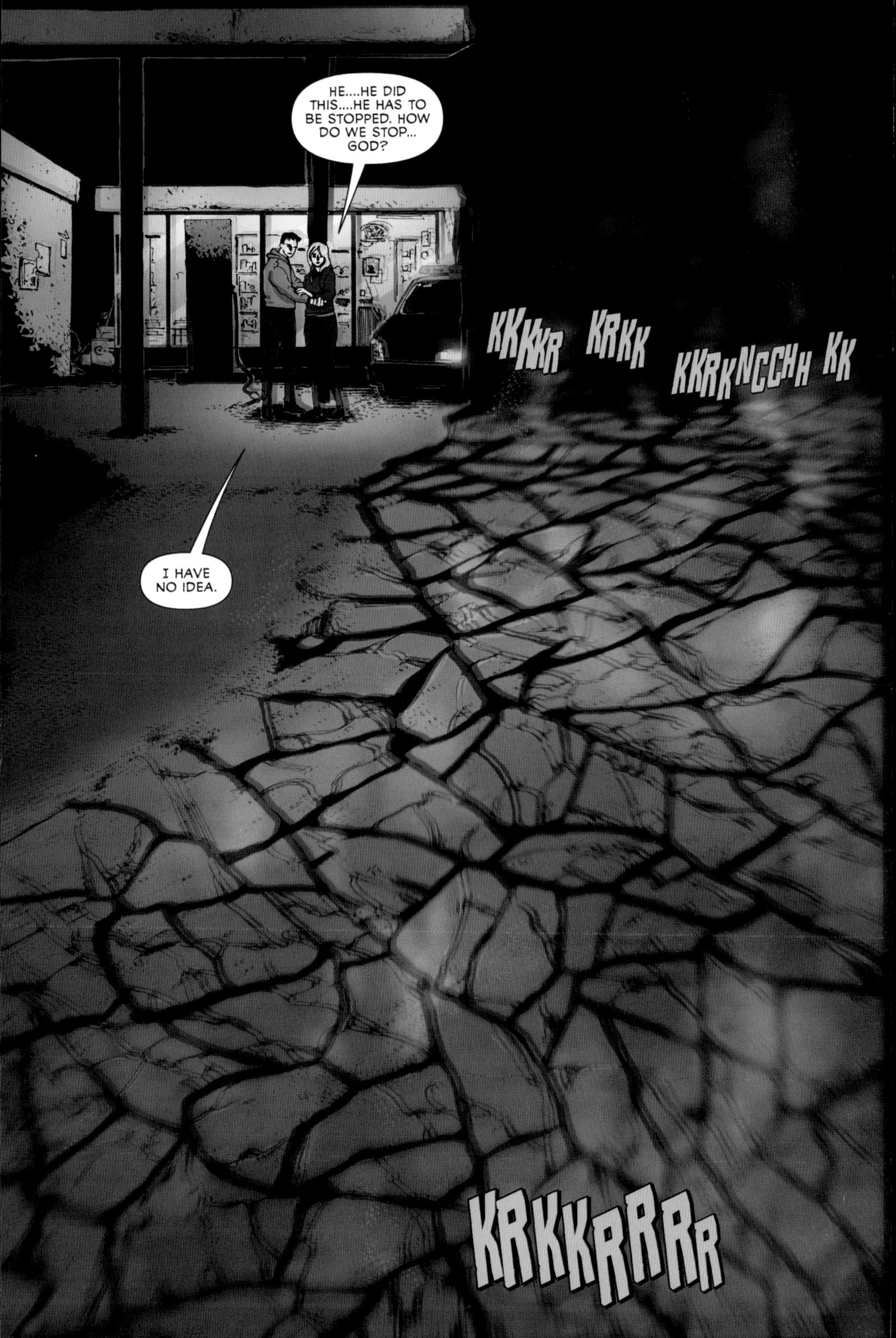
HE....HE DID THIS....HE HAS TO BE STOPPED. HOW DO WE STOP... GOD?
I HAVE NO IDEA.
KKKKR KRKK KKRKNCCHH KK
KRKKRRRR

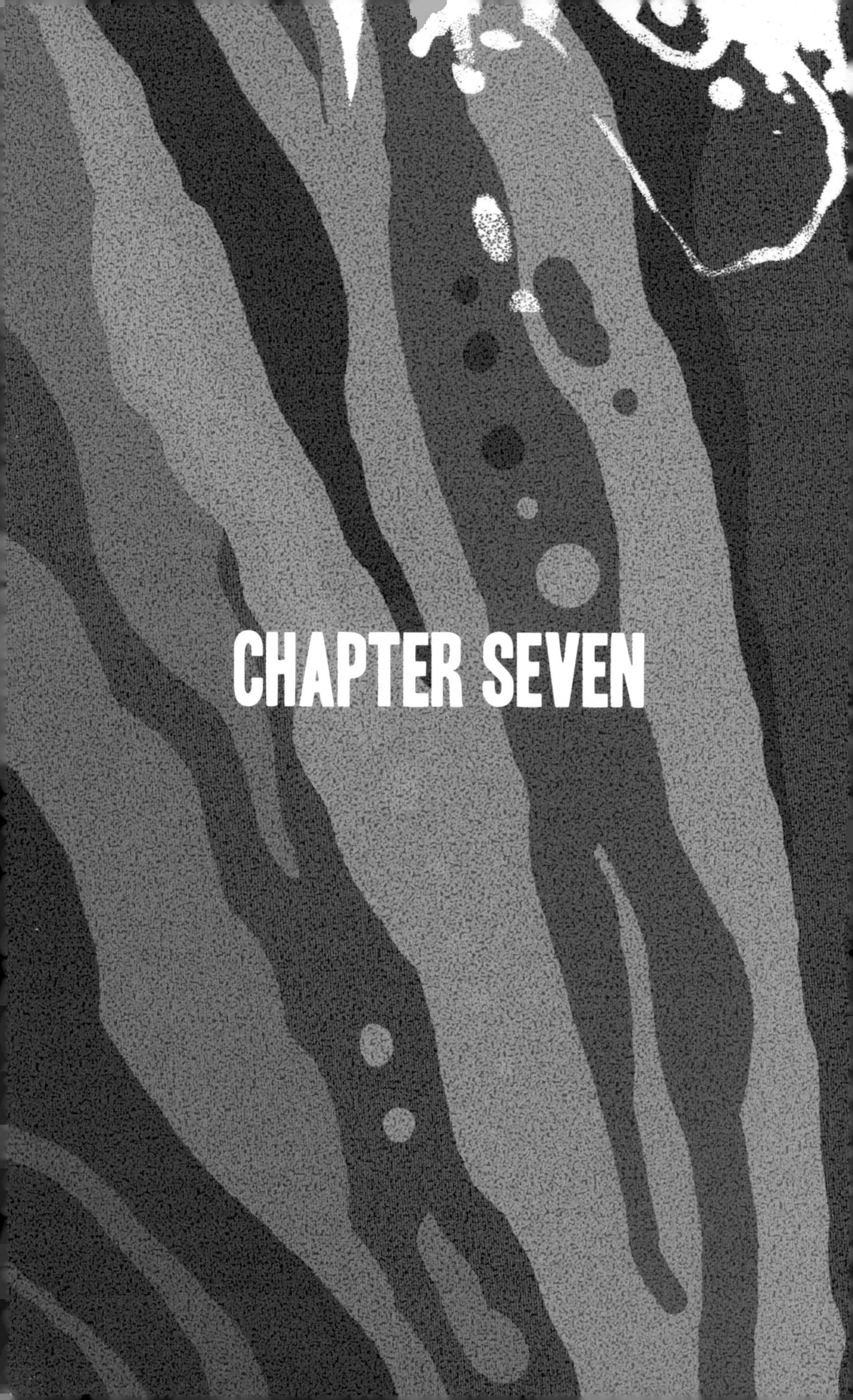

CHAPTER SEVEN

CHAPTER 7: VICIOUS CYCLES

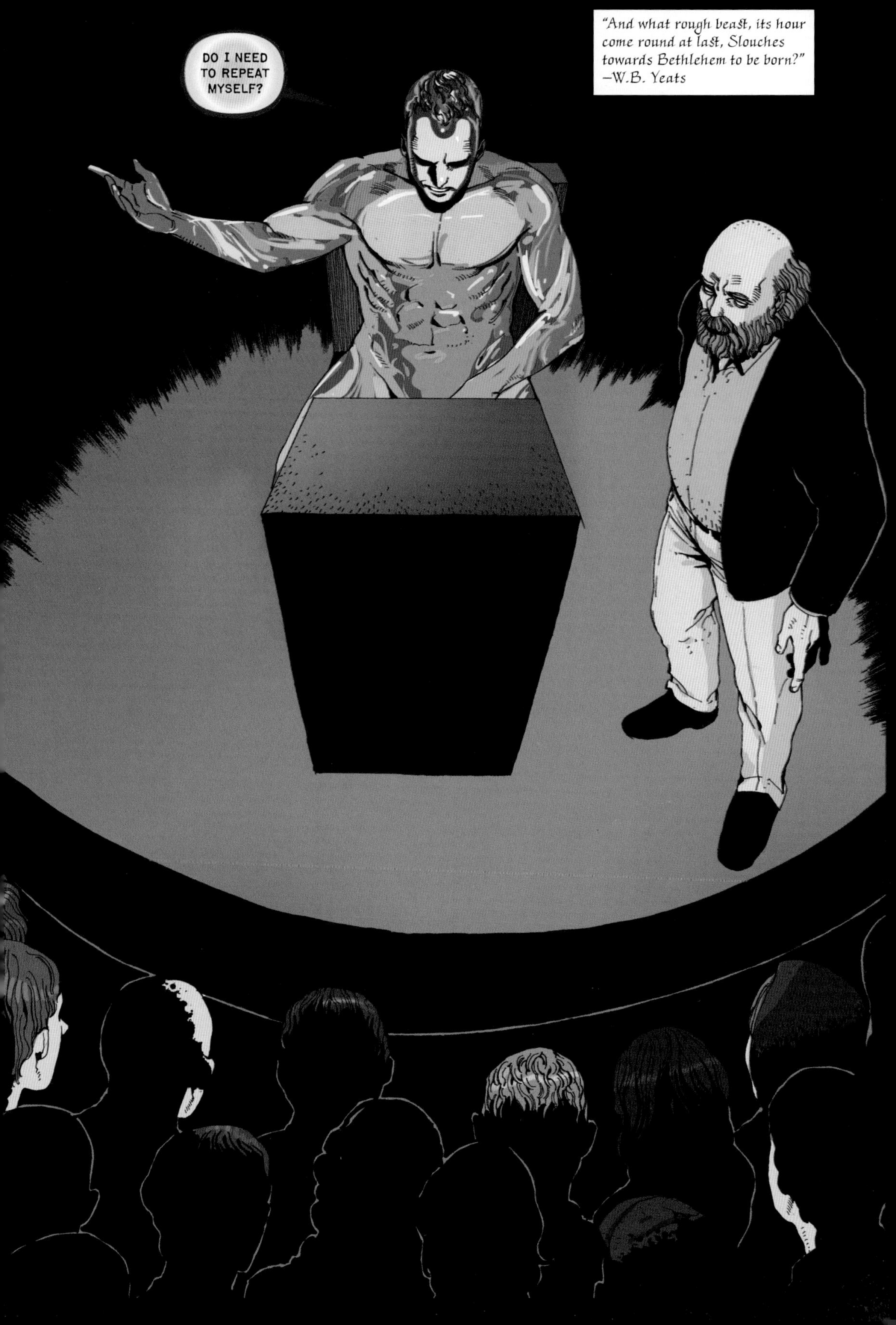
"And what rough beast, its hour come round at last, Slouches towards Bethlehem to be born?" —W.B. Yeats
DO I NEED TO REPEAT MYSELF?

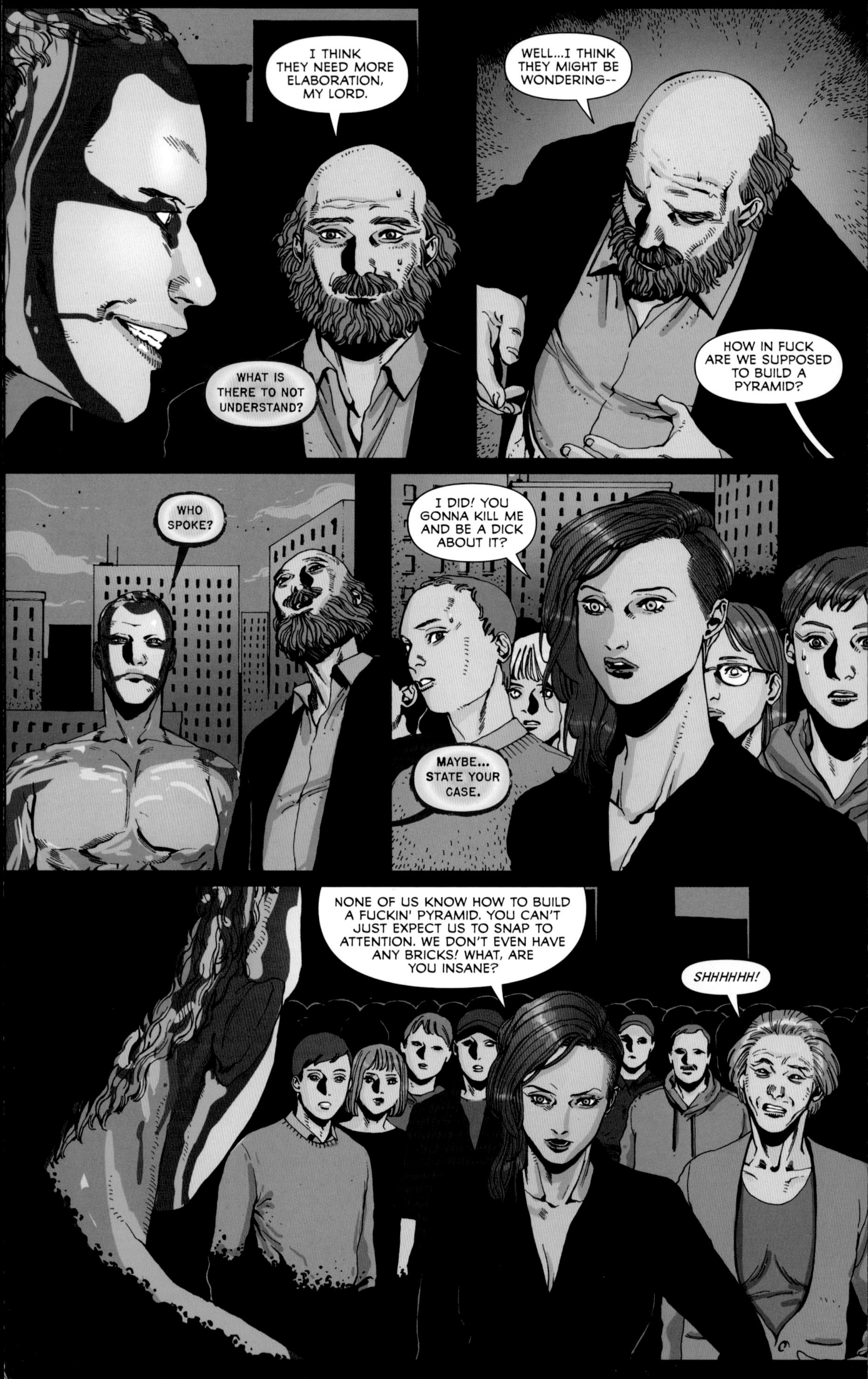
I THINK THEY NEED MORE ELABORATION, MY LORD.
WHAT IS THERE TO NOT UNDERSTAND?
WELL...I THINK THEY MIGHT BE WONDERING--
HOW IN FUCK ARE WE SUPPOSED TO BUILD A PYRAMID?
WHO SPOKE?
I DID! YOU GONNA KILL ME AND BE A DICK ABOUT IT?
MAYBE... STATE YOUR CASE.
NONE OF US KNOW HOW TO BUILD A FUCKIN' PYRAMID. YOU CAN'T JUST EXPECT US TO SNAP TO ATTENTION. WE DON'T EVEN HAVE ANY BRICKS! WHAT, ARE YOU INSANE?
SHHHHHH!

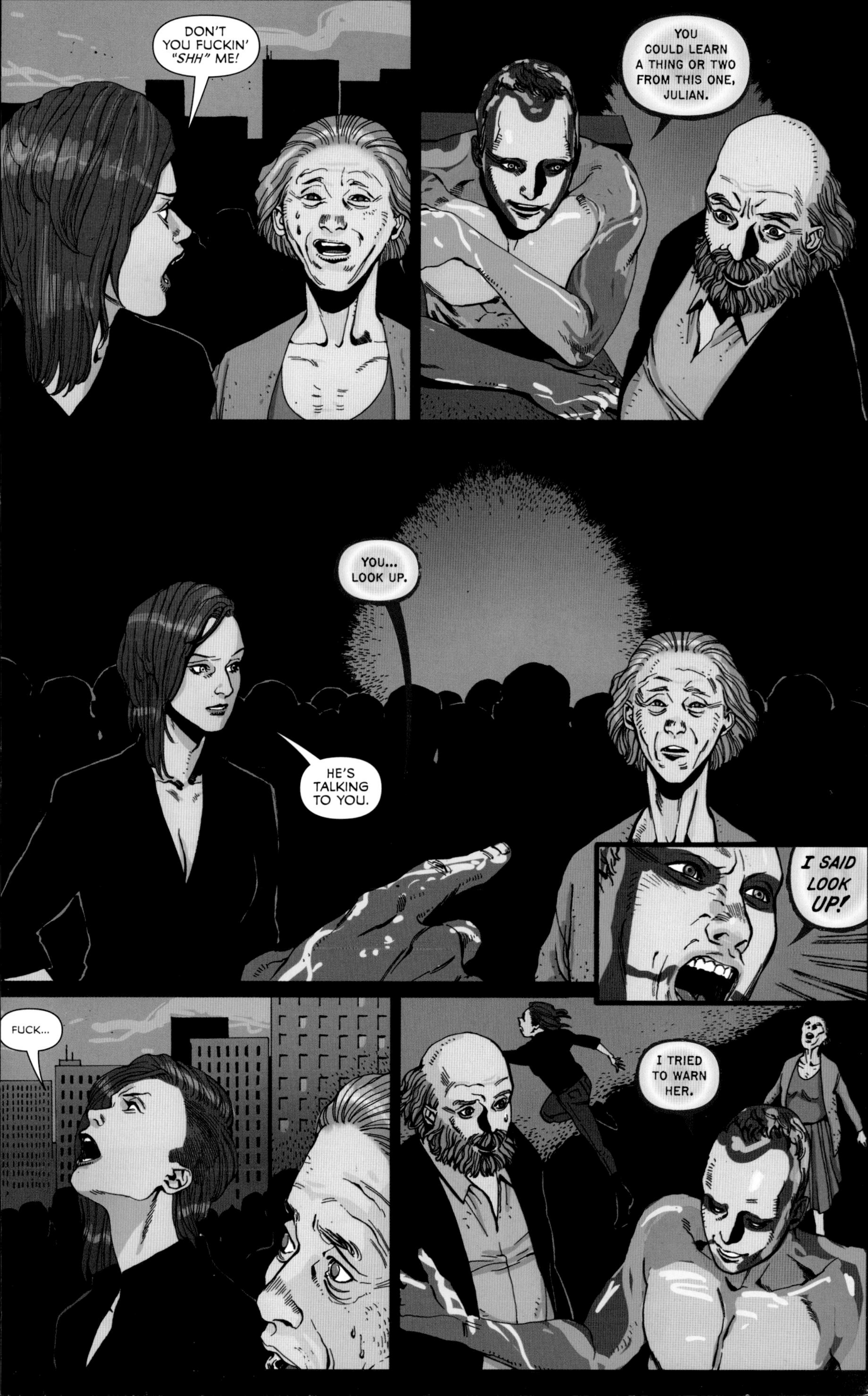
DON'T YOU FUCKIN' "SHH" ME!
YOU COULD LEARN A THING OR TWO FROM THIS ONE, JULIAN.
YOU... LOOK UP.
HE'S TALKING TO YOU.
I SAID LOOK UP!
FUCK...
I TRIED TO WARN HER.

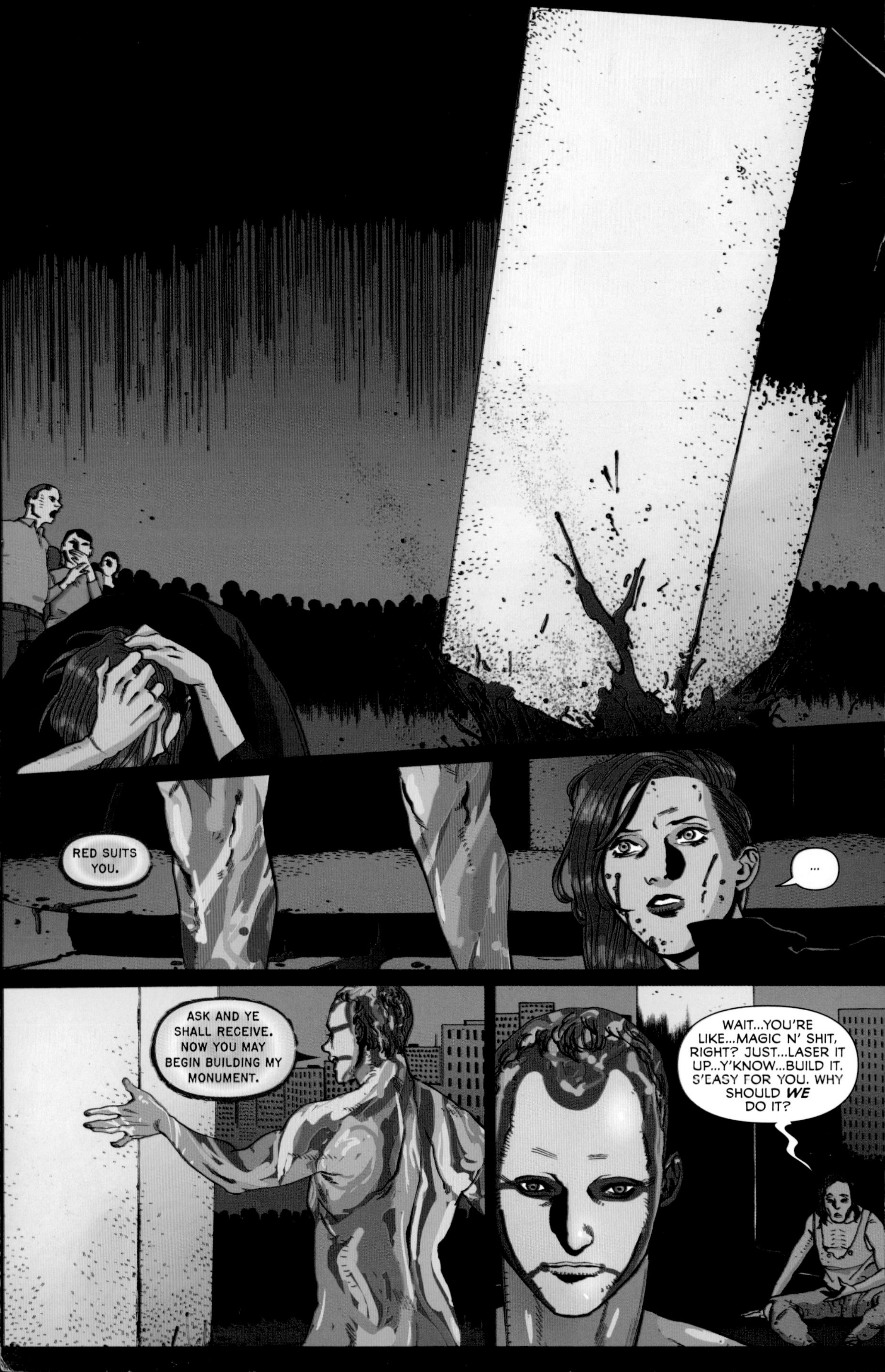
RED SUITS YOU.
...
ASK AND YE SHALL RECEIVE. NOW YOU MAY BEGIN BUILDING MY MONUMENT.
WAIT...YOU'RE LIKE...MAGIC N' SHIT, RIGHT? JUST...LASER IT UP...Y'KNOW...BUILD IT. S'EASY FOR YOU. WHY SHOULD *WE* DO IT?

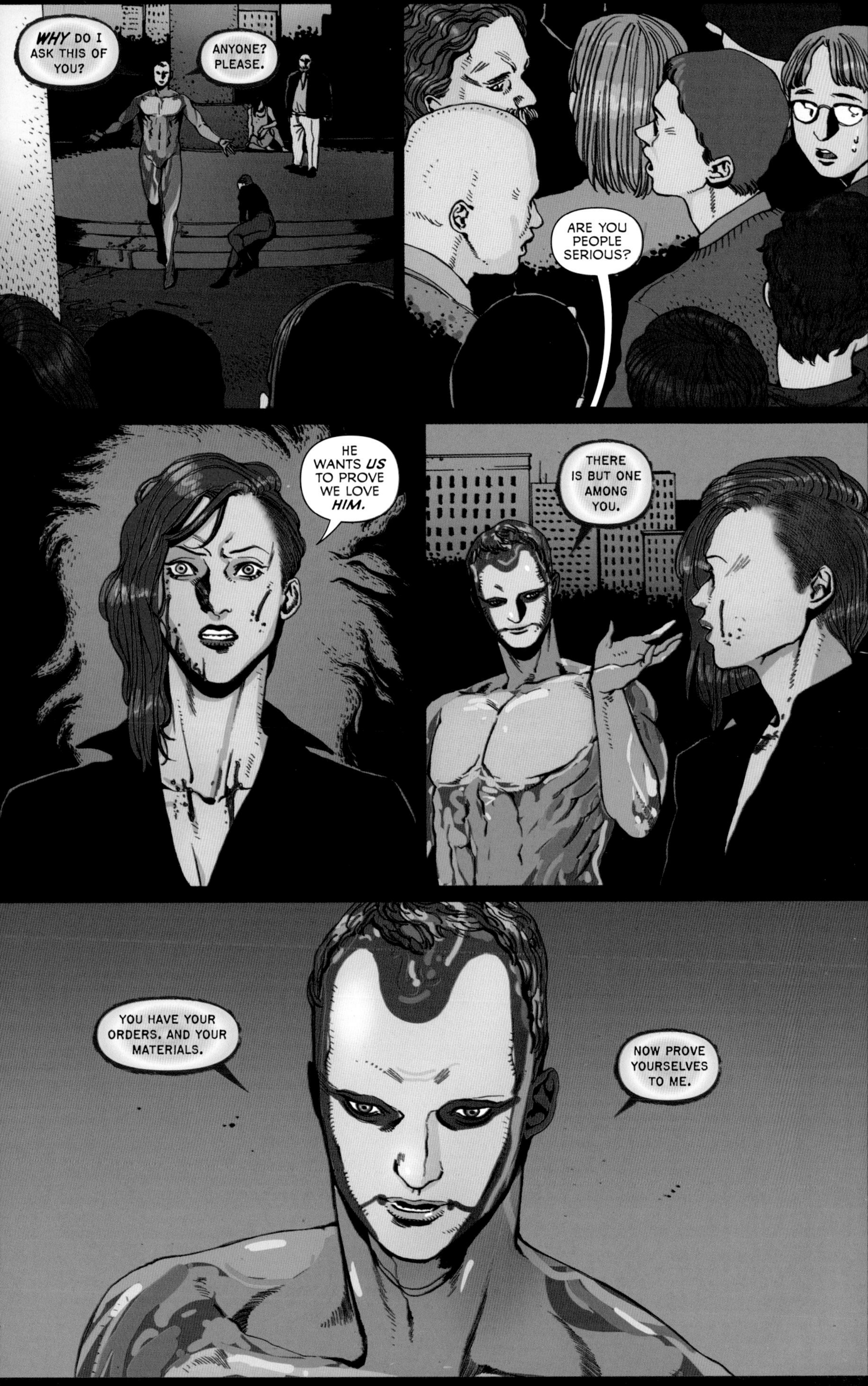
WHY DO I ASK THIS OF YOU?
ANYONE? PLEASE.
ARE YOU PEOPLE SERIOUS?
HE WANTS US TO PROVE WE LOVE HIM.
THERE IS BUT ONE AMONG YOU.
YOU HAVE YOUR ORDERS. AND YOUR MATERIALS.
NOW PROVE YOURSELVES TO ME.

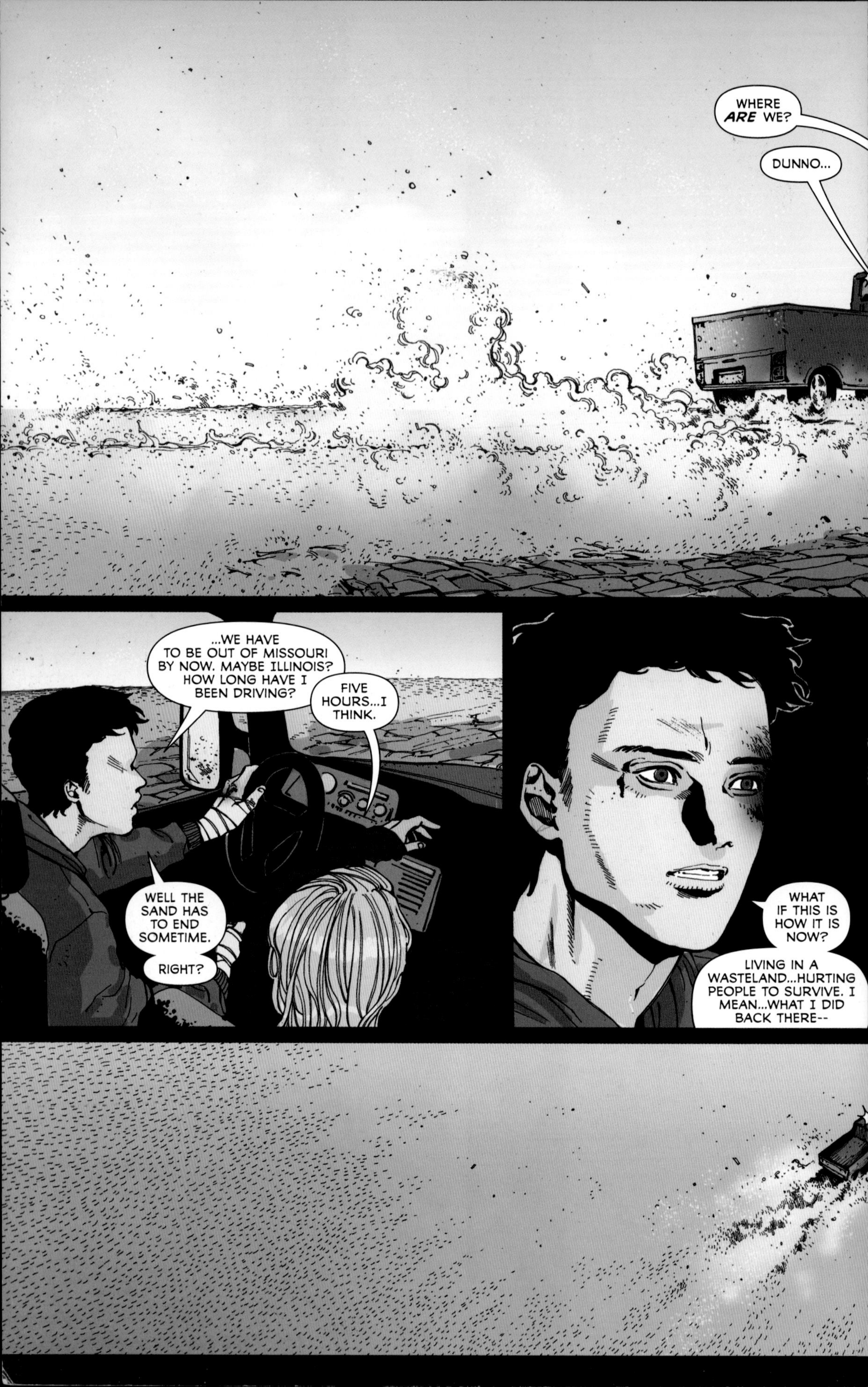
WHERE *ARE* WE?
DUNNO...
...WE HAVE TO BE OUT OF MISSOURI BY NOW. MAYBE ILLINOIS? HOW LONG HAVE I BEEN DRIVING?
FIVE HOURS...I THINK.
WELL THE SAND HAS TO END SOMETIME.
RIGHT?
WHAT IF THIS IS HOW IT IS NOW?
LIVING IN A WASTELAND...HURTING PEOPLE TO SURVIVE. I MEAN...WHAT I DID BACK THERE--

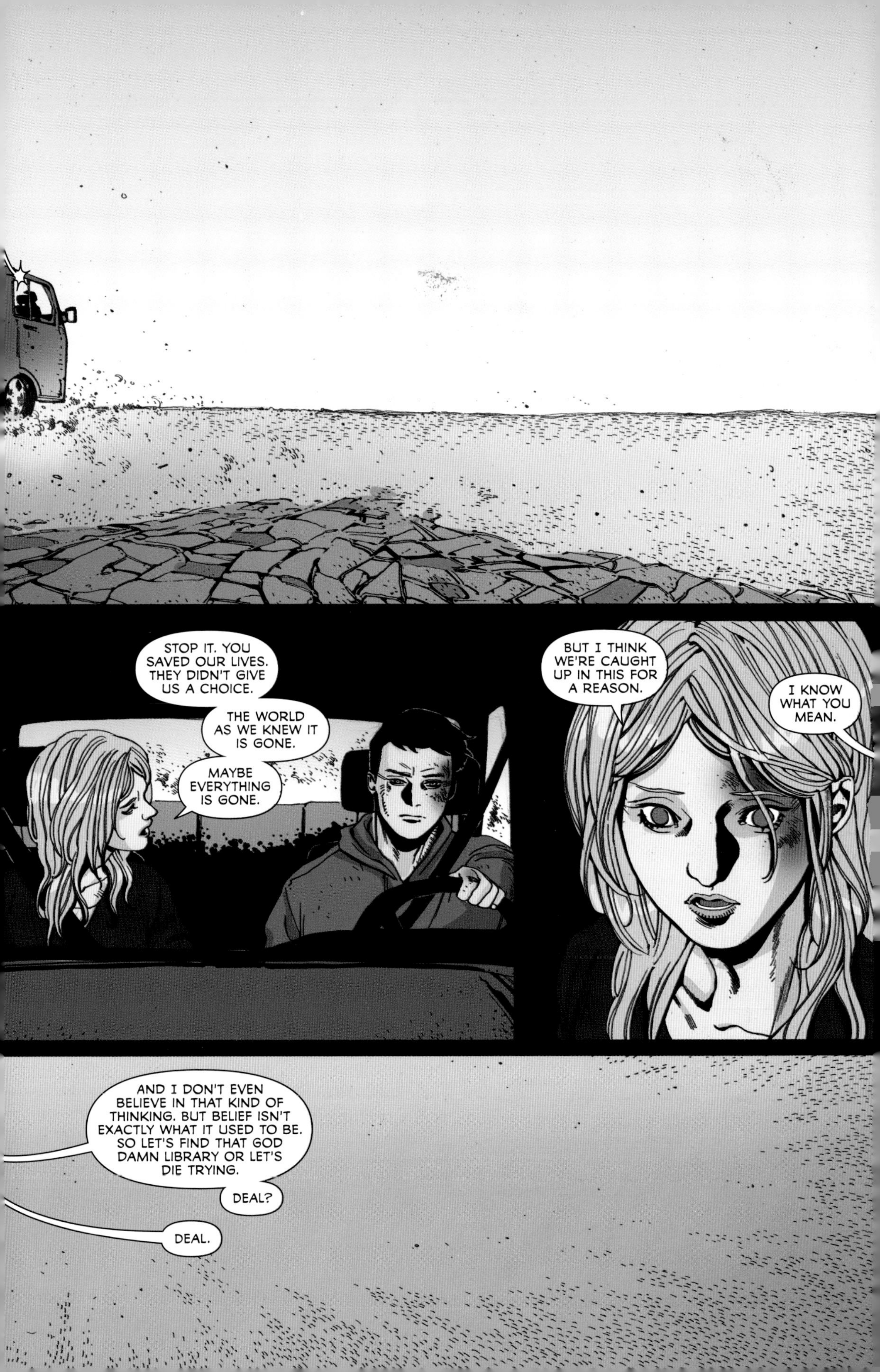
STOP IT. YOU SAVED OUR LIVES. THEY DIDN'T GIVE US A CHOICE.
THE WORLD AS WE KNEW IT IS GONE.
MAYBE EVERYTHING IS GONE.
BUT I THINK WE'RE CAUGHT UP IN THIS FOR A REASON.
I KNOW WHAT YOU MEAN.
AND I DON'T EVEN BELIEVE IN THAT KIND OF THINKING. BUT BELIEF ISN'T EXACTLY WHAT IT USED TO BE. SO LET'S FIND THAT GOD DAMN LIBRARY OR LET'S DIE TRYING.
DEAL?
DEAL.

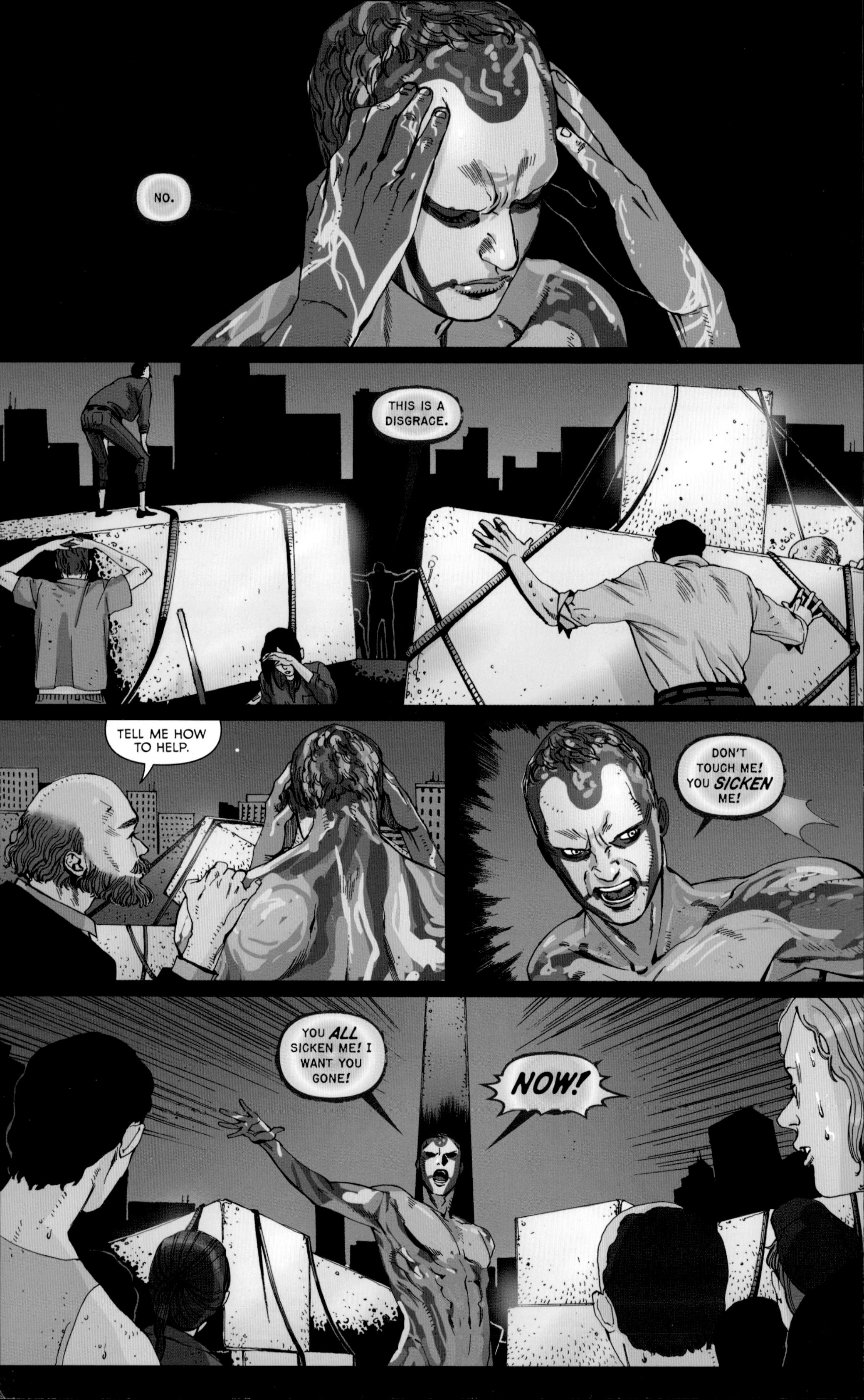
NO.
THIS IS A DISGRACE.
TELL ME HOW TO HELP.
DON'T TOUCH ME! YOU SICKEN ME!
YOU ALL SICKEN ME! I WANT YOU GONE!
NOW!

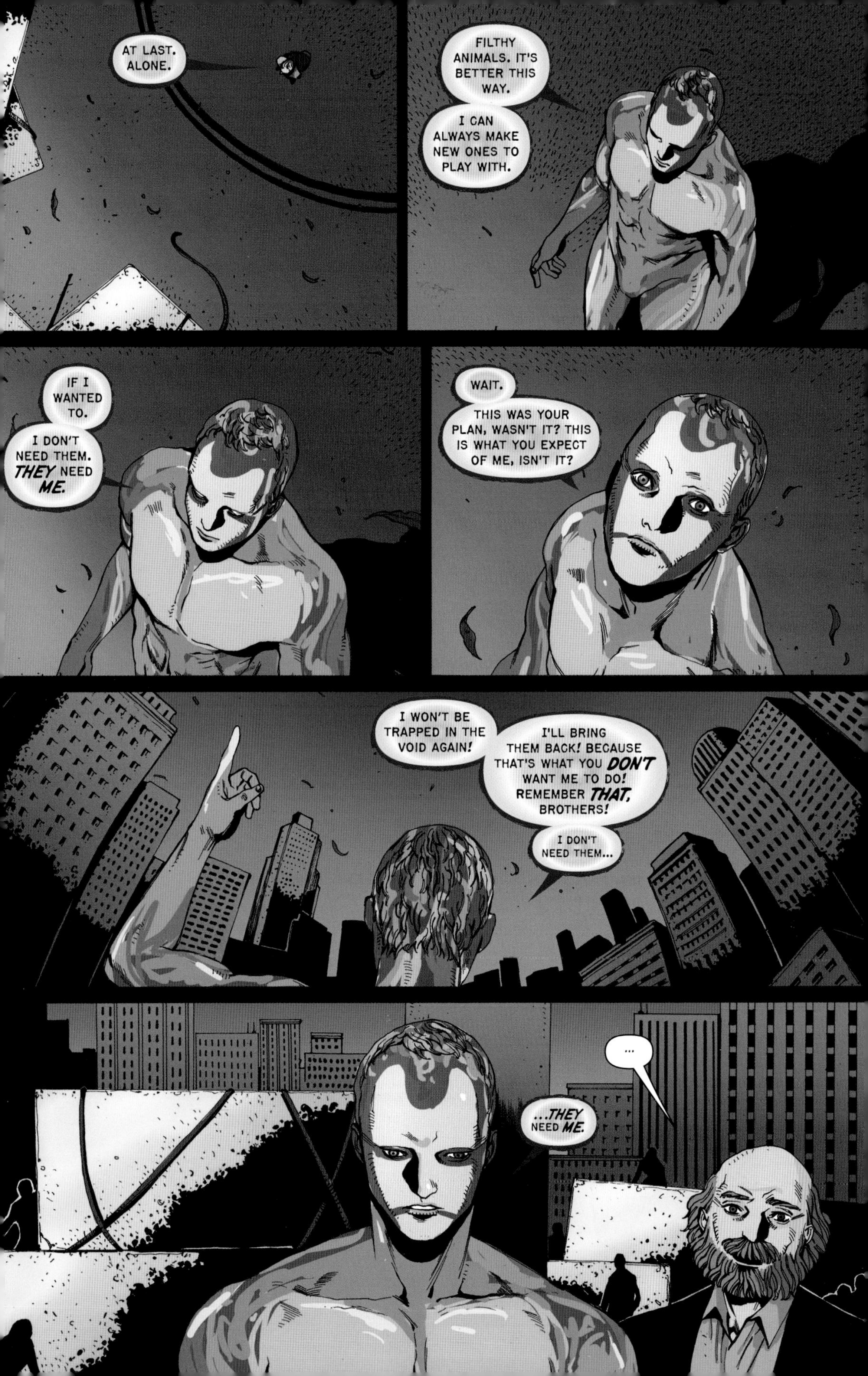
AT LAST. ALONE.
FILTHY ANIMALS. IT'S BETTER THIS WAY.
I CAN ALWAYS MAKE NEW ONES TO PLAY WITH.
IF I WANTED TO.
I DON'T NEED THEM. *THEY* NEED *ME.*
WAIT.
THIS WAS YOUR PLAN, WASN'T IT? THIS IS WHAT YOU EXPECT OF ME, ISN'T IT?
I WON'T BE TRAPPED IN THE VOID AGAIN!
I'LL BRING THEM BACK! BECAUSE THAT'S WHAT YOU *DON'T* WANT ME TO DO! REMEMBER *THAT,* BROTHERS!
I DON'T NEED THEM...
...
...*THEY* NEED *ME.*

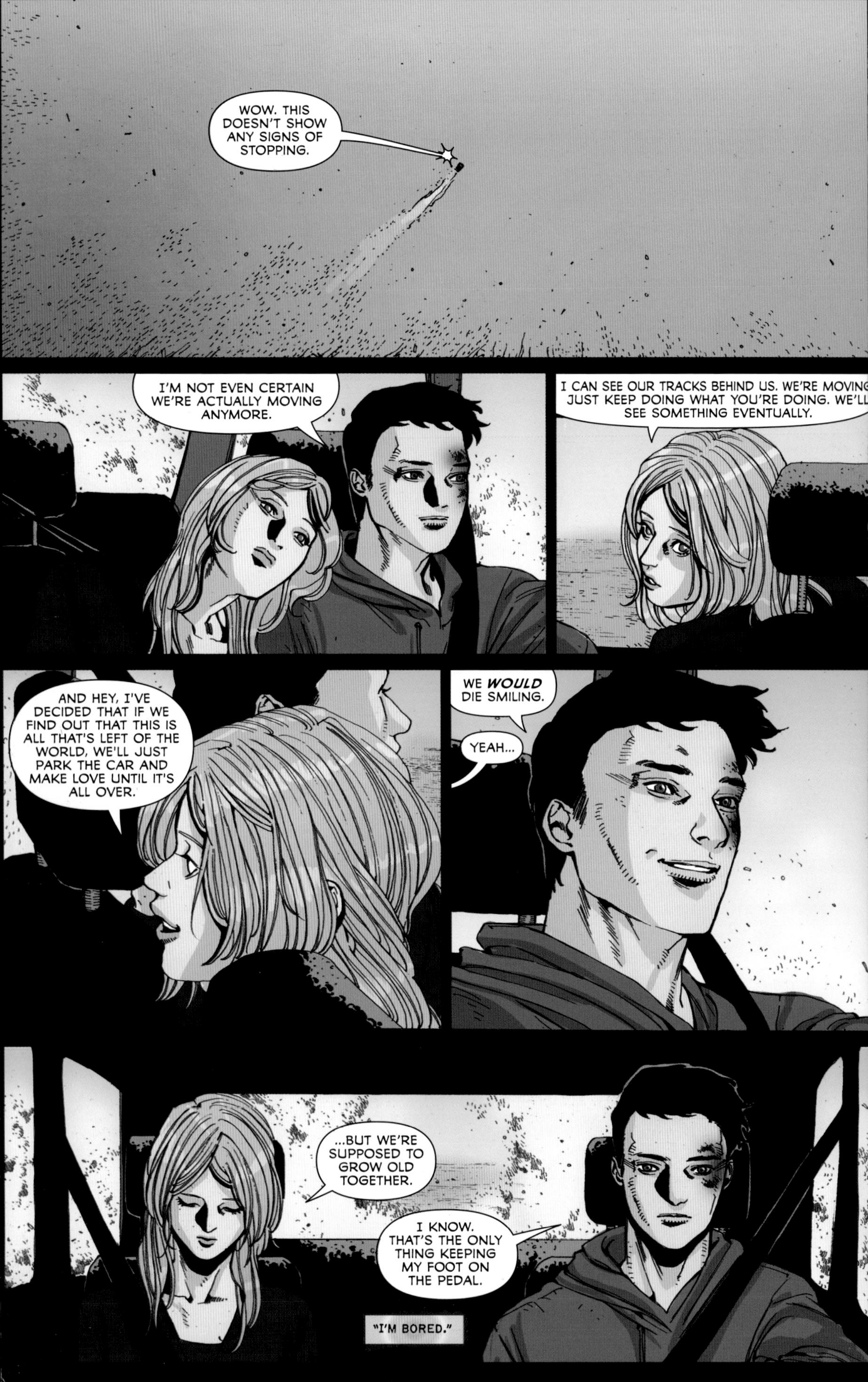
WOW. THIS DOESN'T SHOW ANY SIGNS OF STOPPING.
I'M NOT EVEN CERTAIN WE'RE ACTUALLY MOVING ANYMORE.
I CAN SEE OUR TRACKS BEHIND US. WE'RE MOVING. JUST KEEP DOING WHAT YOU'RE DOING. WE'LL SEE SOMETHING EVENTUALLY.
AND HEY, I'VE DECIDED THAT IF WE FIND OUT THAT THIS IS ALL THAT'S LEFT OF THE WORLD, WE'LL JUST PARK THE CAR AND MAKE LOVE UNTIL IT'S ALL OVER.
WE ***WOULD*** DIE SMILING.
YEAH...
...BUT WE'RE SUPPOSED TO GROW OLD TOGETHER.
I KNOW. THAT'S THE ONLY THING KEEPING MY FOOT ON THE PEDAL.
"I'M BORED."

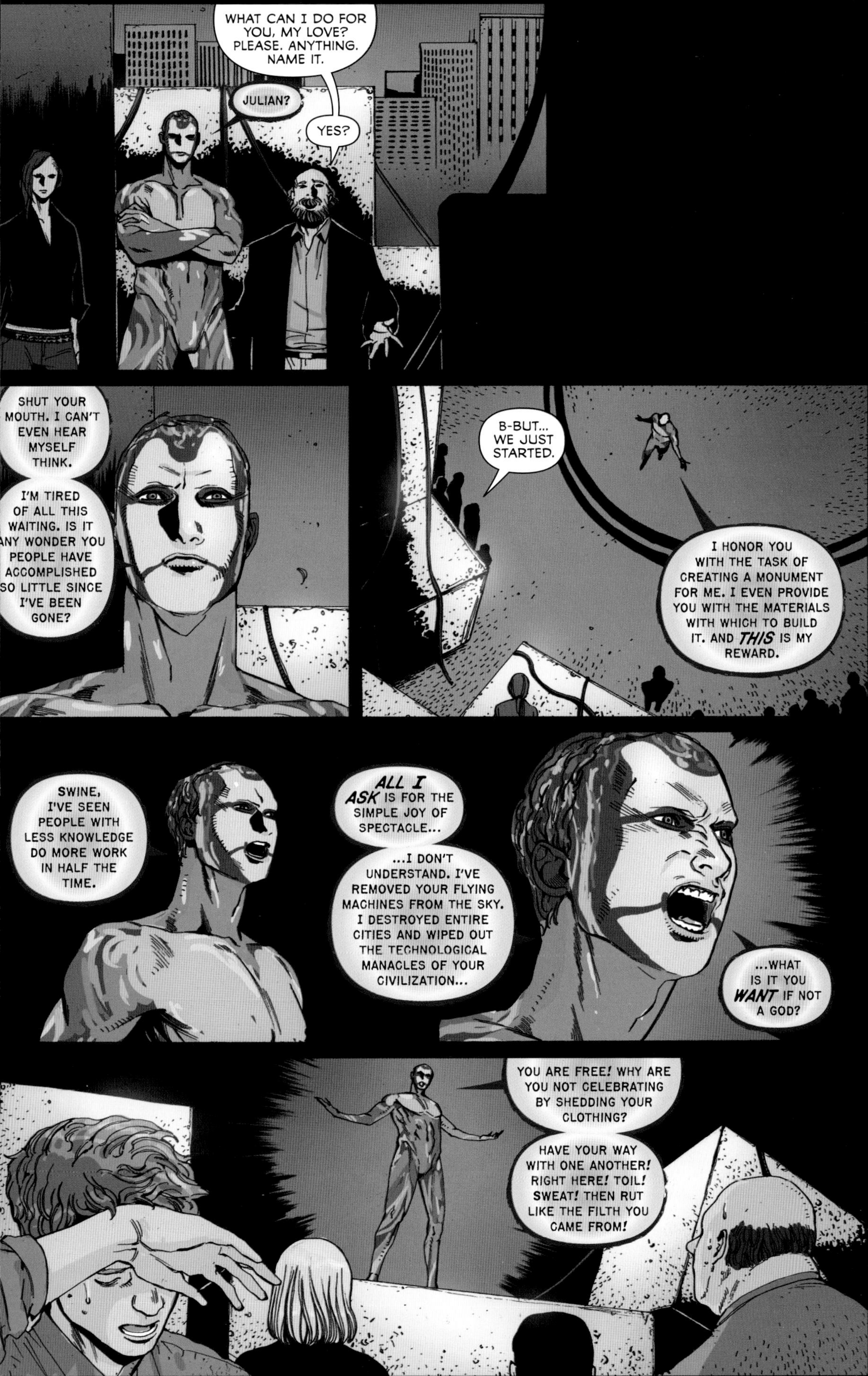
WHAT CAN I DO FOR YOU, MY LOVE? PLEASE. ANYTHING. NAME IT.
JULIAN?
YES?
SHUT YOUR MOUTH. I CAN'T EVEN HEAR MYSELF THINK.
I'M TIRED OF ALL THIS WAITING. IS IT ANY WONDER YOU PEOPLE HAVE ACCOMPLISHED SO LITTLE SINCE I'VE BEEN GONE?
B-BUT... WE JUST STARTED.
I HONOR YOU WITH THE TASK OF CREATING A MONUMENT FOR ME. I EVEN PROVIDE YOU WITH THE MATERIALS WITH WHICH TO BUILD IT. AND THIS IS MY REWARD.
SWINE, I'VE SEEN PEOPLE WITH LESS KNOWLEDGE DO MORE WORK IN HALF THE TIME.
ALL I ASK IS FOR THE SIMPLE JOY OF SPECTACLE...
...I DON'T UNDERSTAND. I'VE REMOVED YOUR FLYING MACHINES FROM THE SKY. I DESTROYED ENTIRE CITIES AND WIPED OUT THE TECHNOLOGICAL MANACLES OF YOUR CIVILIZATION...
...WHAT IS IT YOU WANT IF NOT A GOD?
YOU ARE FREE! WHY ARE YOU NOT CELEBRATING BY SHEDDING YOUR CLOTHING?
HAVE YOUR WAY WITH ONE ANOTHER! RIGHT HERE! TOIL! SWEAT! THEN RUT LIKE THE FILTH YOU CAME FROM!

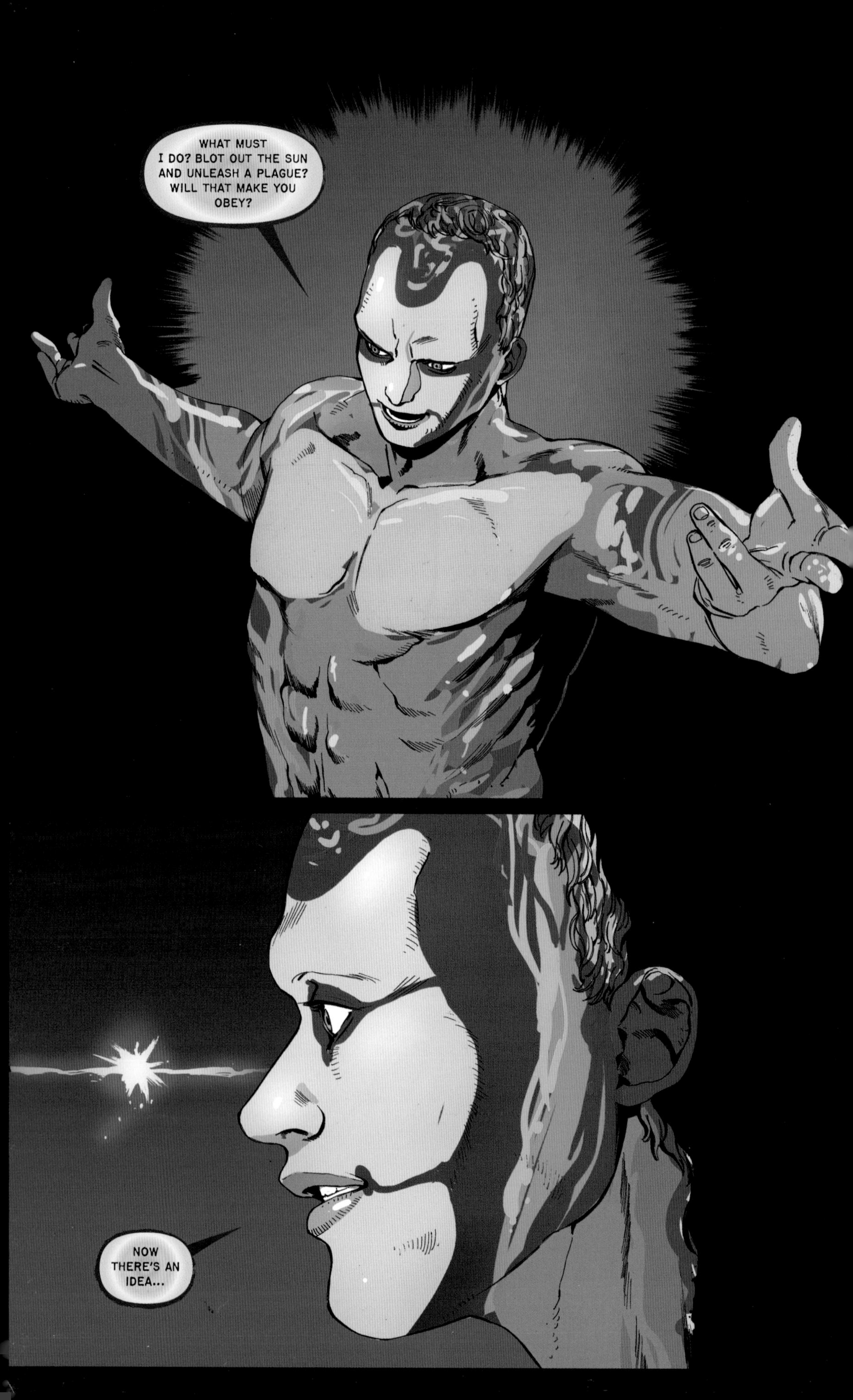
WHAT MUST I DO? BLOT OUT THE SUN AND UNLEASH A PLAGUE? WILL THAT MAKE YOU OBEY?
NOW THERE'S AN IDEA...

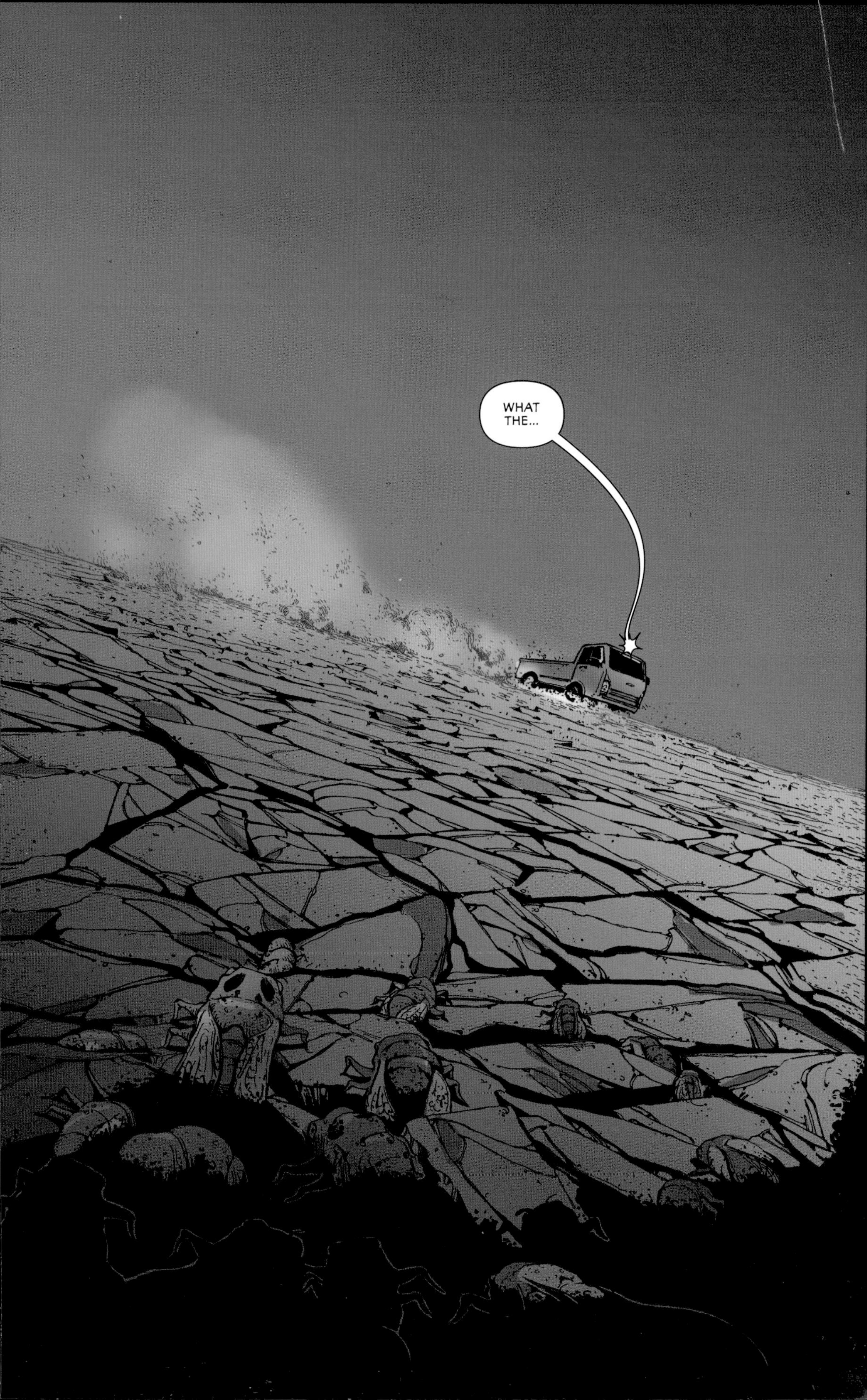
WHAT THE...

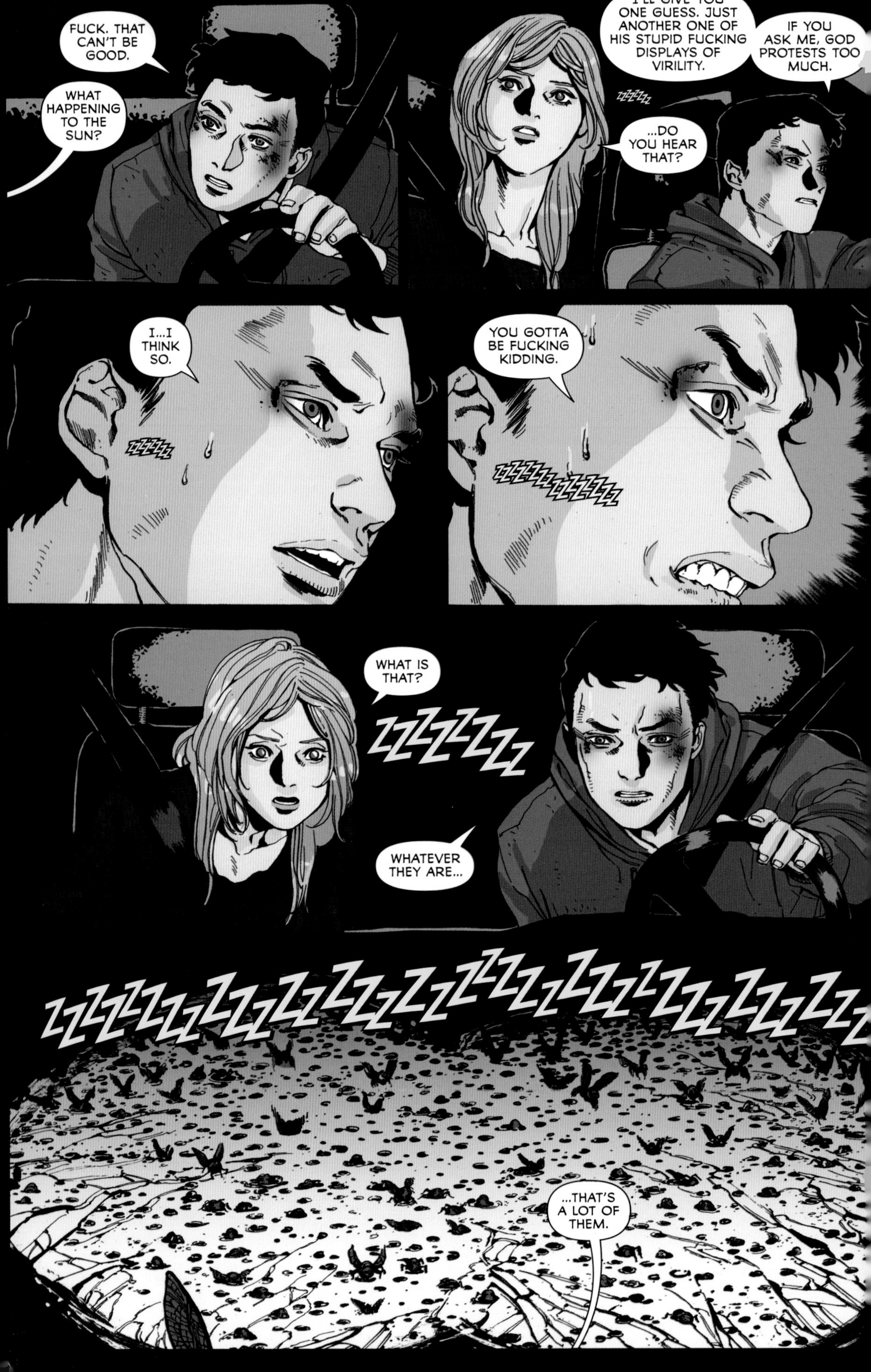
FUCK. THAT CAN'T BE GOOD.
WHAT HAPPENING TO THE SUN?
I'LL GIVE YOU ONE GUESS. JUST ANOTHER ONE OF HIS STUPID FUCKING DISPLAYS OF VIRILITY.
IF YOU ASK ME, GOD PROTESTS TOO MUCH.
ZZZZZ
...DO YOU HEAR THAT?
I...I THINK SO.
ZZZZZZZ
YOU GOTTA BE FUCKING KIDDING.
ZZZZZZZZZZZZZZ
WHAT IS THAT?
ZZZZZZZZ
WHATEVER THEY ARE...
ZZZZZZZZZZZZZZZZZZZZZZZZZZZZZZZZZZZZZ
...THAT'S A LOT OF THEM.

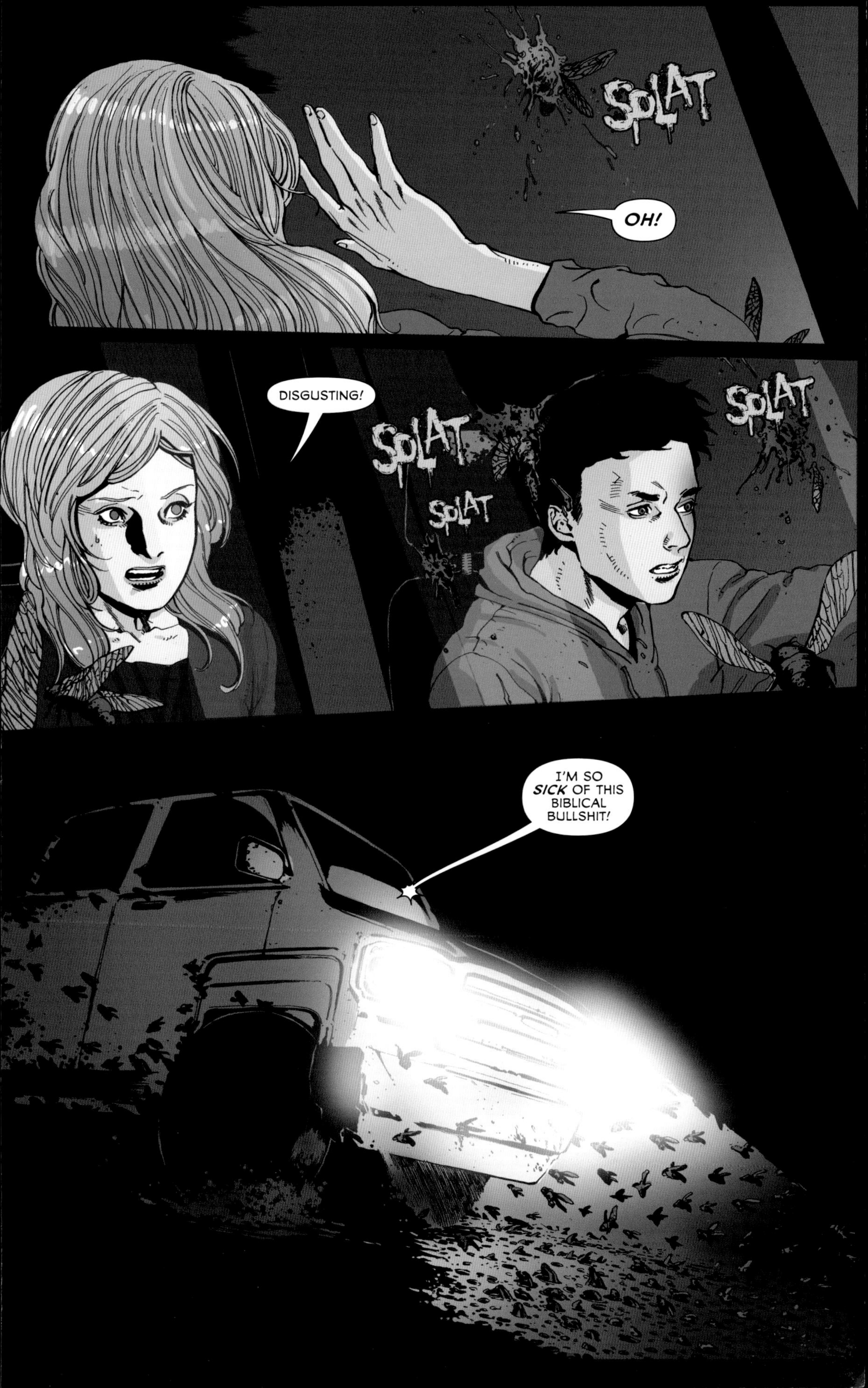
SPLAT
OH!
DISGUSTING!
SPLAT
SPLAT
SPLAT
I'M SO SICK OF THIS BIBLICAL BULLSHIT!

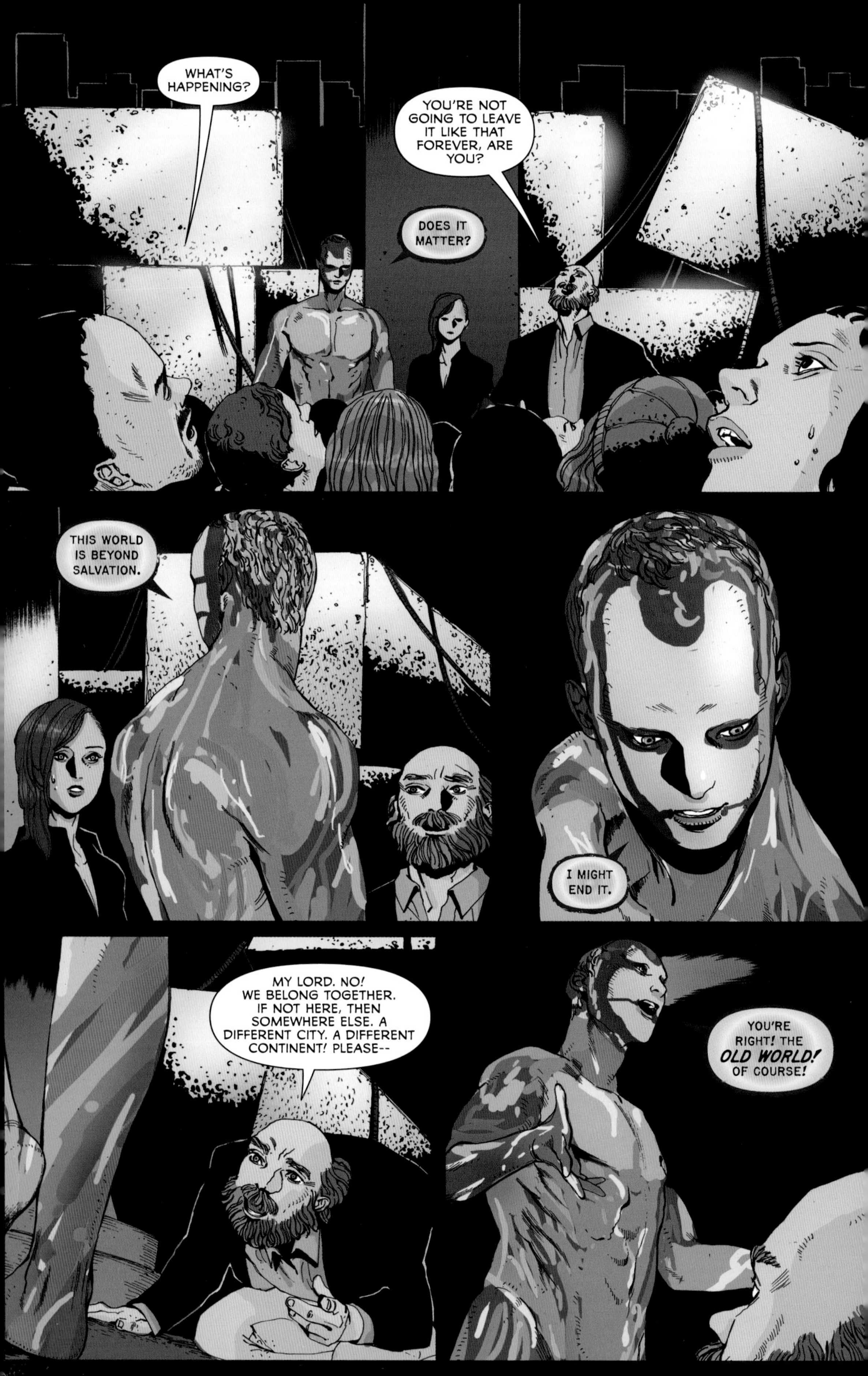
WHAT'S HAPPENING?
YOU'RE NOT GOING TO LEAVE IT LIKE THAT FOREVER, ARE YOU?
DOES IT MATTER?
THIS WORLD IS BEYOND SALVATION.
I MIGHT END IT.
MY LORD. NO! WE BELONG TOGETHER. IF NOT HERE, THEN SOMEWHERE ELSE. A DIFFERENT CITY. A DIFFERENT CONTINENT! PLEASE--
YOU'RE RIGHT! THE OLD WORLD! OF COURSE!

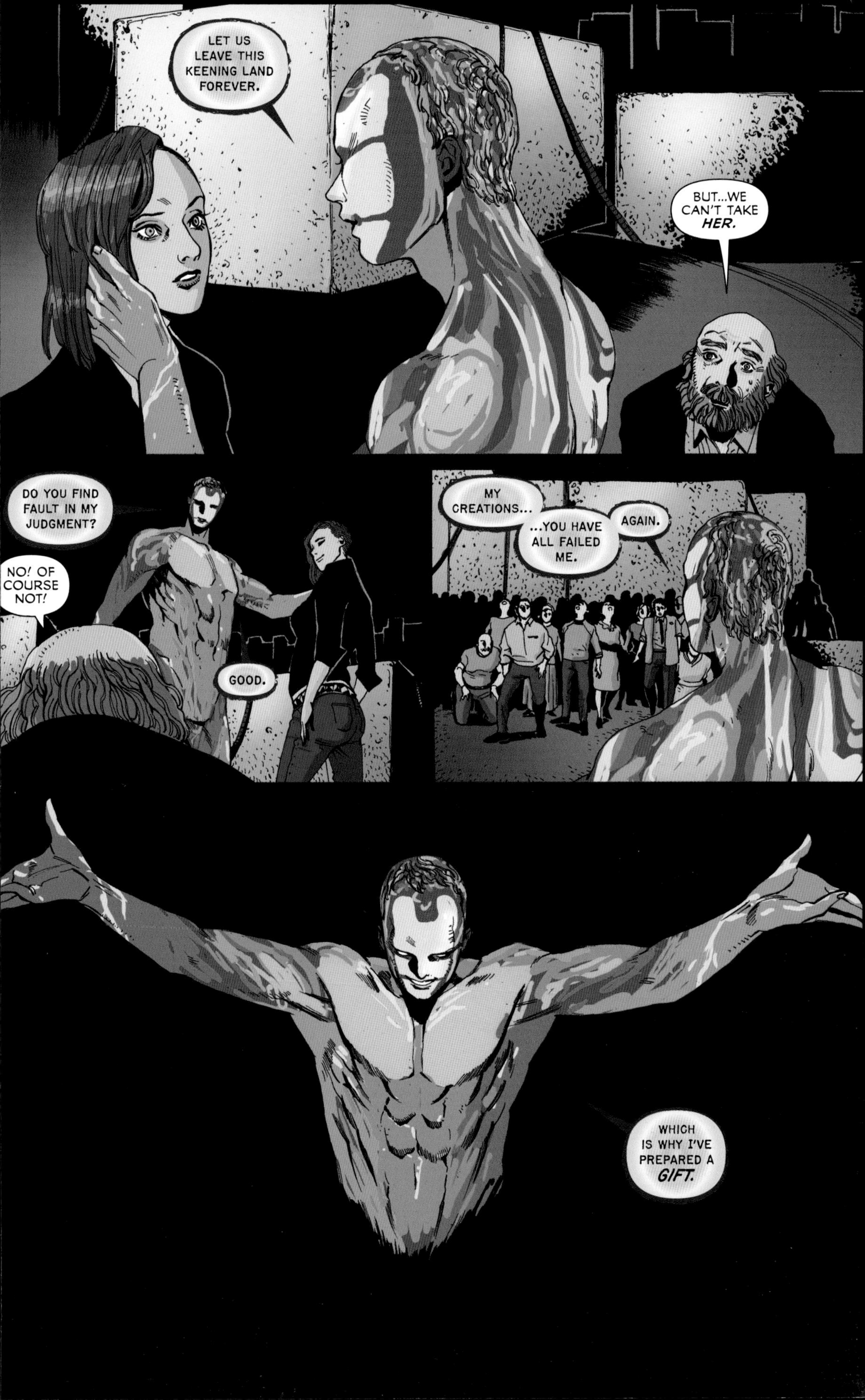
LET US LEAVE THIS KEENING LAND FOREVER.
BUT...WE CAN'T TAKE *HER.*
DO YOU FIND FAULT IN MY JUDGMENT?
NO! OF COURSE NOT!
GOOD.
MY CREATIONS...
...YOU HAVE ALL FAILED ME.
AGAIN.
WHICH IS WHY I'VE PREPARED A *GIFT.*

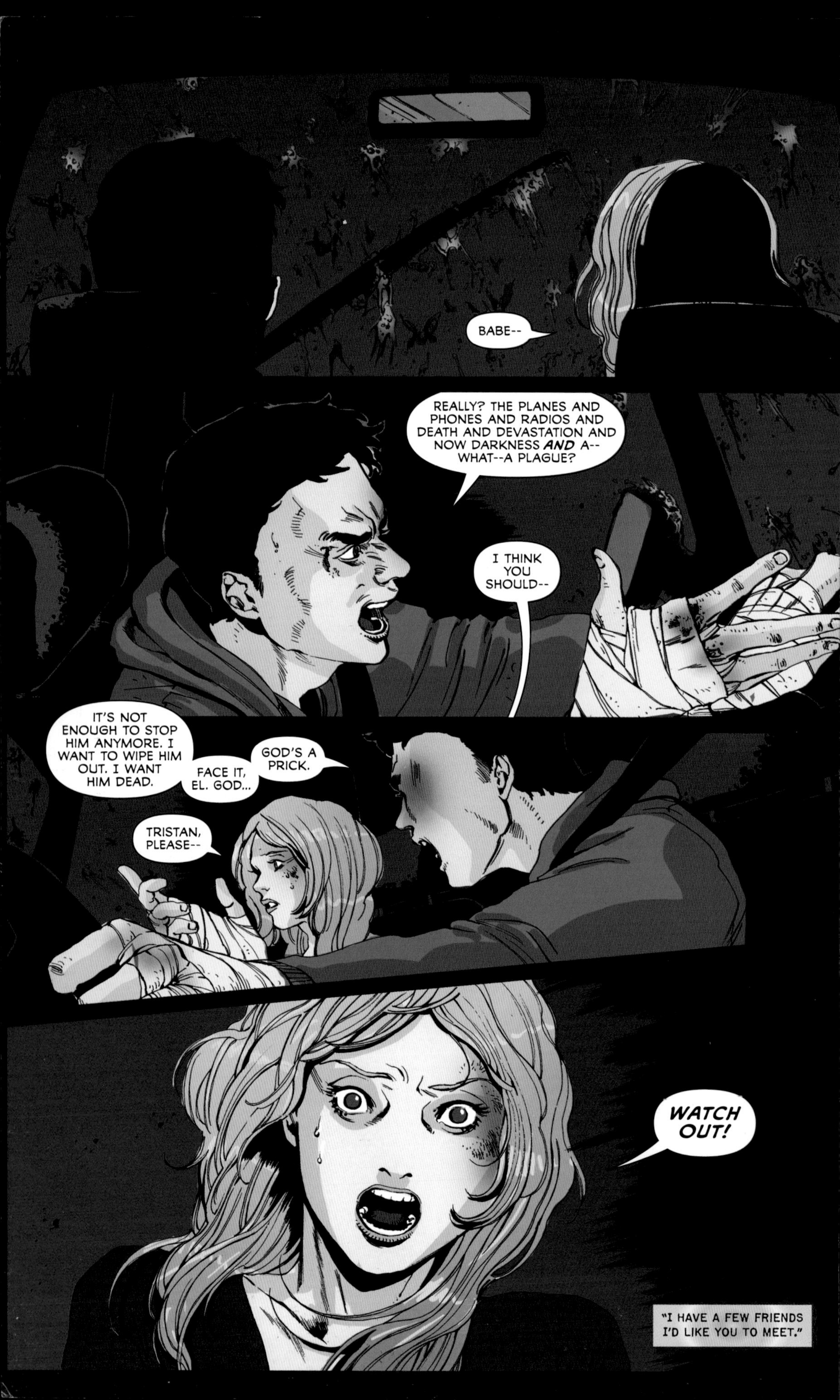
BABE--
REALLY? THE PLANES AND PHONES AND RADIOS AND DEATH AND DEVASTATION AND NOW DARKNESS AND A-- WHAT--A PLAGUE?
I THINK YOU SHOULD--
IT'S NOT ENOUGH TO STOP HIM ANYMORE. I WANT TO WIPE HIM OUT. I WANT HIM DEAD.
FACE IT, EL. GOD...
GOD'S A PRICK.
TRISTAN, PLEASE--
WATCH OUT!
"I HAVE A FEW FRIENDS I'D LIKE YOU TO MEET."

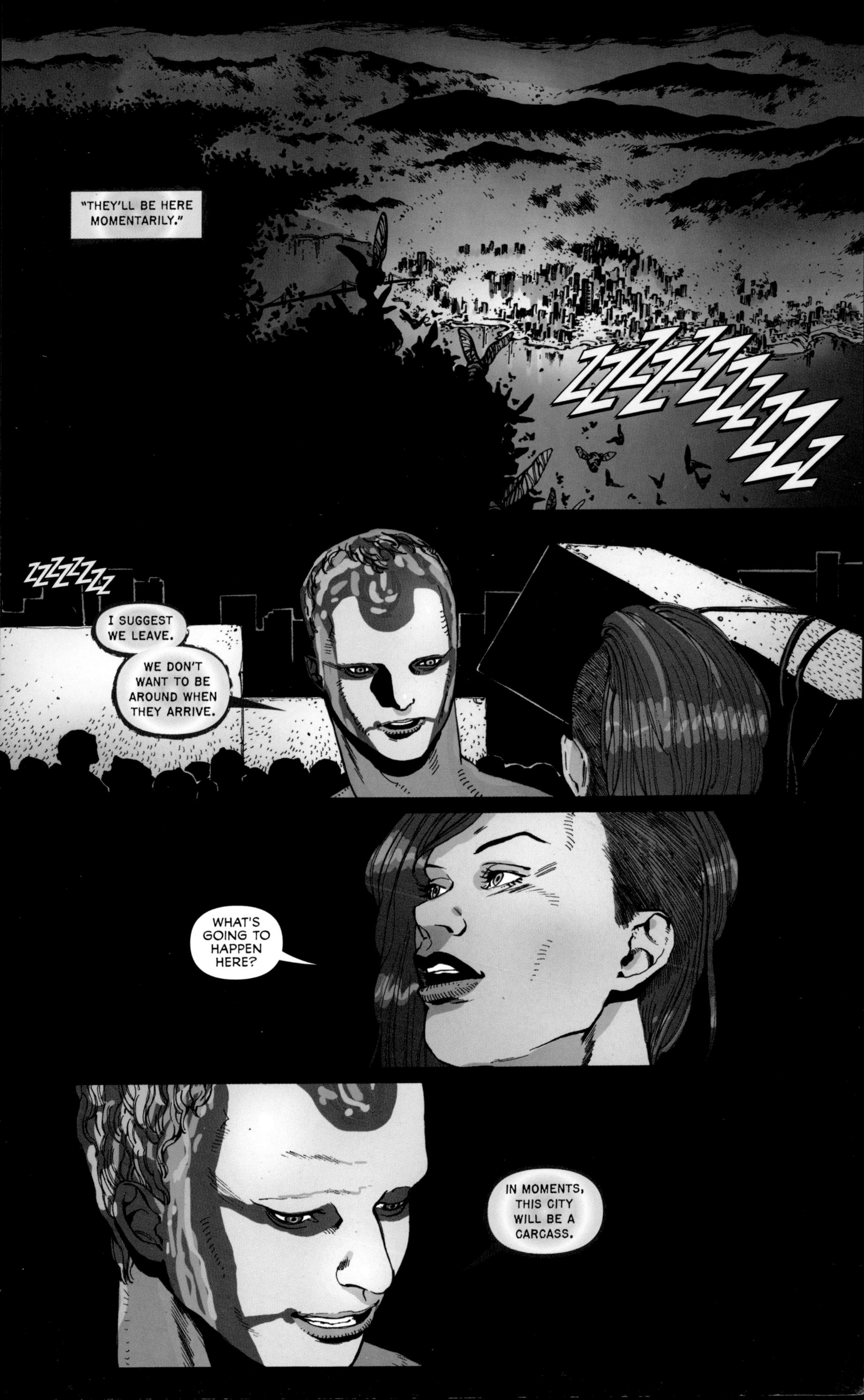
"THEY'LL BE HERE MOMENTARILY."
ZZZZZZZZZZ
ZZZZZZZZ
I SUGGEST WE LEAVE.
WE DON'T WANT TO BE AROUND WHEN THEY ARRIVE.
WHAT'S GOING TO HAPPEN HERE?
IN MOMENTS, THIS CITY WILL BE A CARCASS.

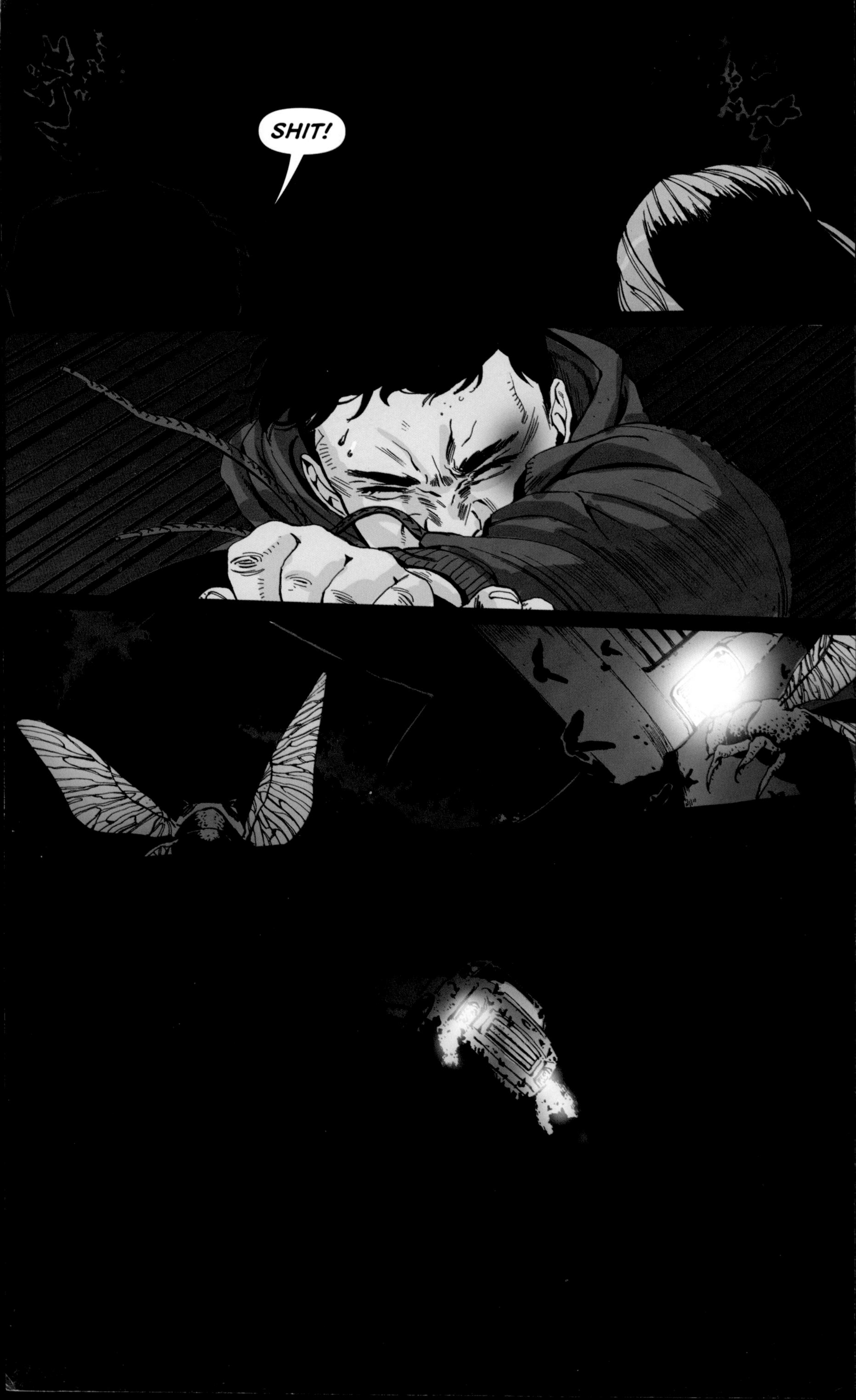
SHIT!

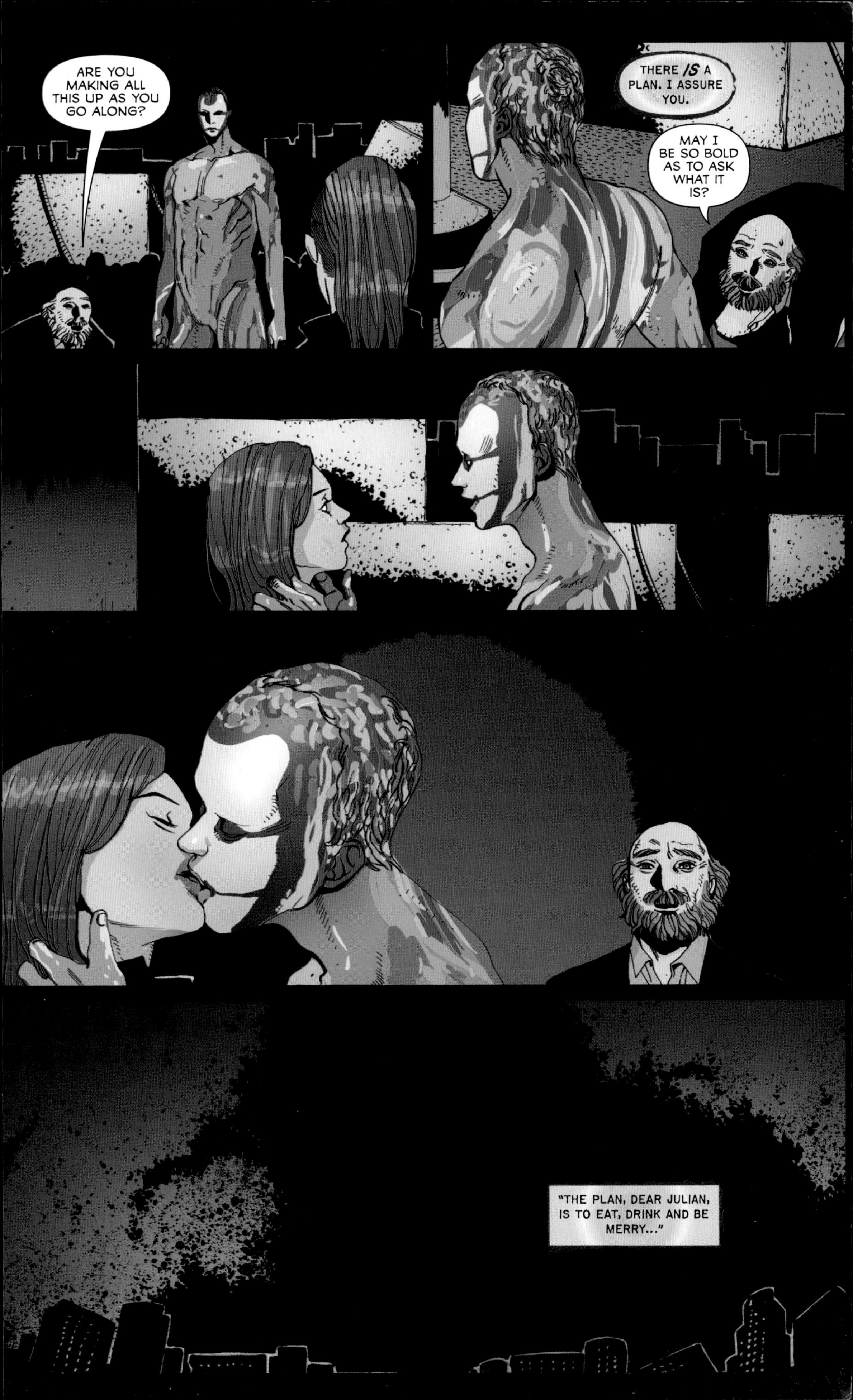
ARE YOU MAKING ALL THIS UP AS YOU GO ALONG?
THERE IS A PLAN. I ASSURE YOU.
MAY I BE SO BOLD AS TO ASK WHAT IT IS?
"THE PLAN, DEAR JULIAN, IS TO EAT, DRINK AND BE MERRY..."

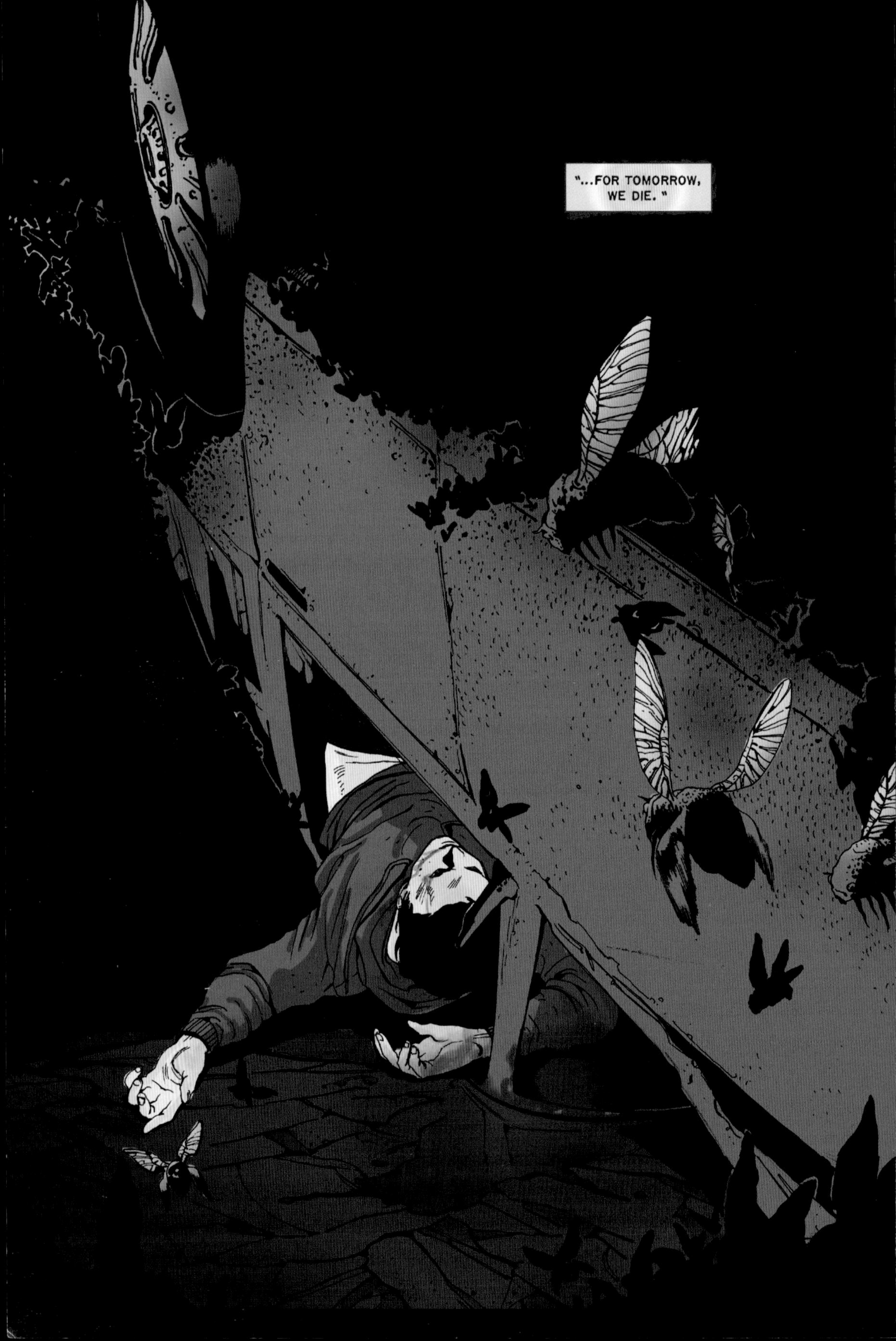
"...FOR TOMORROW, WE DIE."

CHAPTER EIGHT

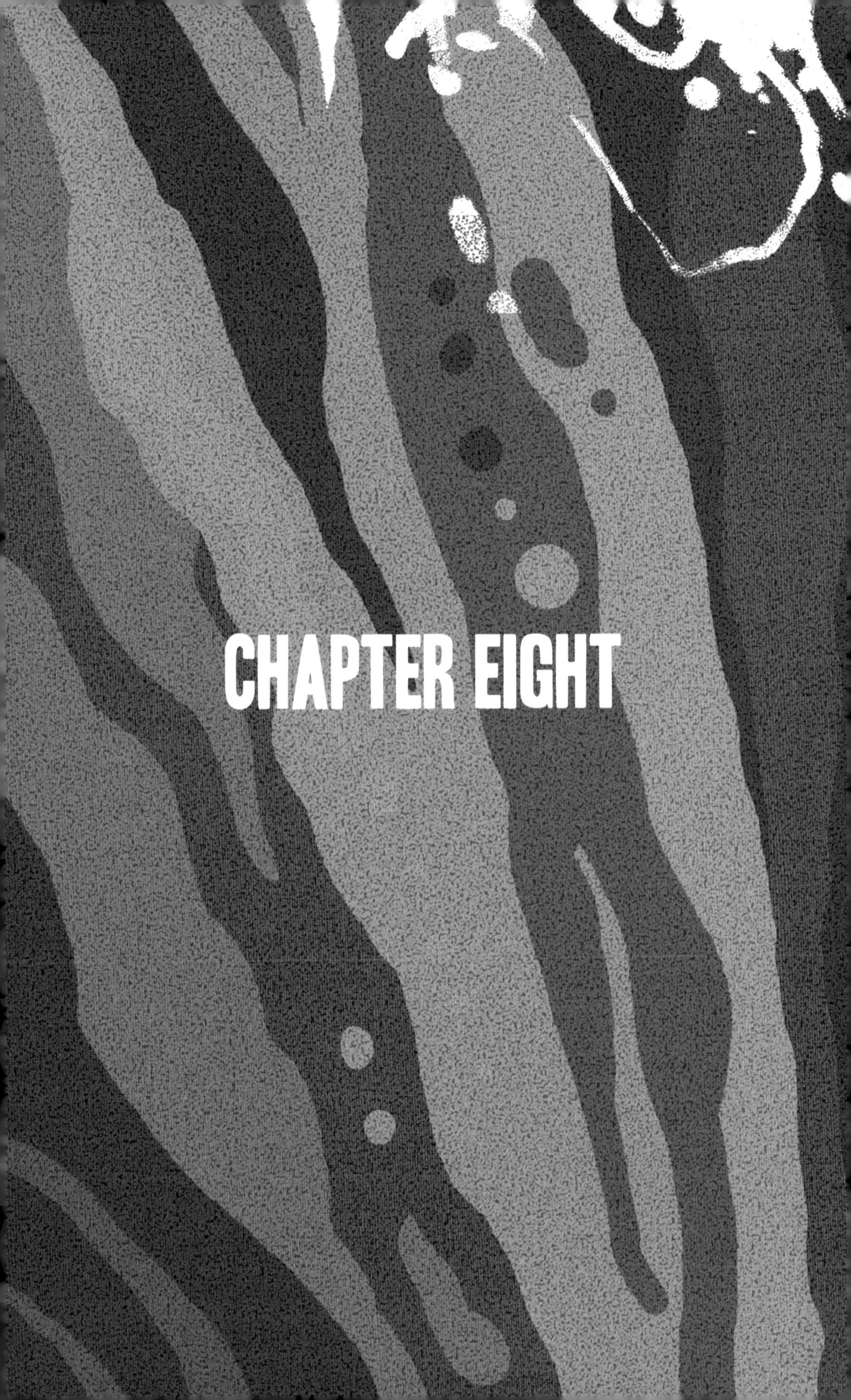

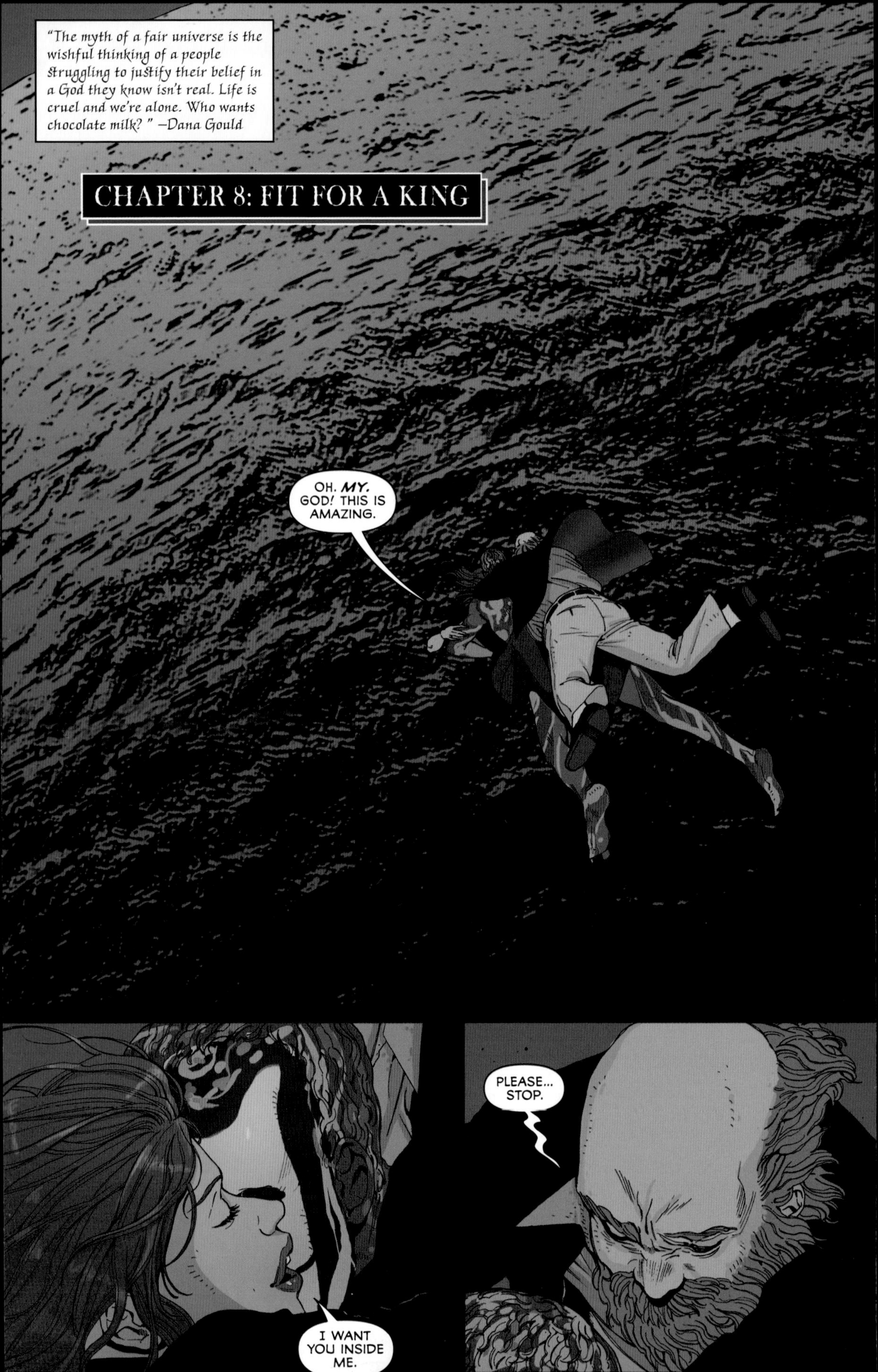
"The myth of a fair universe is the wishful thinking of a people struggling to justify their belief in a God they know isn't real. Life is cruel and we're alone. Who wants chocolate milk? " —Dana Gould
CHAPTER 8: FIT FOR A KING
OH. MY. GOD! THIS IS AMAZING.
I WANT YOU INSIDE ME.
PLEASE... STOP.

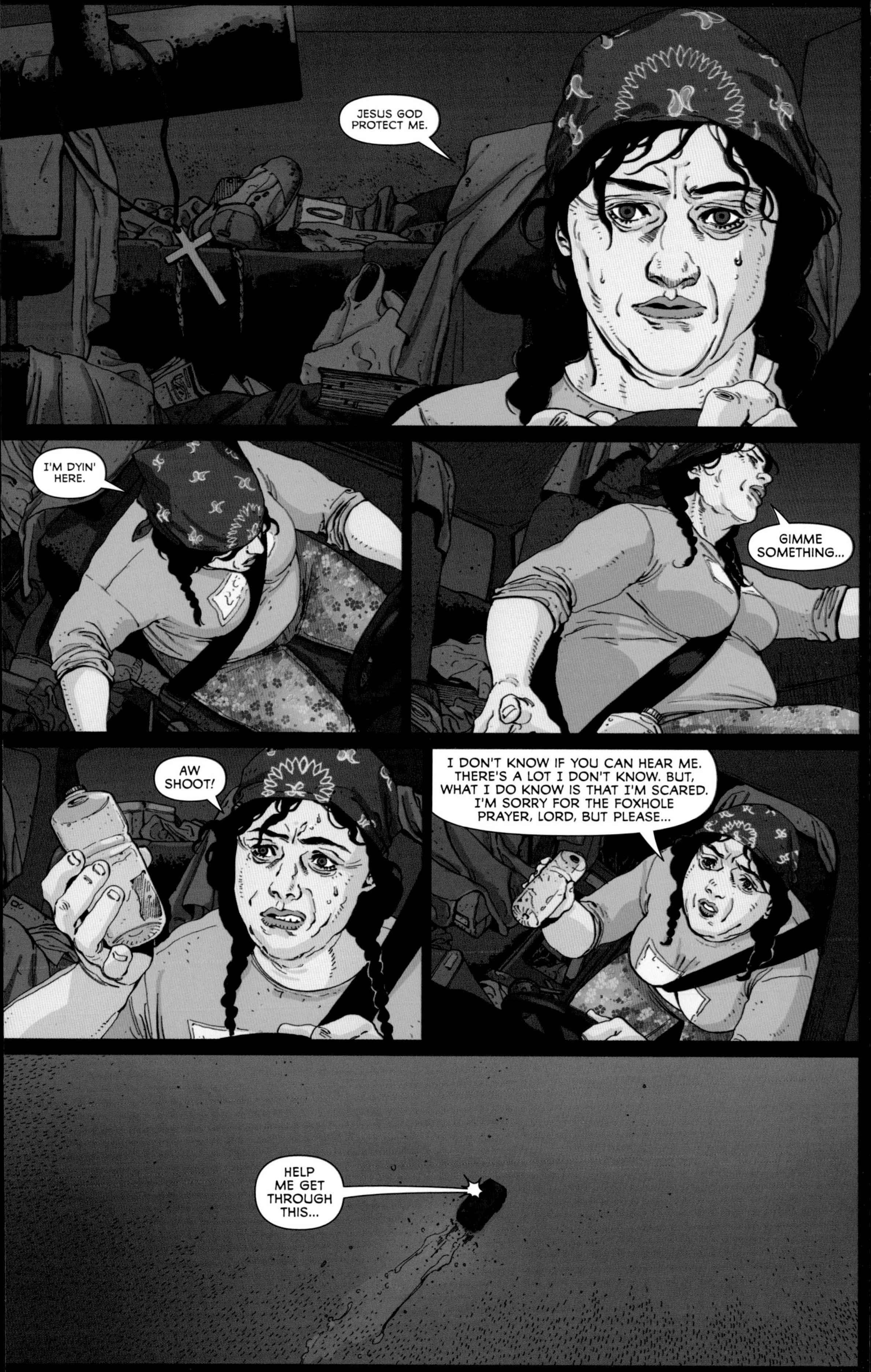
JESUS GOD PROTECT ME.
I'M DYIN' HERE.
GIMME SOMETHING...
AW SHOOT!
I DON'T KNOW IF YOU CAN HEAR ME. THERE'S A LOT I DON'T KNOW. BUT, WHAT I DO KNOW IS THAT I'M SCARED. I'M SORRY FOR THE FOXHOLE PRAYER, LORD, BUT PLEASE...
HELP ME GET THROUGH THIS...

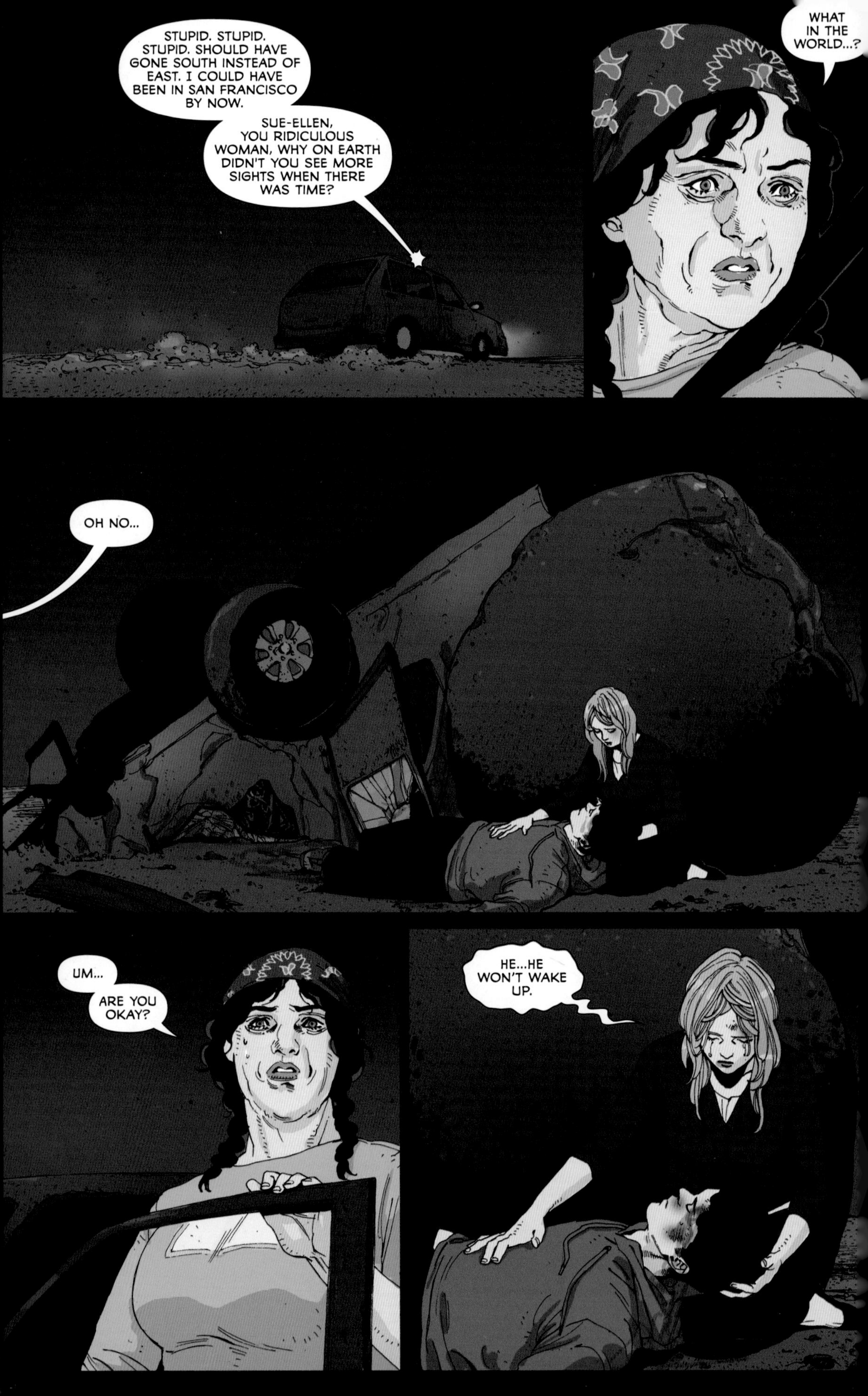
STUPID. STUPID. STUPID. SHOULD HAVE GONE SOUTH INSTEAD OF EAST. I COULD HAVE BEEN IN SAN FRANCISCO BY NOW.
SUE-ELLEN, YOU RIDICULOUS WOMAN, WHY ON EARTH DIDN'T YOU SEE MORE SIGHTS WHEN THERE WAS TIME?
WHAT IN THE WORLD...?
OH NO...
UM...
ARE YOU OKAY?
HE...HE WON'T WAKE UP.

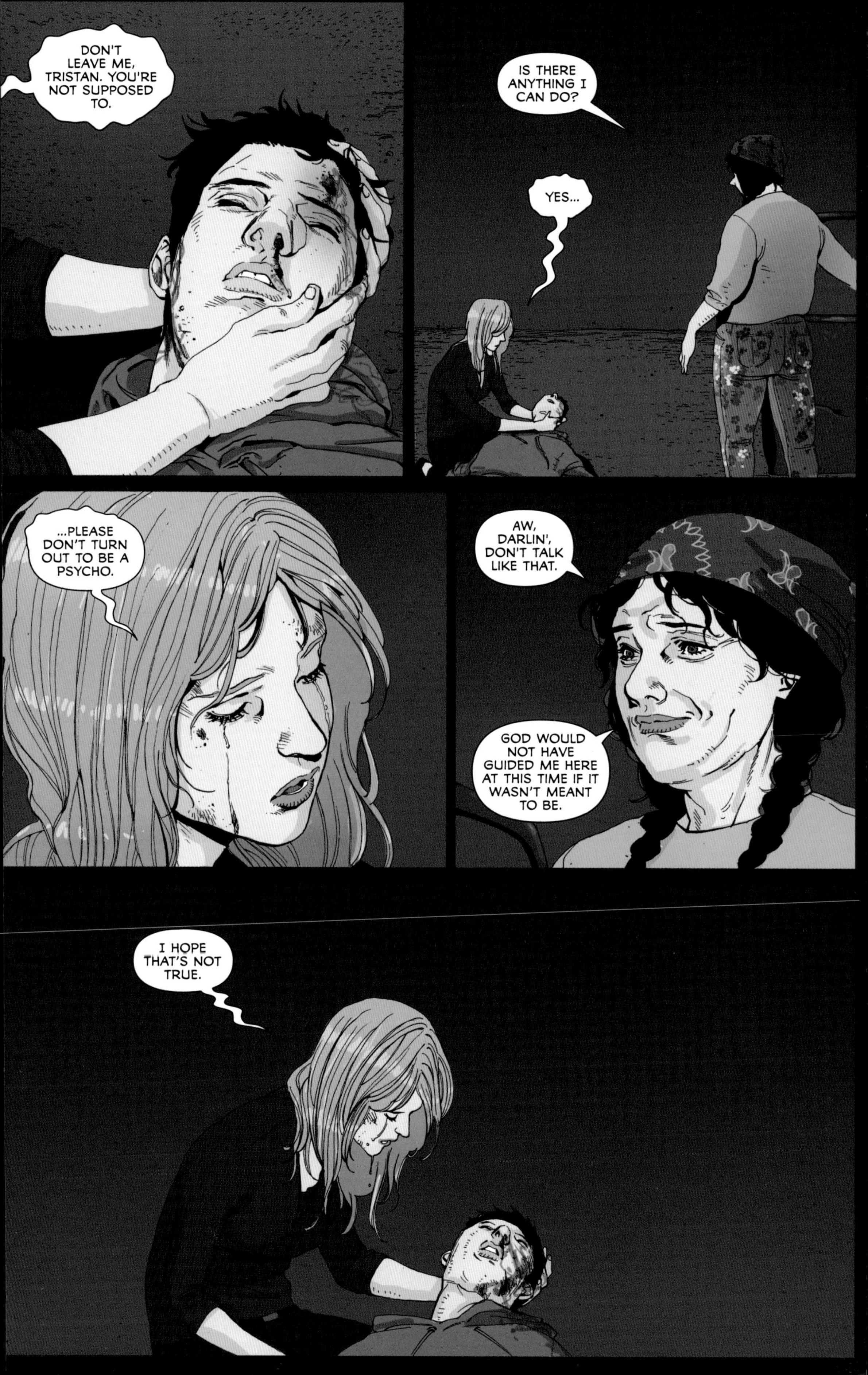
DON'T LEAVE ME, TRISTAN. YOU'RE NOT SUPPOSED TO.
IS THERE ANYTHING I CAN DO?
YES...
...PLEASE DON'T TURN OUT TO BE A PSYCHO.
AW, DARLIN', DON'T TALK LIKE THAT.
GOD WOULD NOT HAVE GUIDED ME HERE AT THIS TIME IF IT WASN'T MEANT TO BE.
I HOPE THAT'S NOT TRUE.

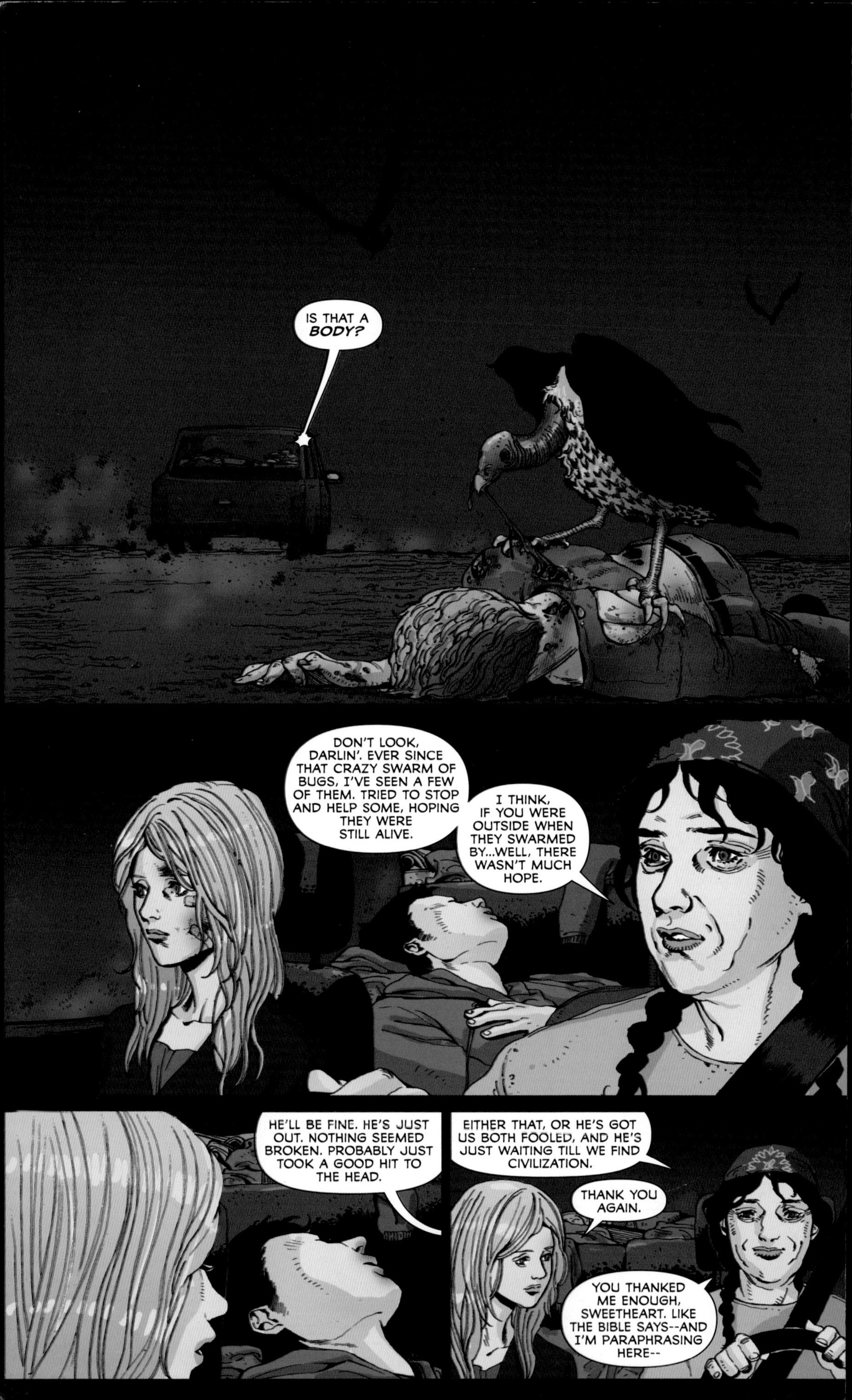

IS THAT A *BODY?*
DON'T LOOK, DARLIN'. EVER SINCE THAT CRAZY SWARM OF BUGS, I'VE SEEN A FEW OF THEM. TRIED TO STOP AND HELP SOME, HOPING THEY WERE STILL ALIVE.
I THINK, IF YOU WERE OUTSIDE WHEN THEY SWARMED BY...WELL, THERE WASN'T MUCH HOPE.
HE'LL BE FINE. HE'S JUST OUT. NOTHING SEEMED BROKEN. PROBABLY JUST TOOK A GOOD HIT TO THE HEAD.
EITHER THAT, OR HE'S GOT US BOTH FOOLED, AND HE'S JUST WAITING TILL WE FIND CIVILIZATION.
THANK YOU AGAIN.
YOU THANKED ME ENOUGH, SWEETHEART. LIKE THE BIBLE SAYS--AND I'M PARAPHRASING HERE--

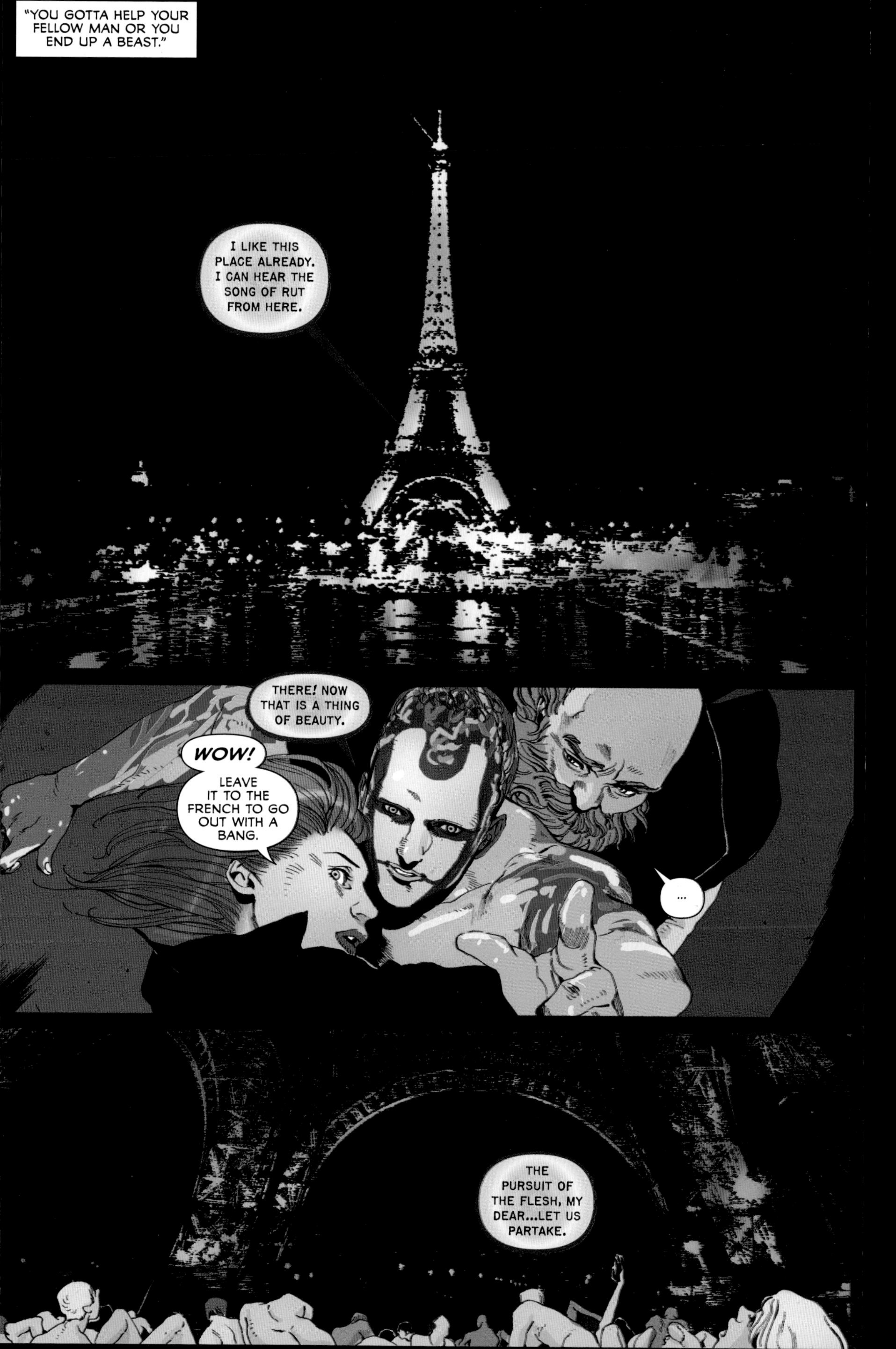

"YOU GOTTA HELP YOUR FELLOW MAN OR YOU END UP A BEAST."
I LIKE THIS PLACE ALREADY. I CAN HEAR THE SONG OF RUT FROM HERE.
THERE! NOW THAT IS A THING OF BEAUTY.
WOW!
LEAVE IT TO THE FRENCH TO GO OUT WITH A BANG.
...
THE PURSUIT OF THE FLESH, MY DEAR...LET US PARTAKE.

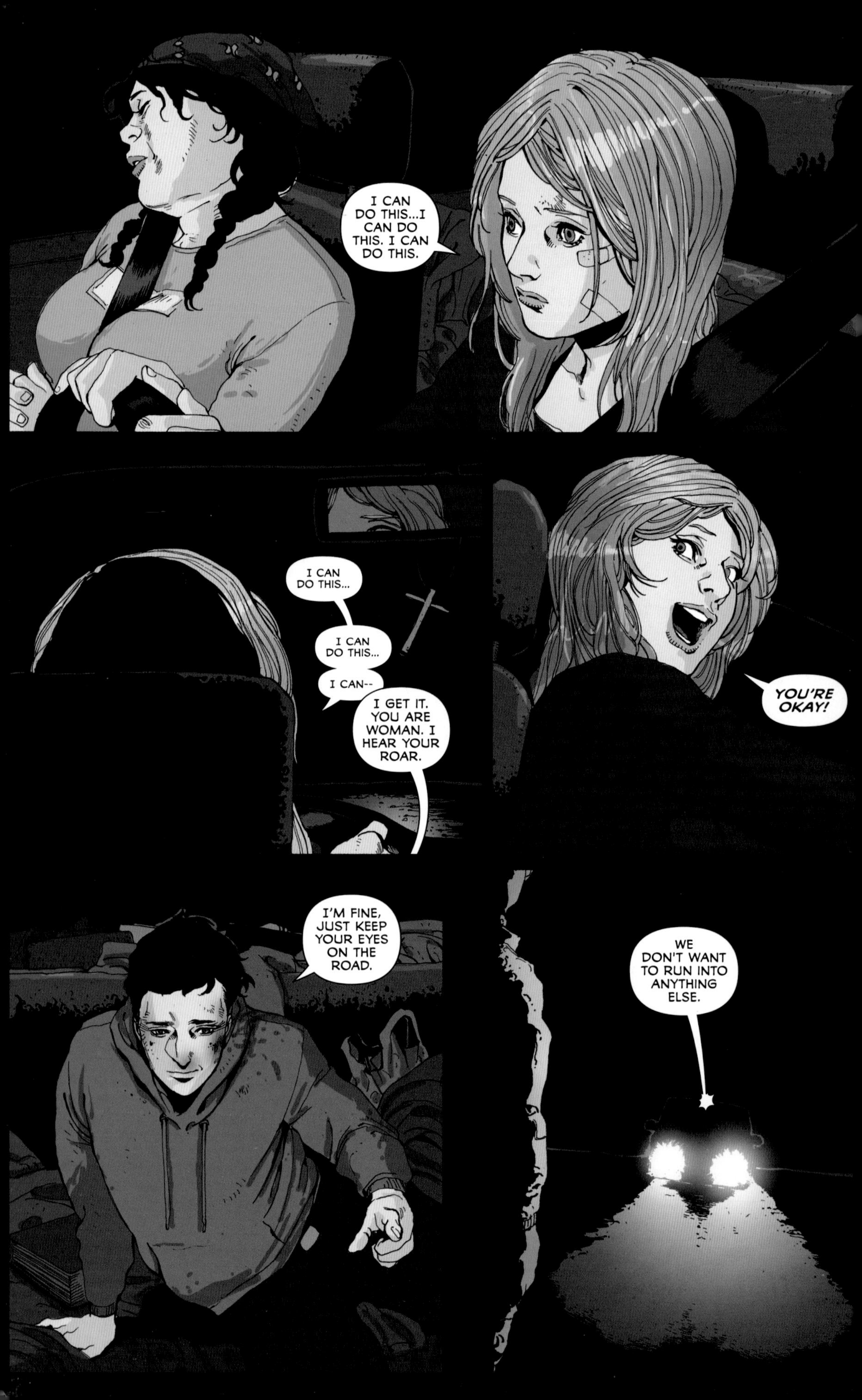
I CAN DO THIS...I CAN DO THIS. I CAN DO THIS.
I CAN DO THIS...
I CAN DO THIS...
I CAN--
I GET IT. YOU ARE WOMAN. I HEAR YOUR ROAR.
YOU'RE OKAY!
I'M FINE, JUST KEEP YOUR EYES ON THE ROAD.
WE DON'T WANT TO RUN INTO ANYTHING ELSE.

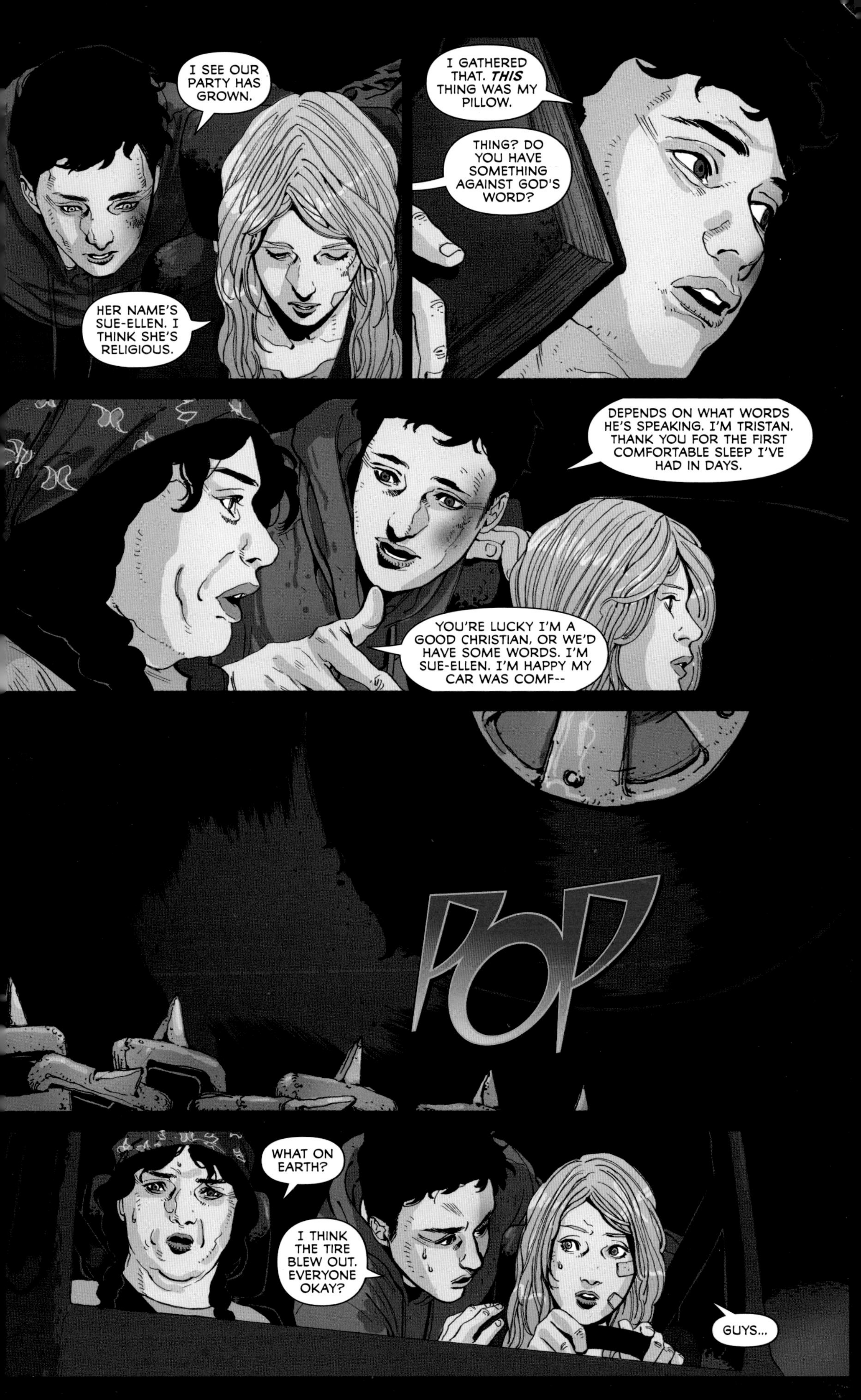
I SEE OUR PARTY HAS GROWN.
HER NAME'S SUE-ELLEN. I THINK SHE'S RELIGIOUS.
I GATHERED THAT. *THIS* THING WAS MY PILLOW.
THING? DO YOU HAVE SOMETHING AGAINST GOD'S WORD?
DEPENDS ON WHAT WORDS HE'S SPEAKING. I'M TRISTAN. THANK YOU FOR THE FIRST COMFORTABLE SLEEP I'VE HAD IN DAYS.
YOU'RE LUCKY I'M A GOOD CHRISTIAN, OR WE'D HAVE SOME WORDS. I'M SUE-ELLEN. I'M HAPPY MY CAR WAS COMF--
POP
WHAT ON EARTH?
I THINK THE TIRE BLEW OUT. EVERYONE OKAY?
GUYS...

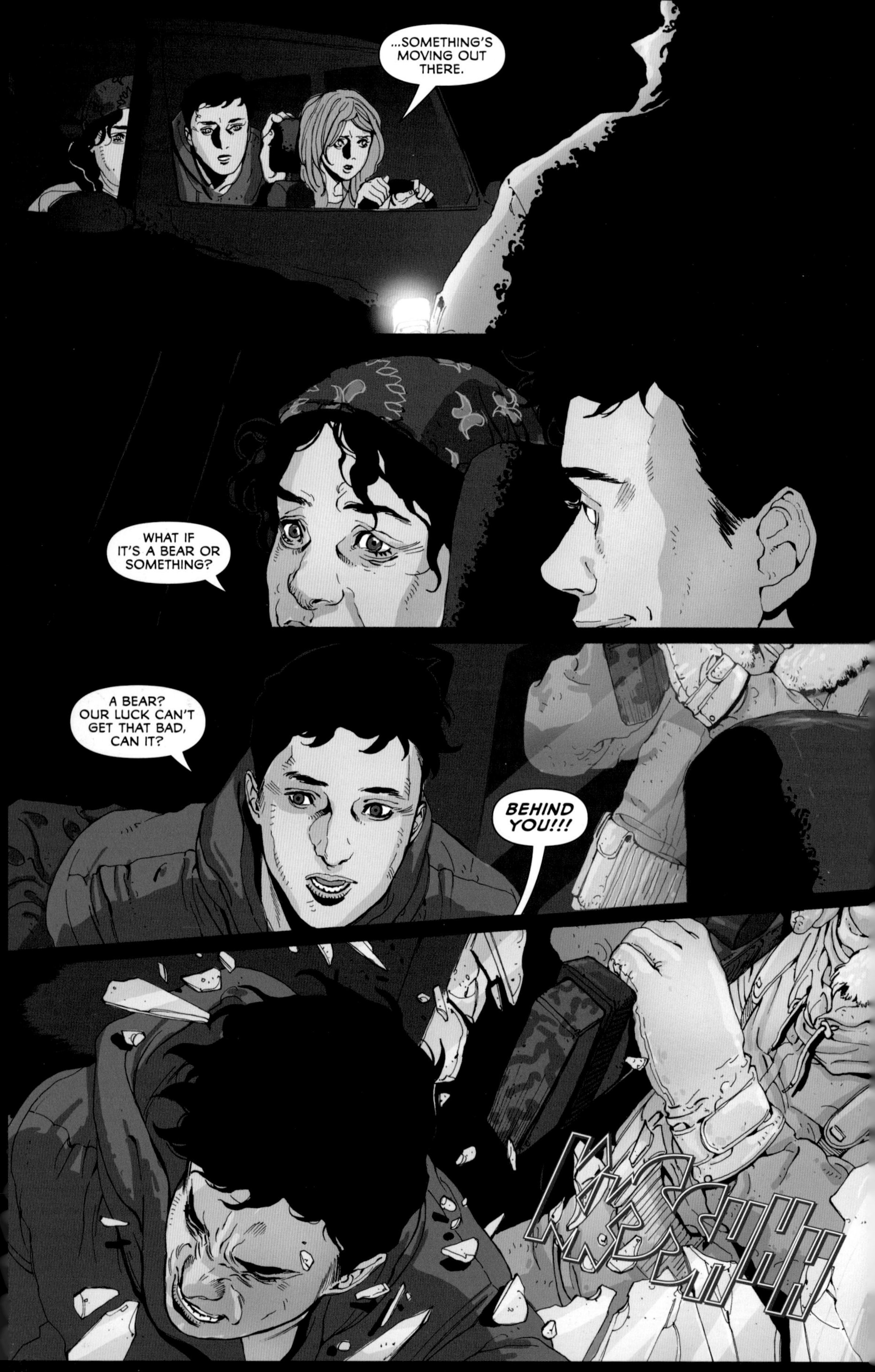
...SOMETHING'S MOVING OUT THERE.
WHAT IF IT'S A BEAR OR SOMETHING?
A BEAR? OUR LUCK CAN'T GET THAT BAD, CAN IT?
BEHIND YOU!!!

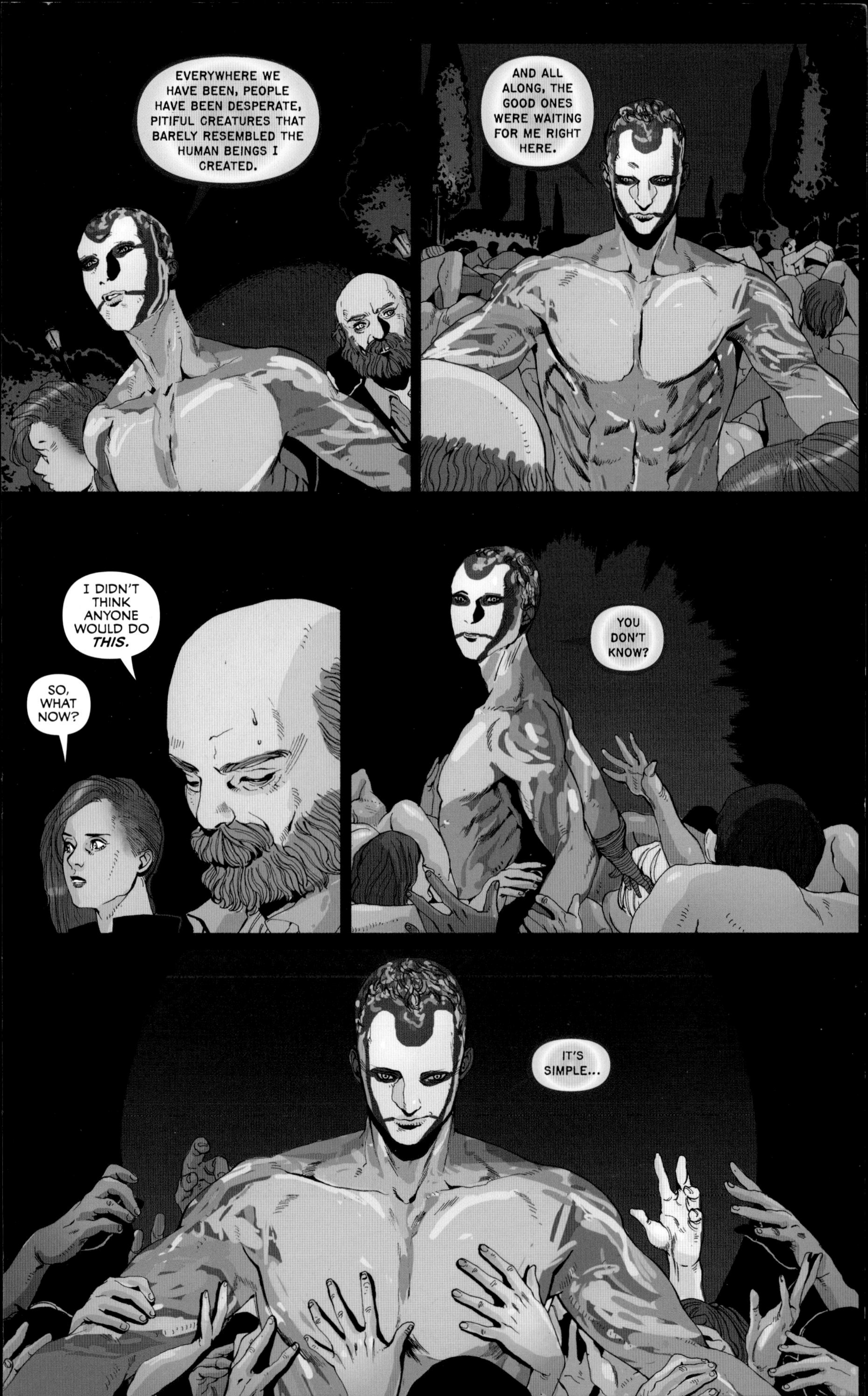
EVERYWHERE WE HAVE BEEN, PEOPLE HAVE BEEN DESPERATE, PITIFUL CREATURES THAT BARELY RESEMBLED THE HUMAN BEINGS I CREATED.
AND ALL ALONG, THE GOOD ONES WERE WAITING FOR ME RIGHT HERE.
I DIDN'T THINK ANYONE WOULD DO *THIS.*
SO, WHAT NOW?
YOU DON'T KNOW?
IT'S SIMPLE...

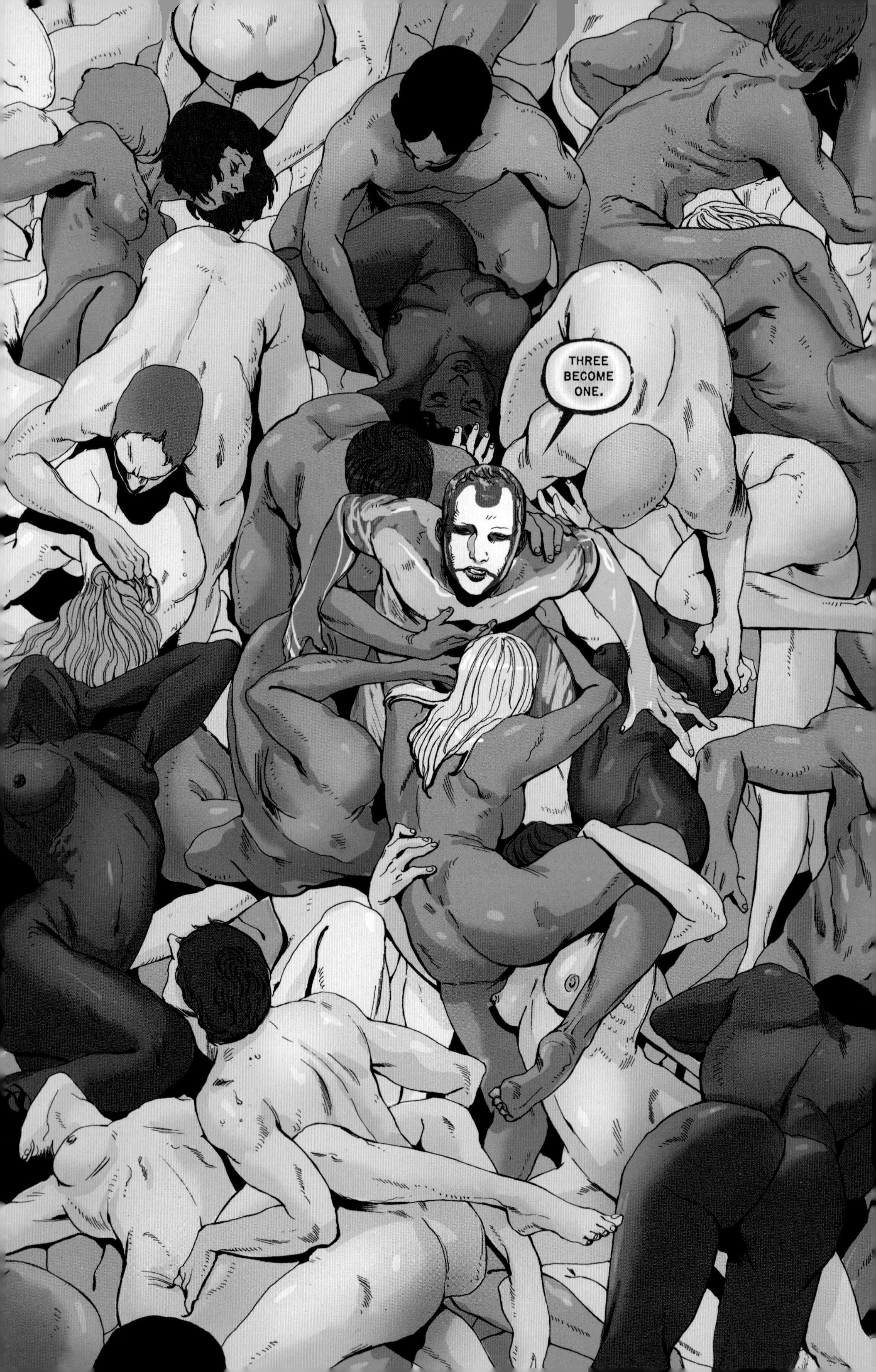
THREE BECOME ONE.

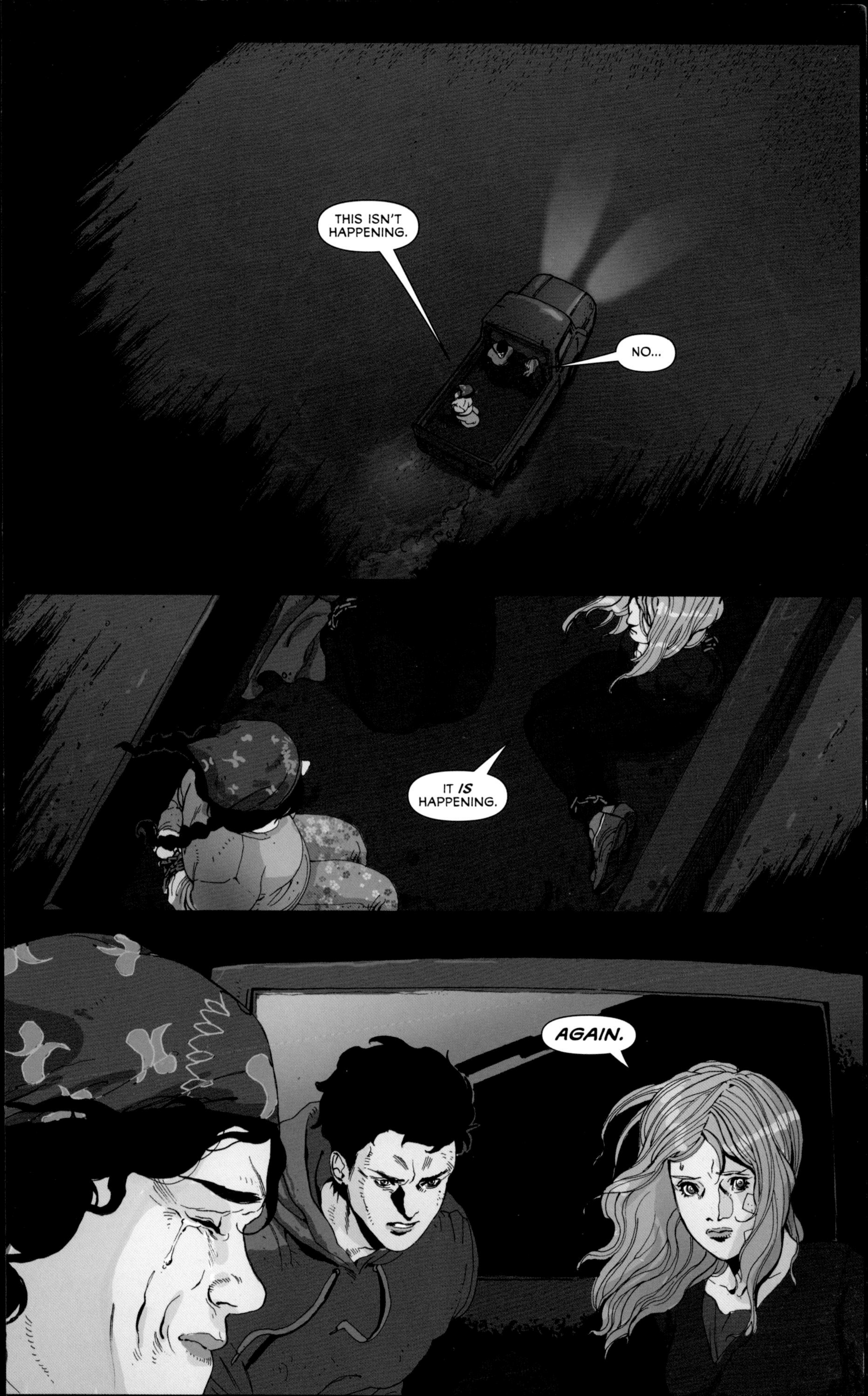
THIS ISN'T HAPPENING.
NO...
IT *IS* HAPPENING.
AGAIN.

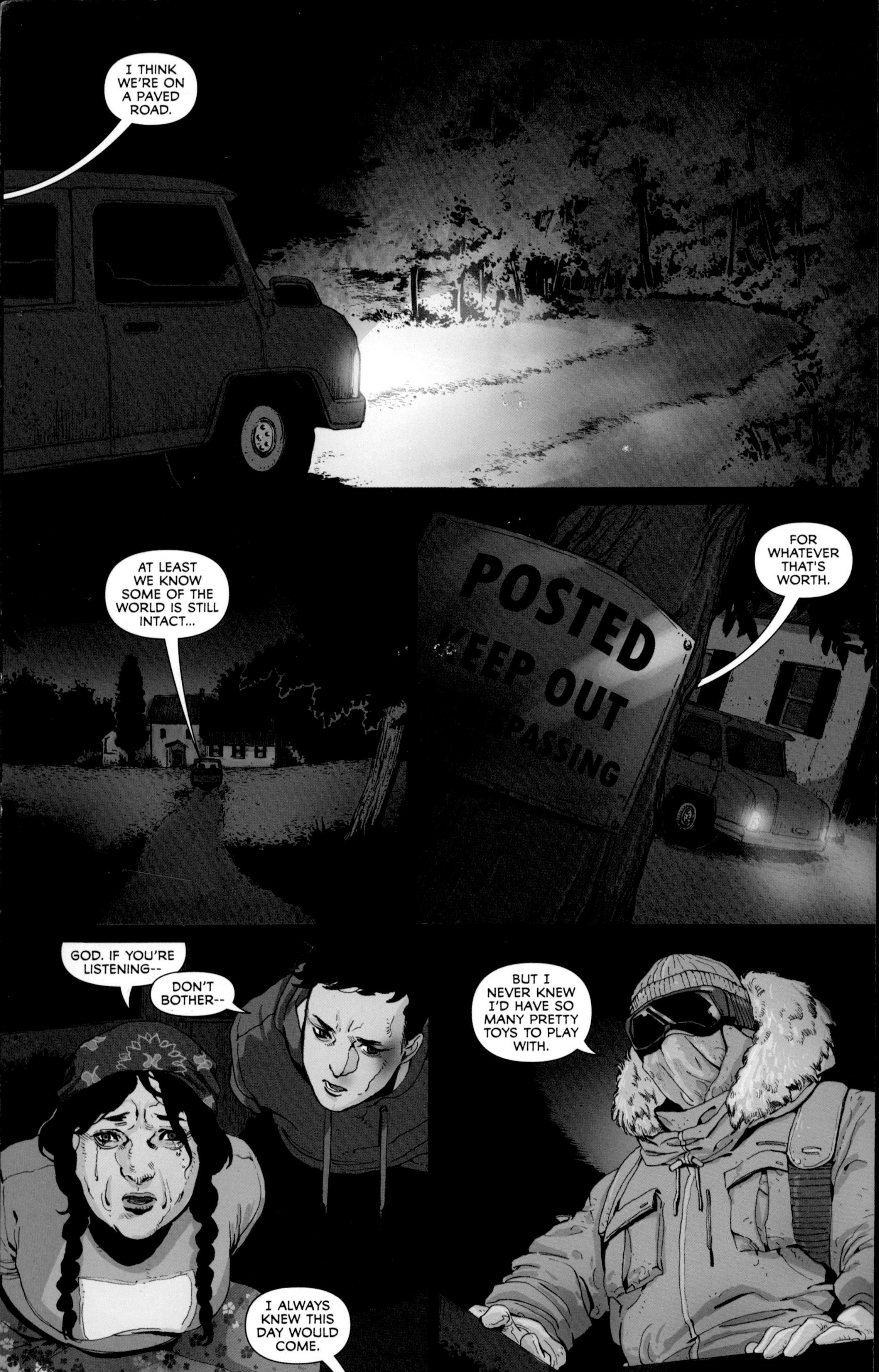
I THINK WE'RE ON A PAVED ROAD.
AT LEAST WE KNOW SOME OF THE WORLD IS STILL INTACT...
POSTED
EEP OUT
PASSING
FOR WHATEVER THAT'S WORTH.
GOD. IF YOU'RE LISTENING--
DON'T BOTHER--
I ALWAYS KNEW THIS DAY WOULD COME.
BUT I NEVER KNEW I'D HAVE SO MANY PRETTY TOYS TO PLAY WITH.

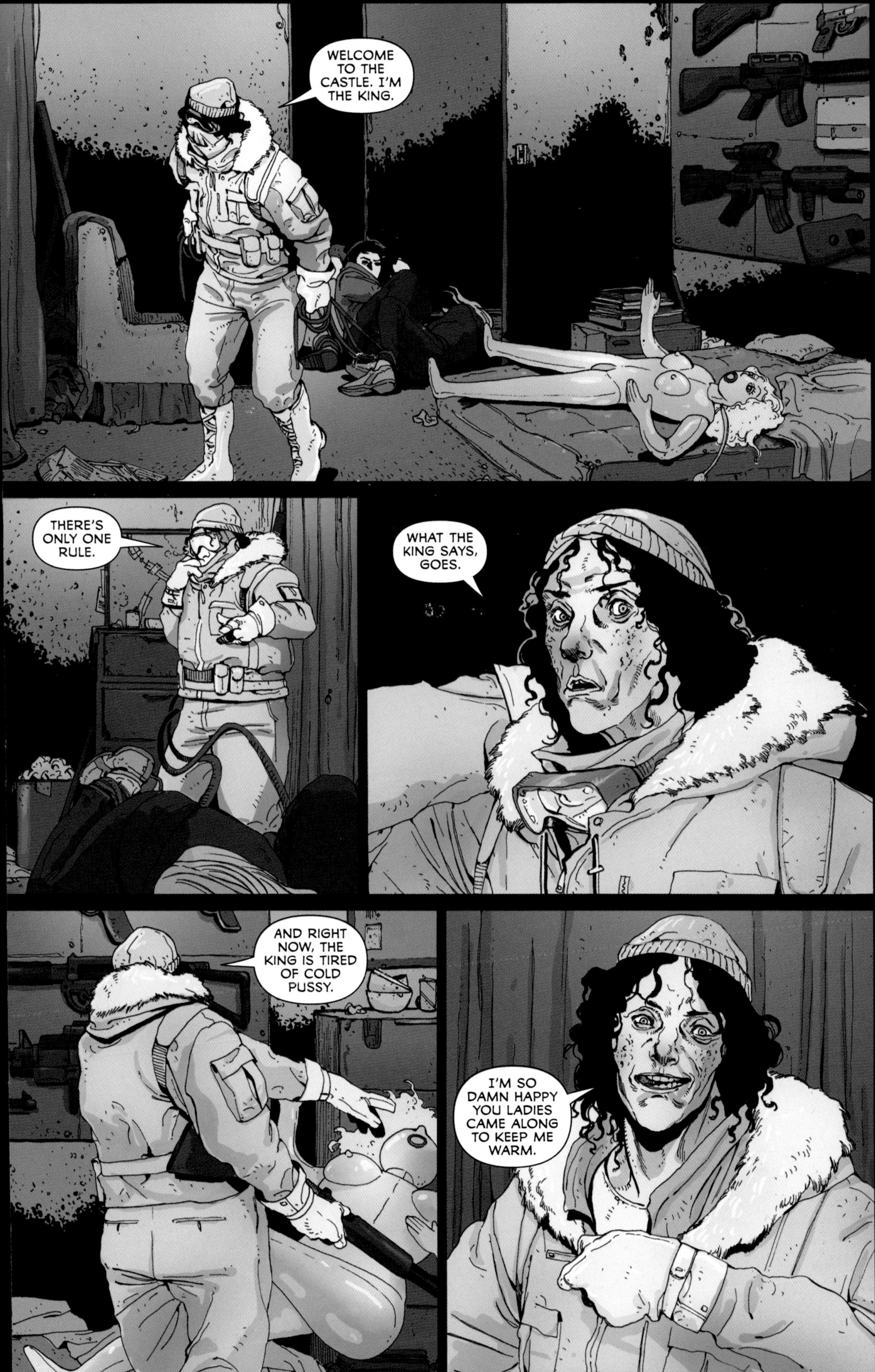
WELCOME TO THE CASTLE. I'M THE KING.
THERE'S ONLY ONE RULE.
WHAT THE KING SAYS, GOES.
AND RIGHT NOW, THE KING IS TIRED OF COLD PUSSY.
I'M SO DAMN HAPPY YOU LADIES CAME ALONG TO KEEP ME WARM.

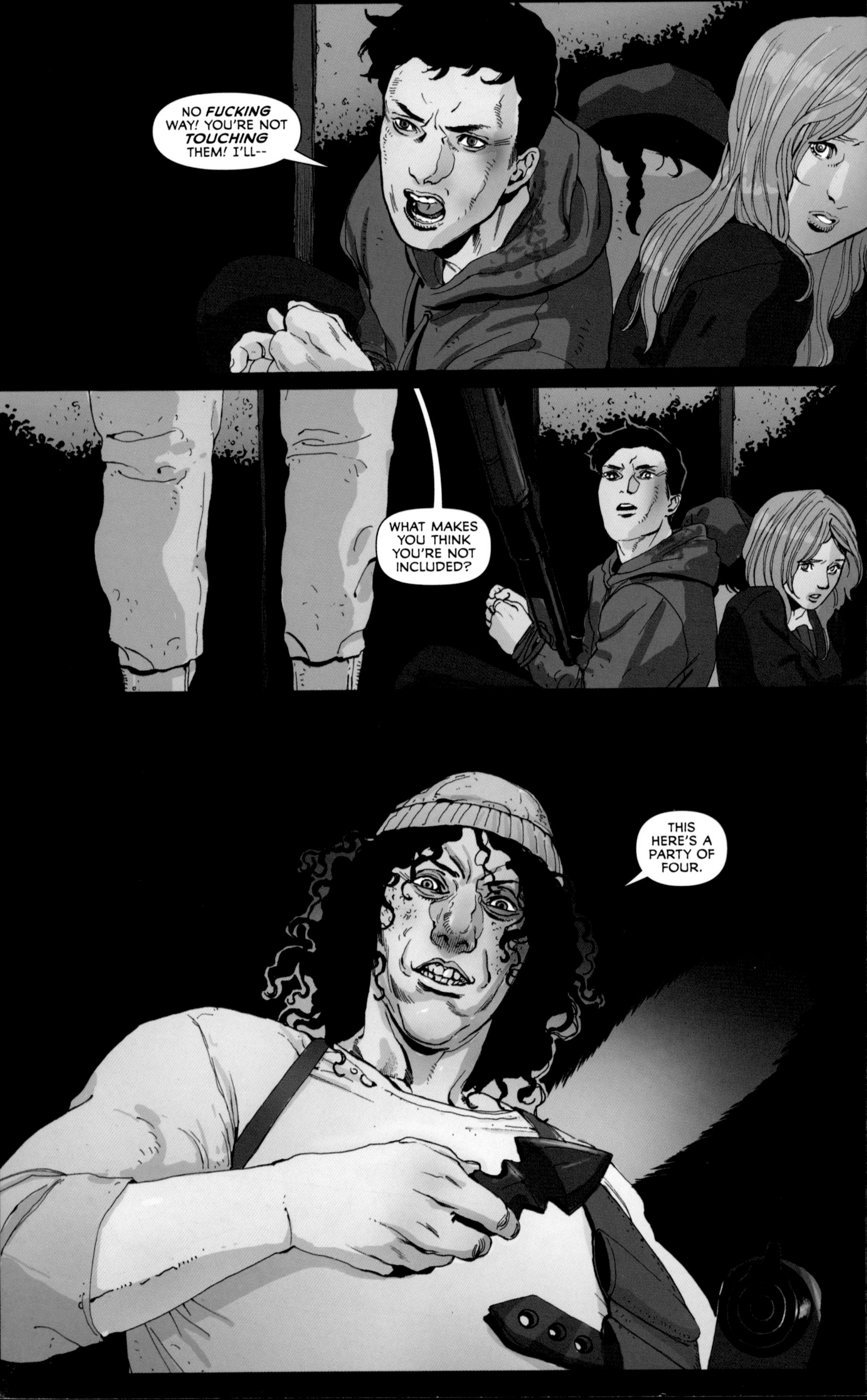
NO *FUCKING* WAY! YOU'RE NOT *TOUCHING* THEM! I'LL--
WHAT MAKES YOU THINK YOU'RE NOT INCLUDED?
THIS HERE'S A PARTY OF FOUR.

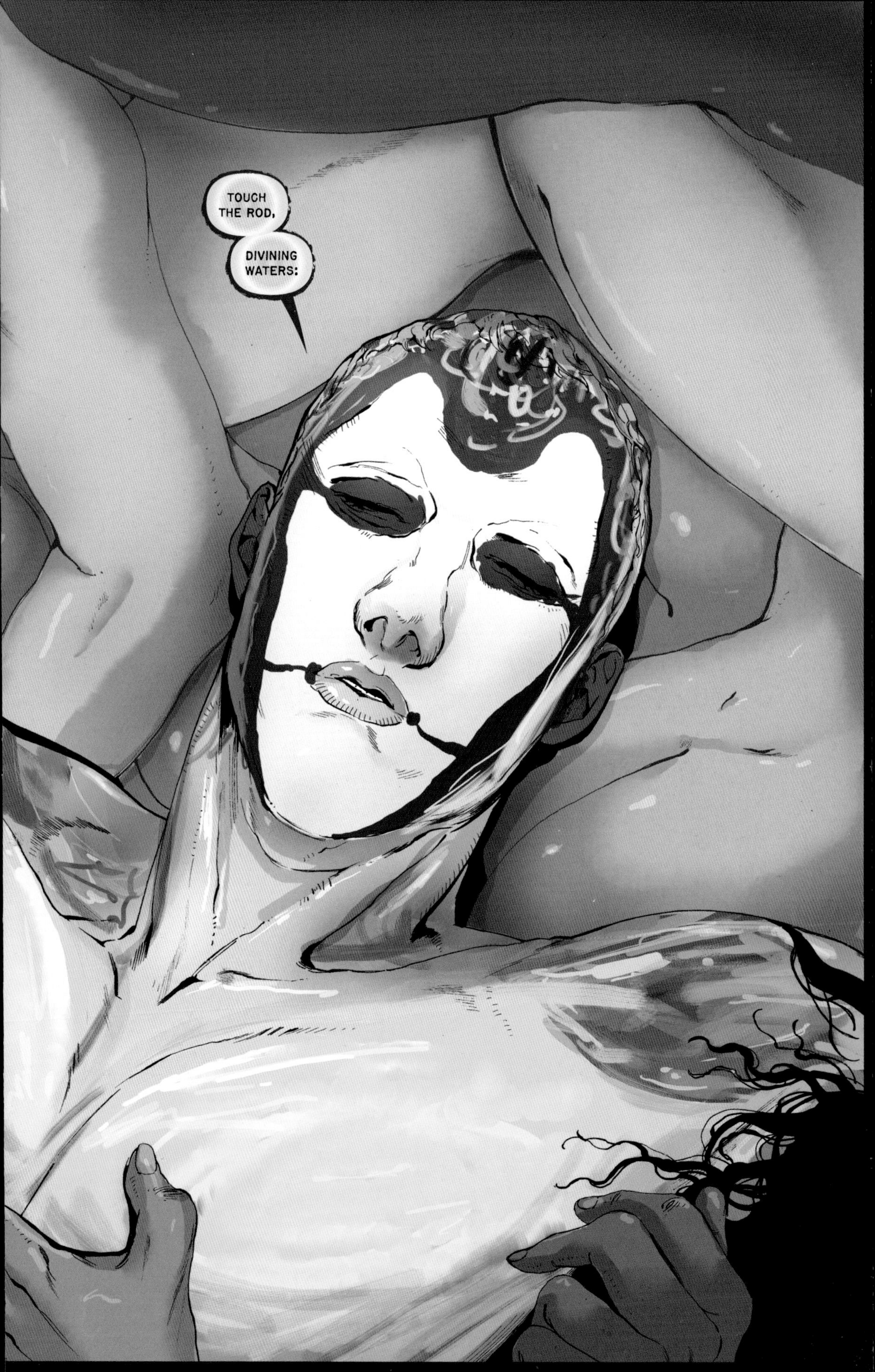
TOUCH THE ROD,
DIVINING WATERS:

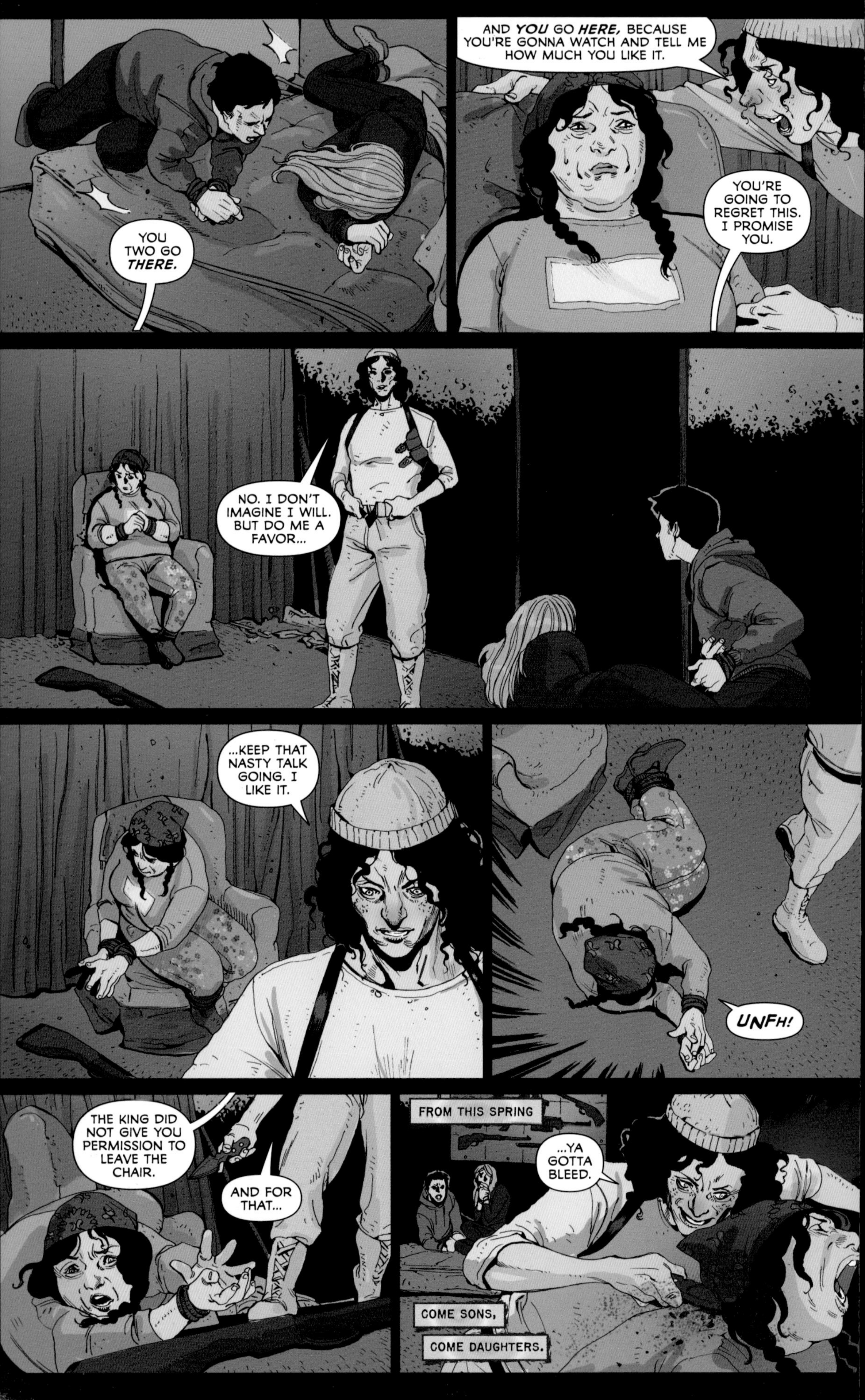
YOU TWO GO *THERE.*
AND *YOU* GO *HERE,* BECAUSE YOU'RE GONNA WATCH AND TELL ME HOW MUCH YOU LIKE IT.
YOU'RE GOING TO REGRET THIS. I PROMISE YOU.
NO. I DON'T IMAGINE I WILL. BUT DO ME A FAVOR...
...KEEP THAT NASTY TALK GOING. I LIKE IT.
UNFH!
THE KING DID NOT GIVE YOU PERMISSION TO LEAVE THE CHAIR.
AND FOR THAT...
FROM THIS SPRING
...YA GOTTA BLEED.
COME SONS,
COME DAUGHTERS.

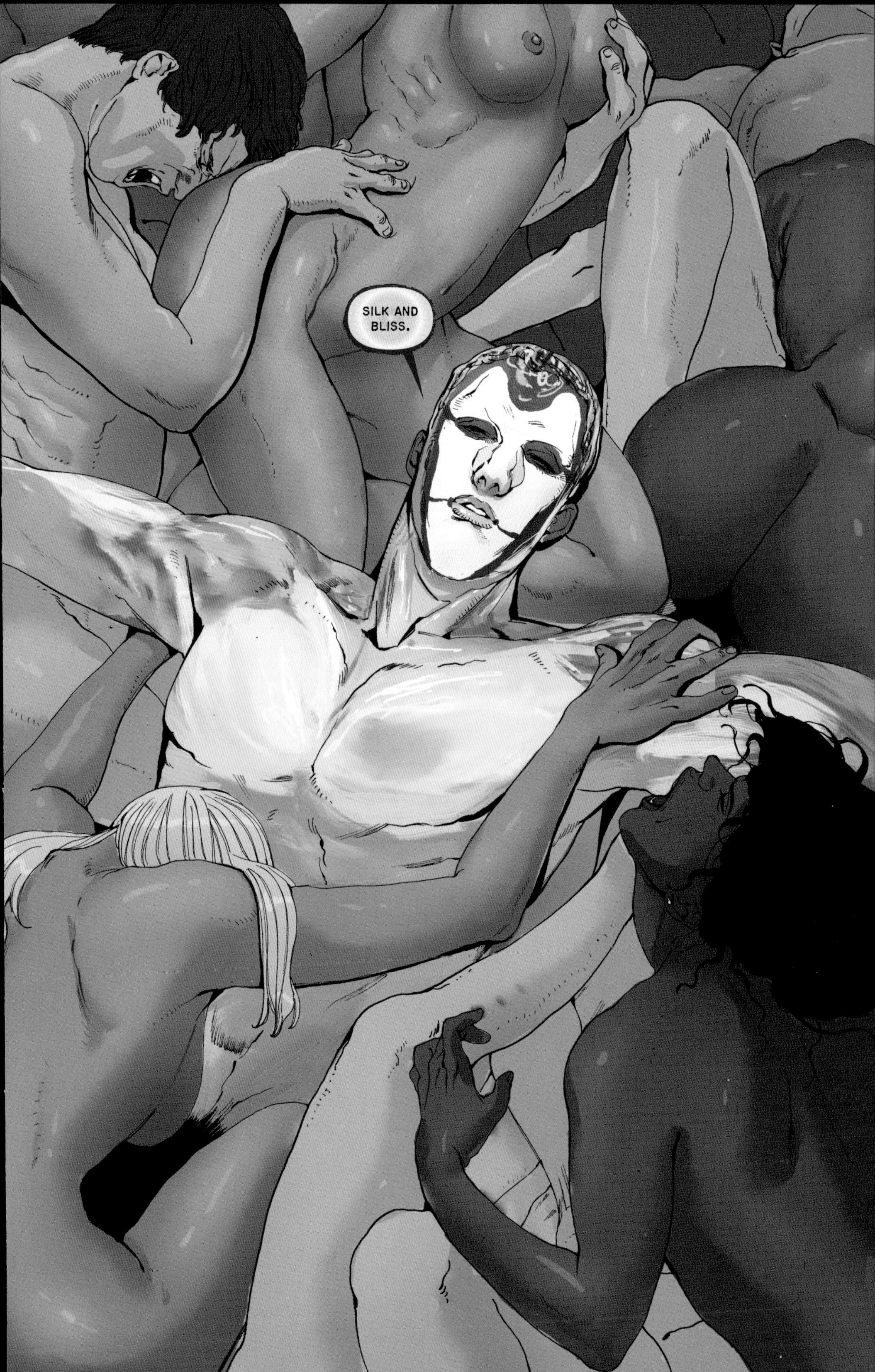
SILK AND BLISS.

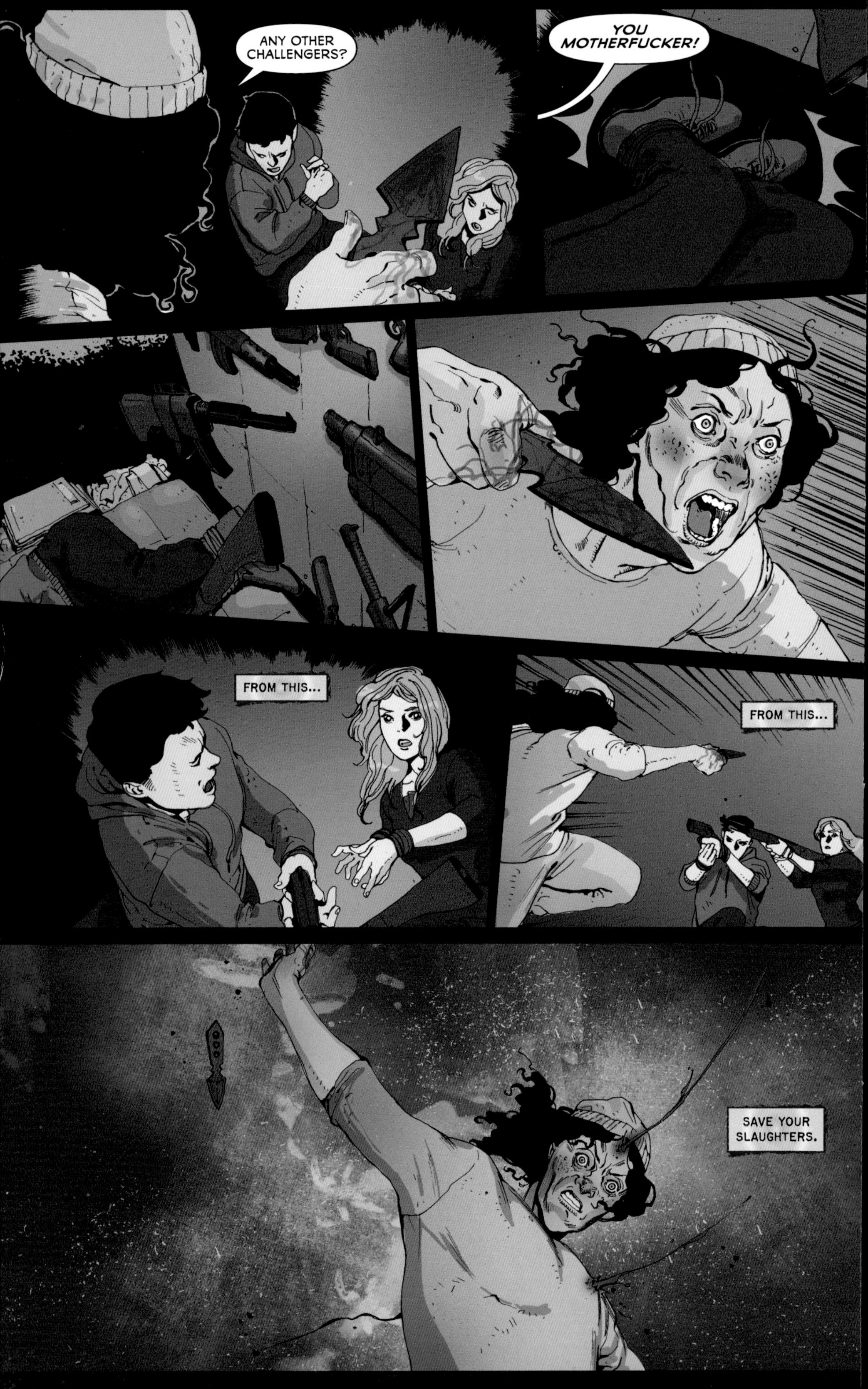
ANY OTHER CHALLENGERS?
YOU MOTHERFUCKER!
FROM THIS...
FROM THIS...
SAVE YOUR SLAUGHTERS.

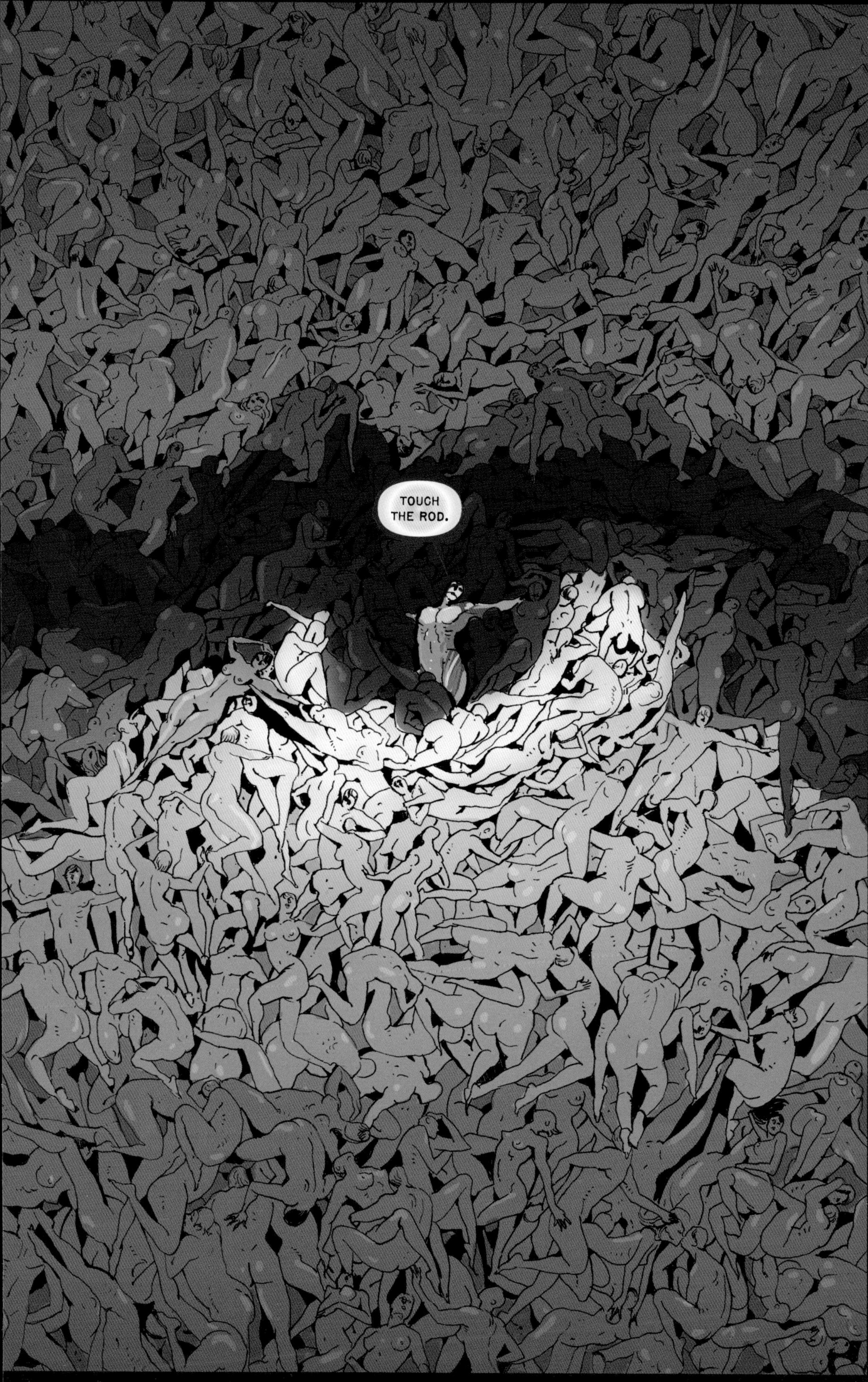
TOUCH THE ROD.

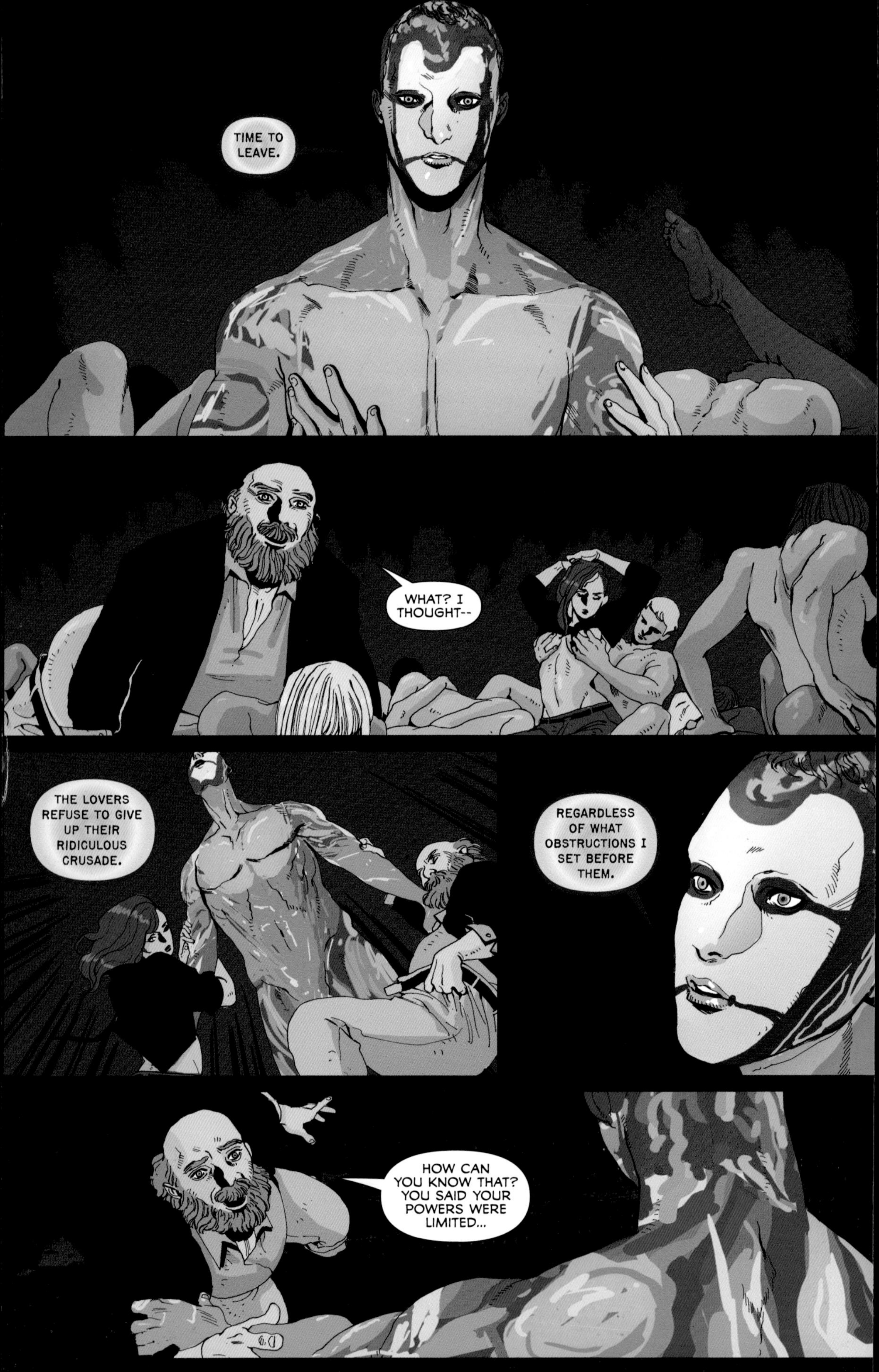
TIME TO LEAVE.
WHAT? I THOUGHT--
THE LOVERS REFUSE TO GIVE UP THEIR RIDICULOUS CRUSADE.
REGARDLESS OF WHAT OBSTRUCTIONS I SET BEFORE THEM.
HOW CAN YOU KNOW THAT? YOU SAID YOUR POWERS WERE LIMITED...

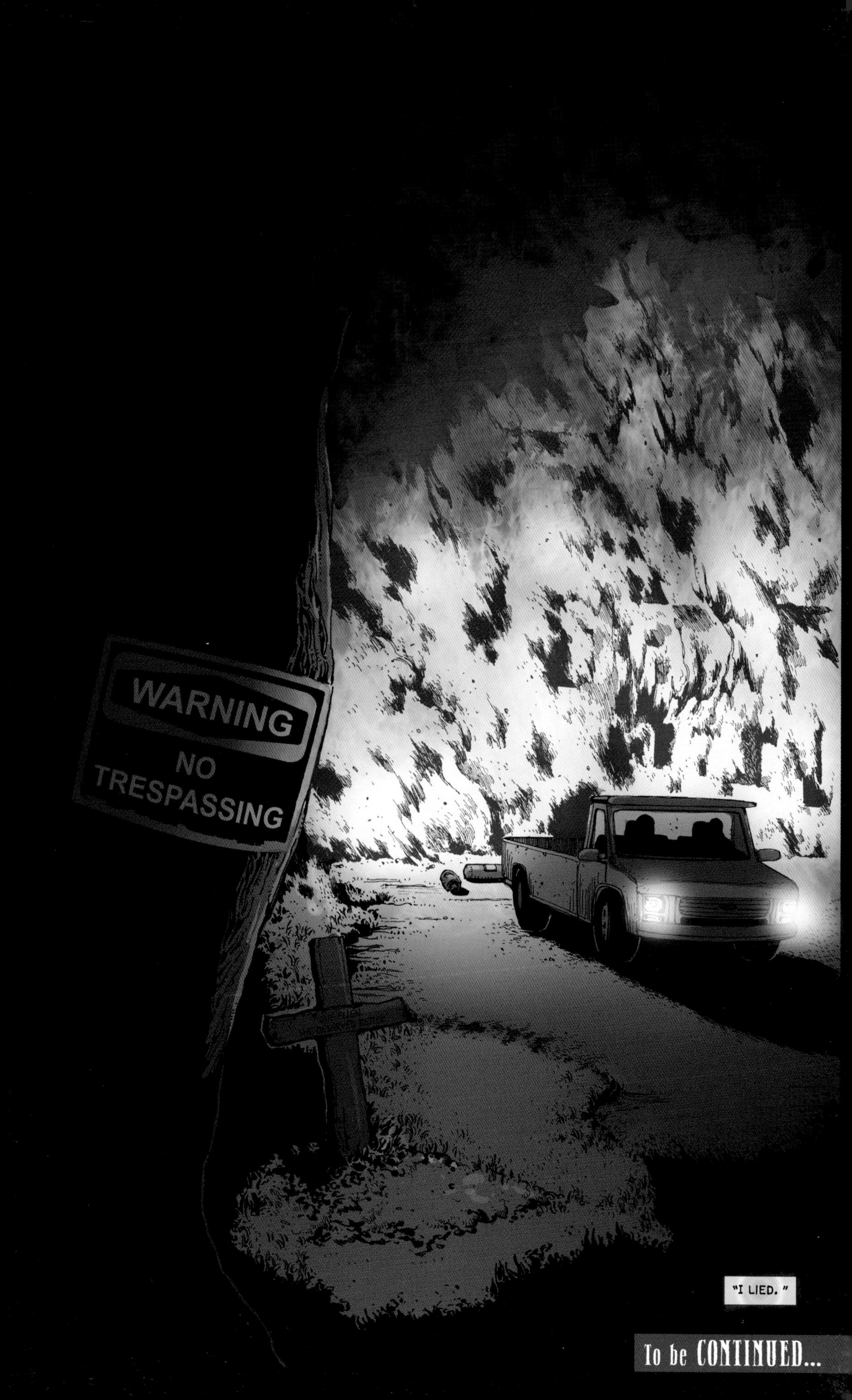
WARNING
NO TRESPASSING
"I LIED."
To be CONTINUED...

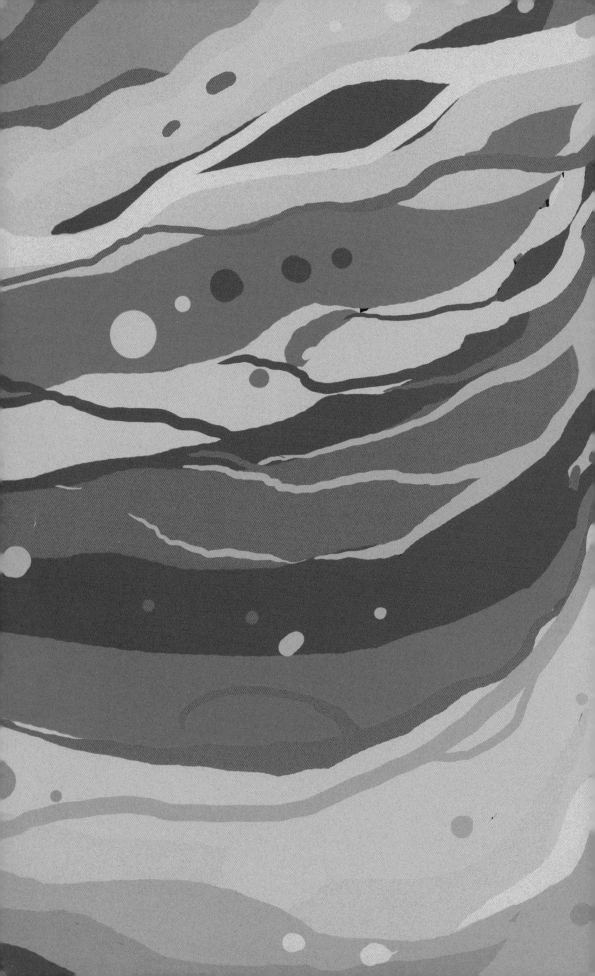

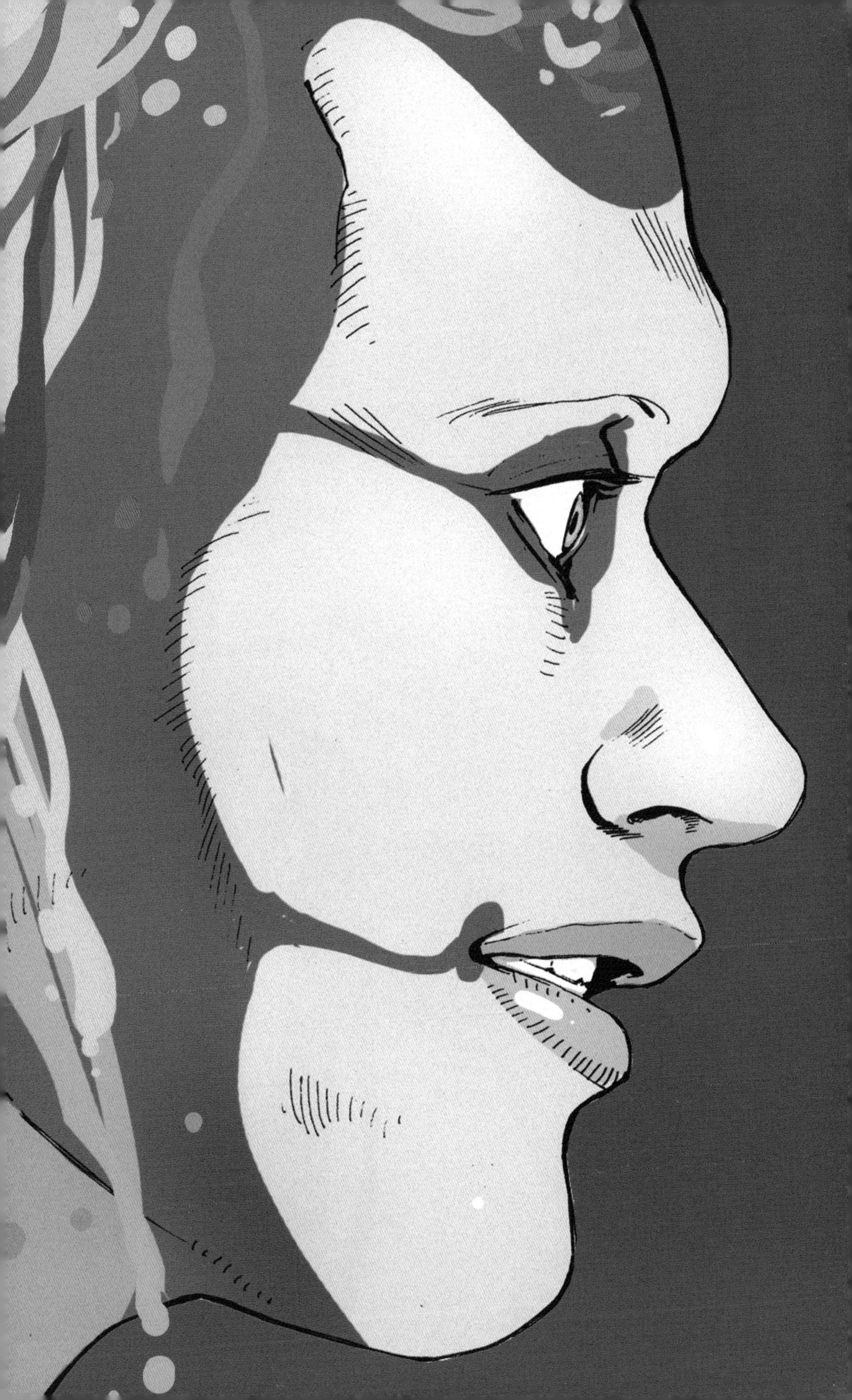

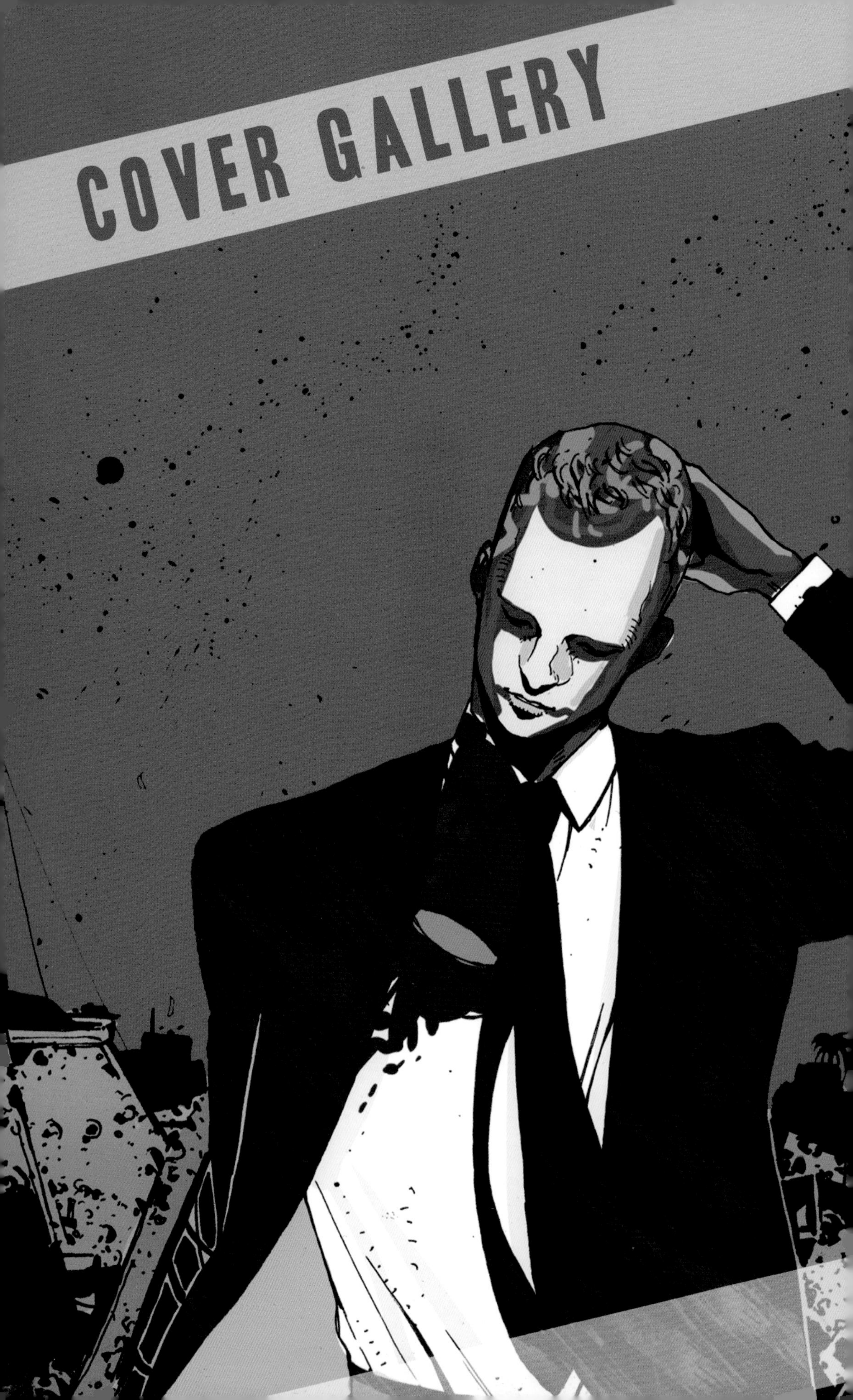
COVER GALLERY

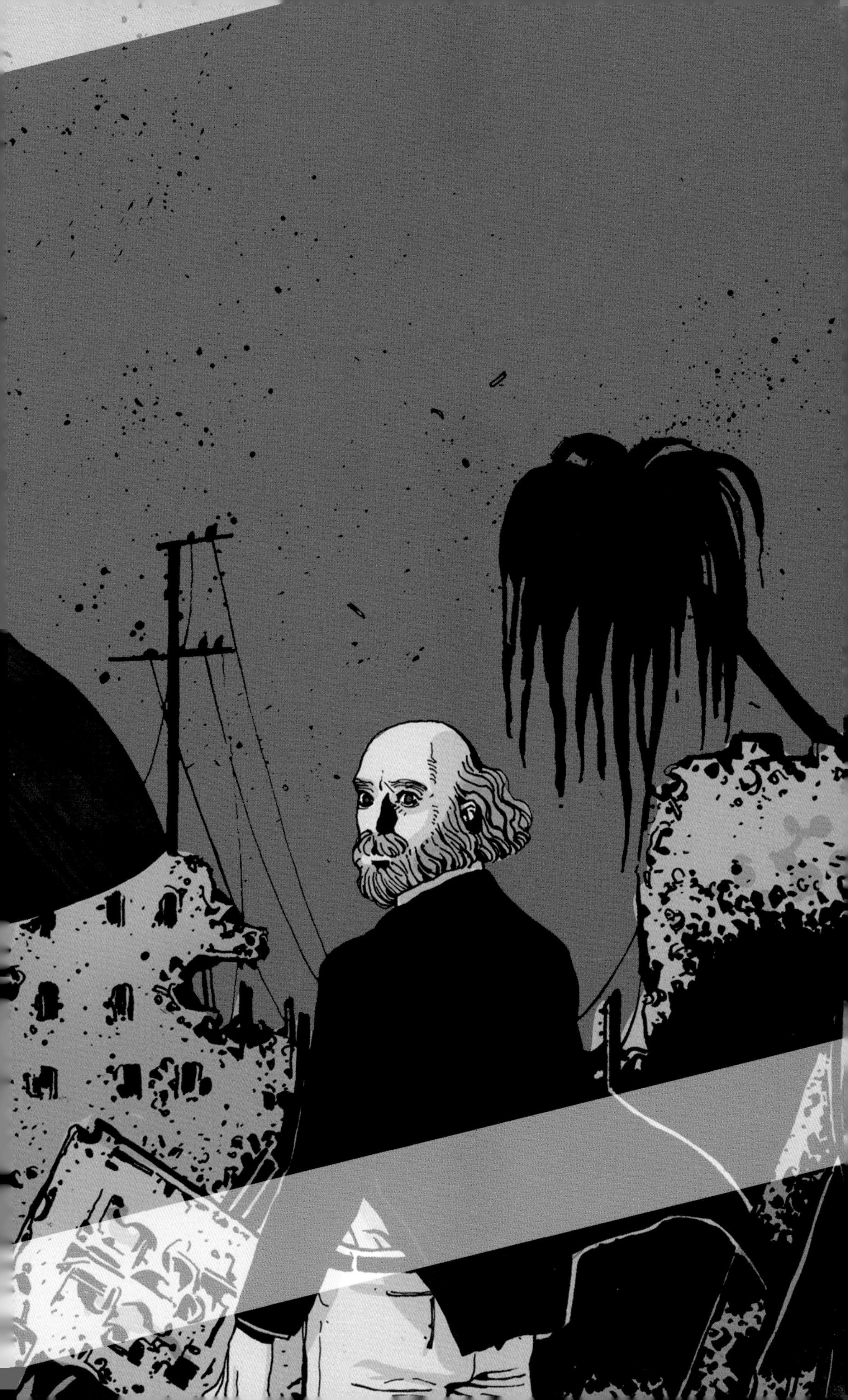

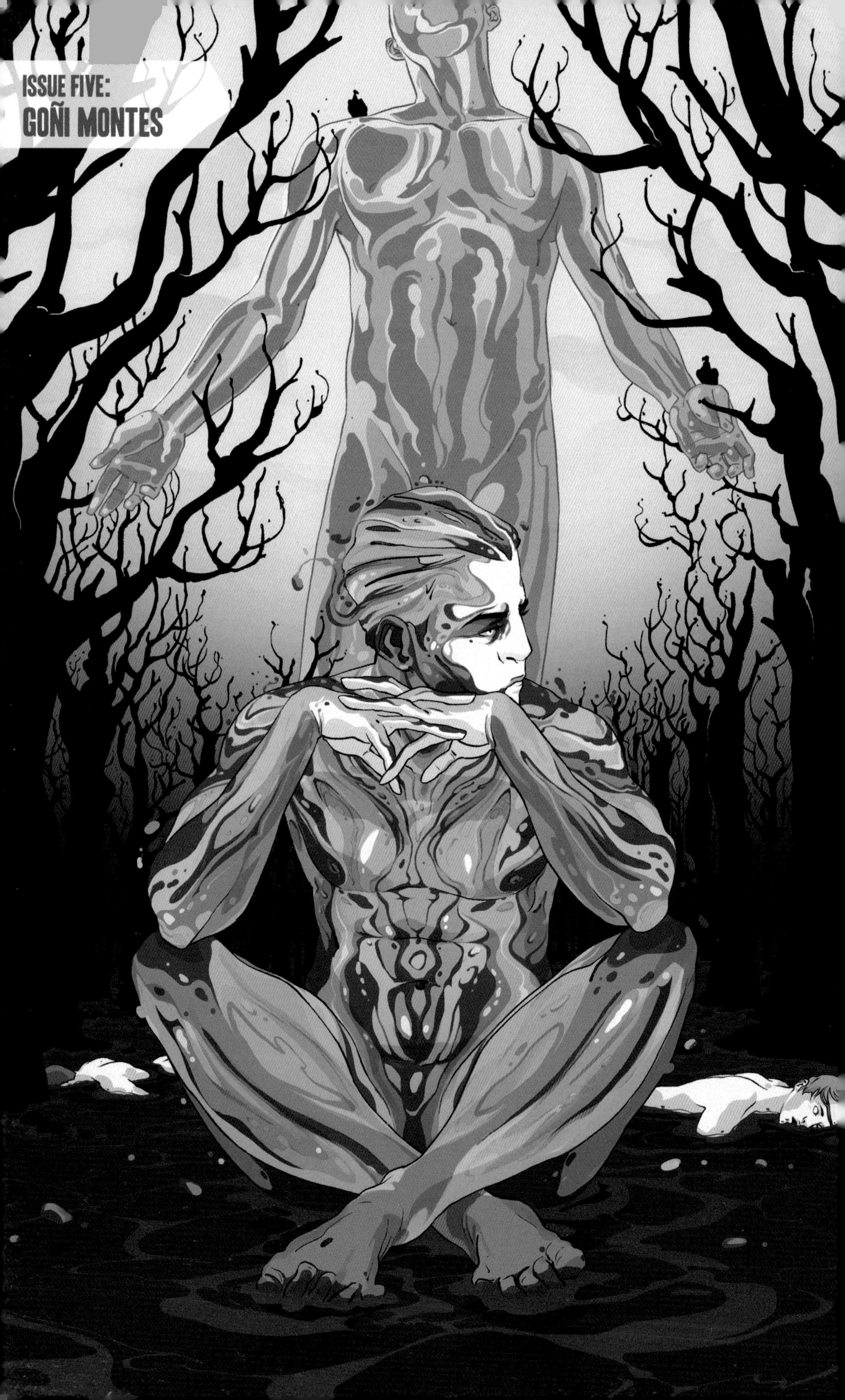

ISSUE FIVE:
GOÑI MONTES

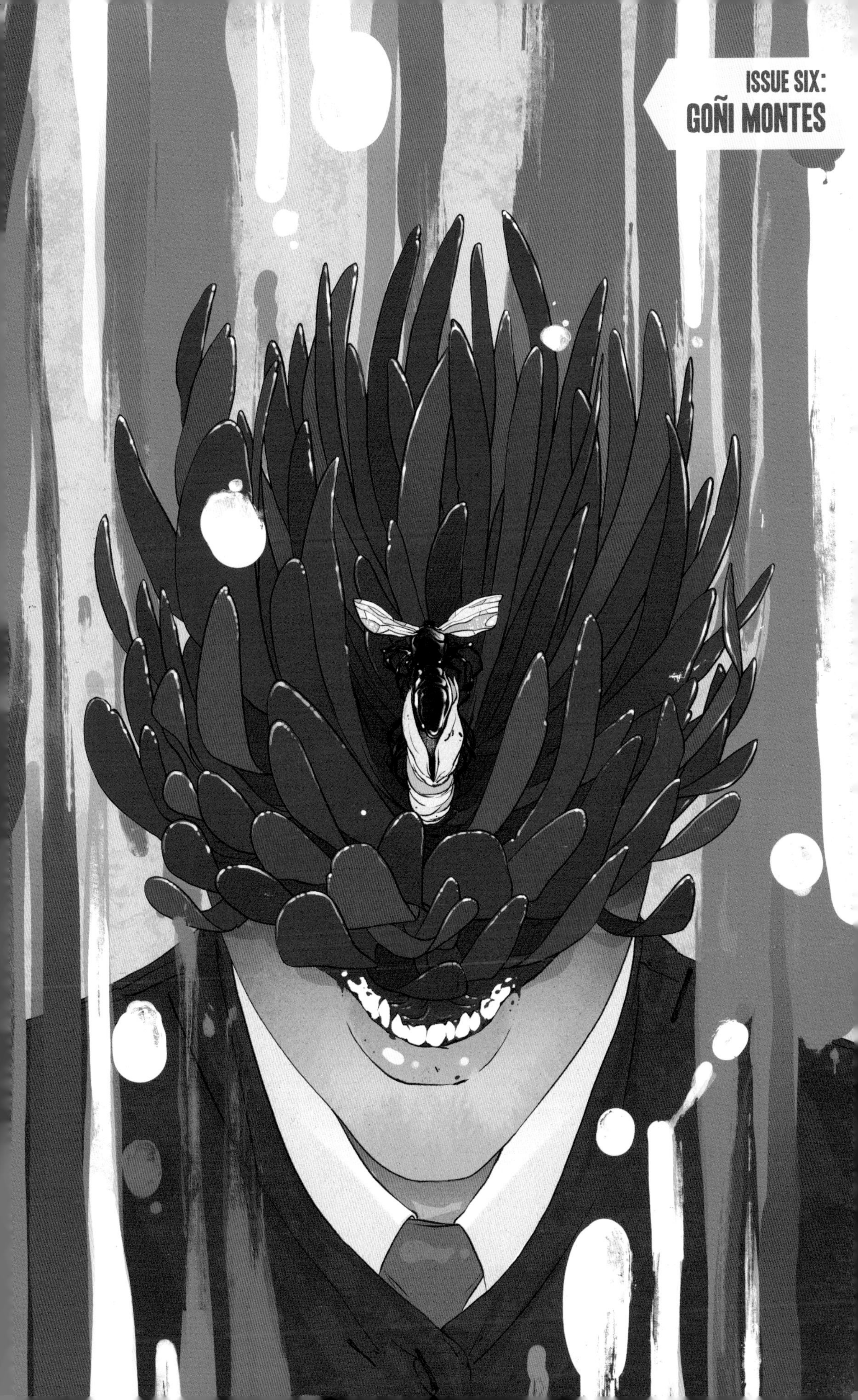
ISSUE SIX:
GOÑI MONTES

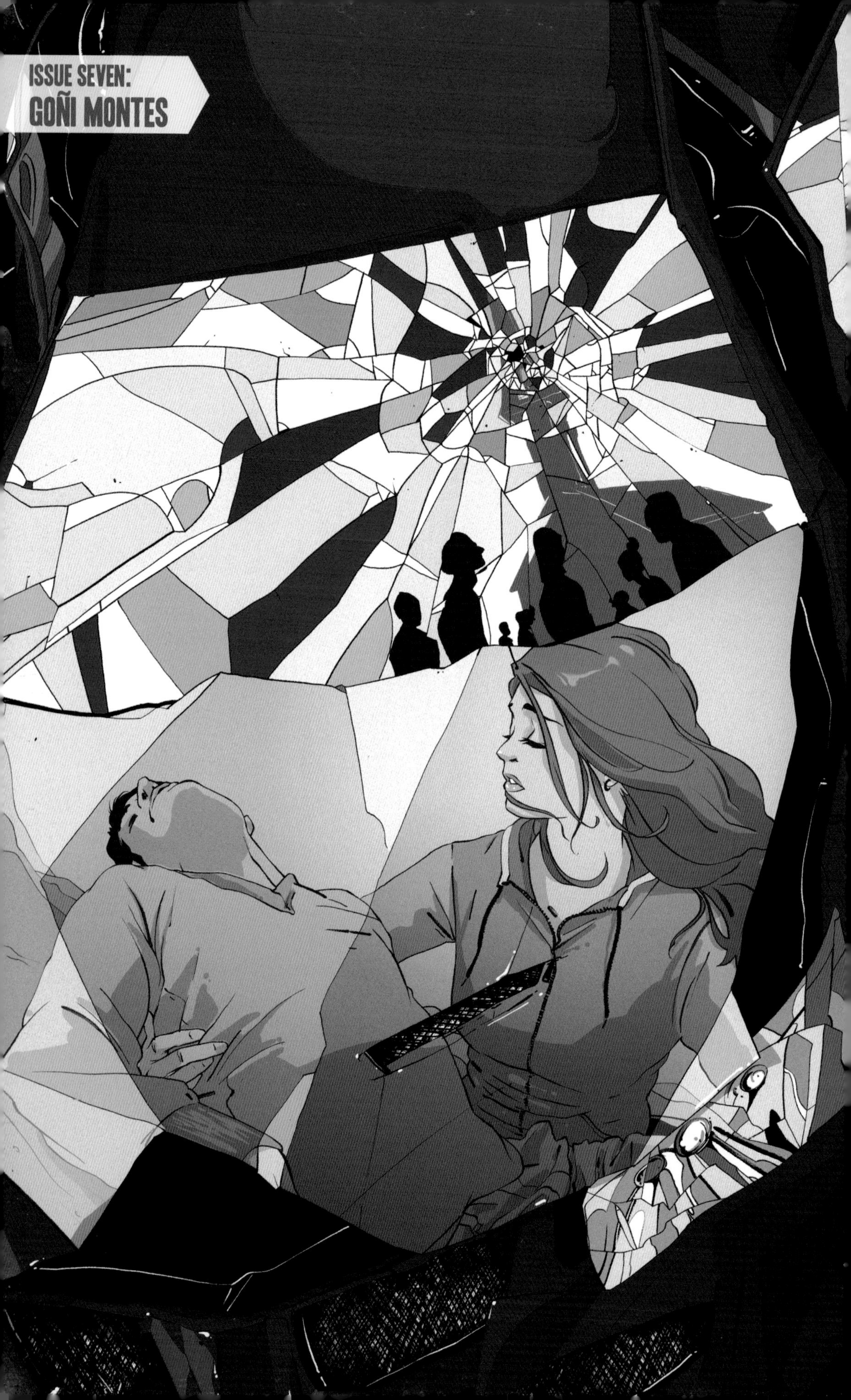
ISSUE SEVEN:
GOÑI MONTES

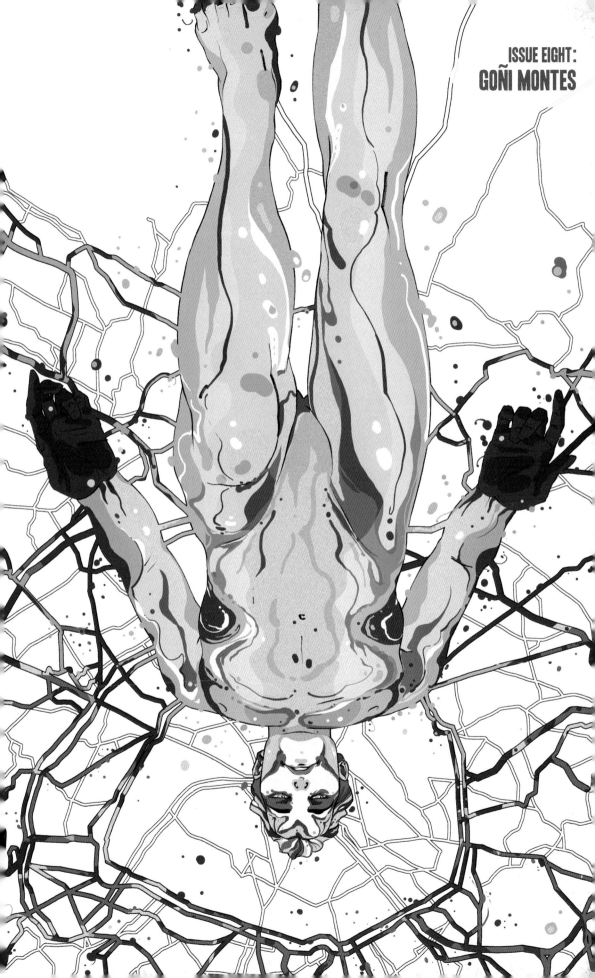

ISSUE EIGHT:
GOÑI MONTES

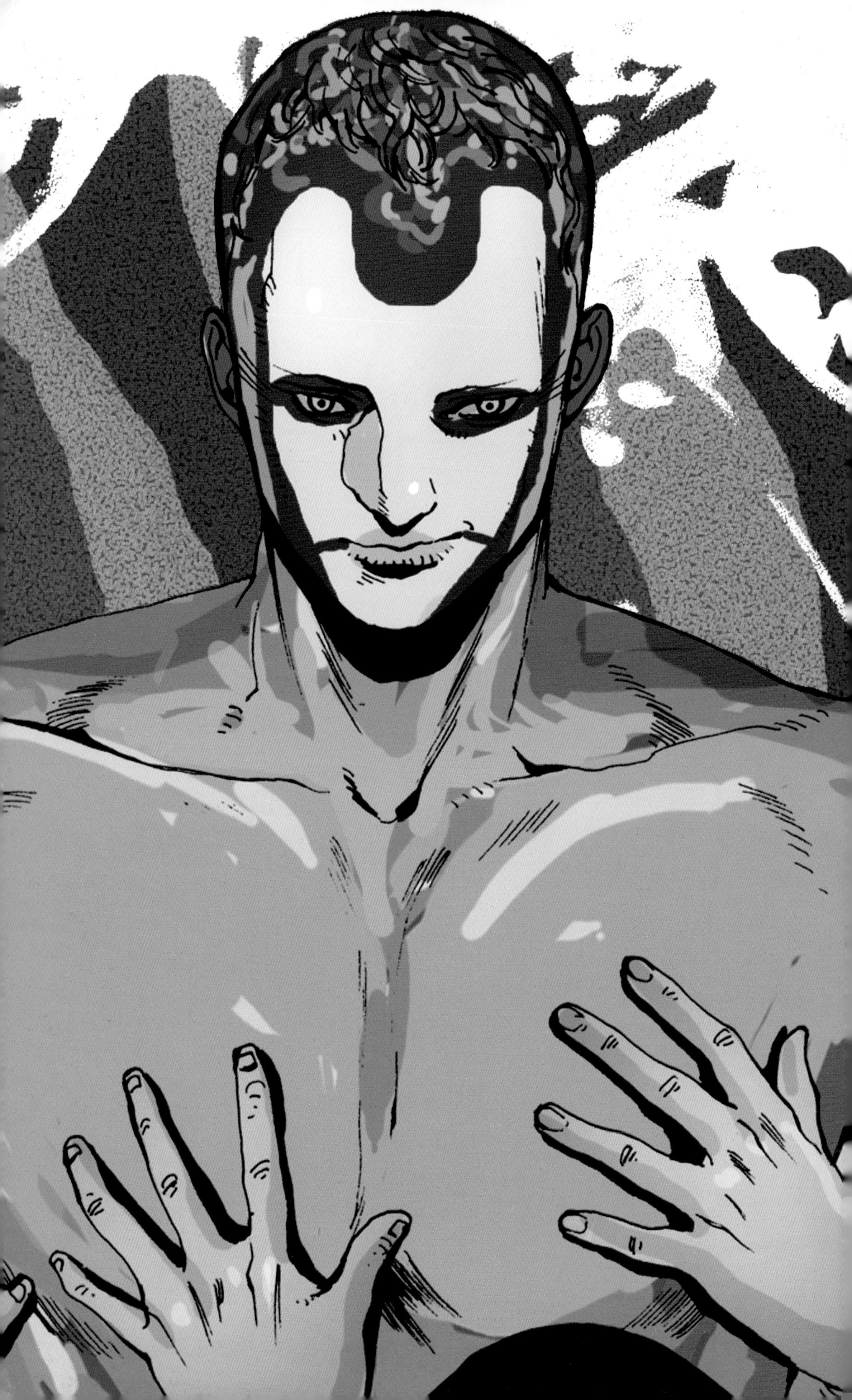

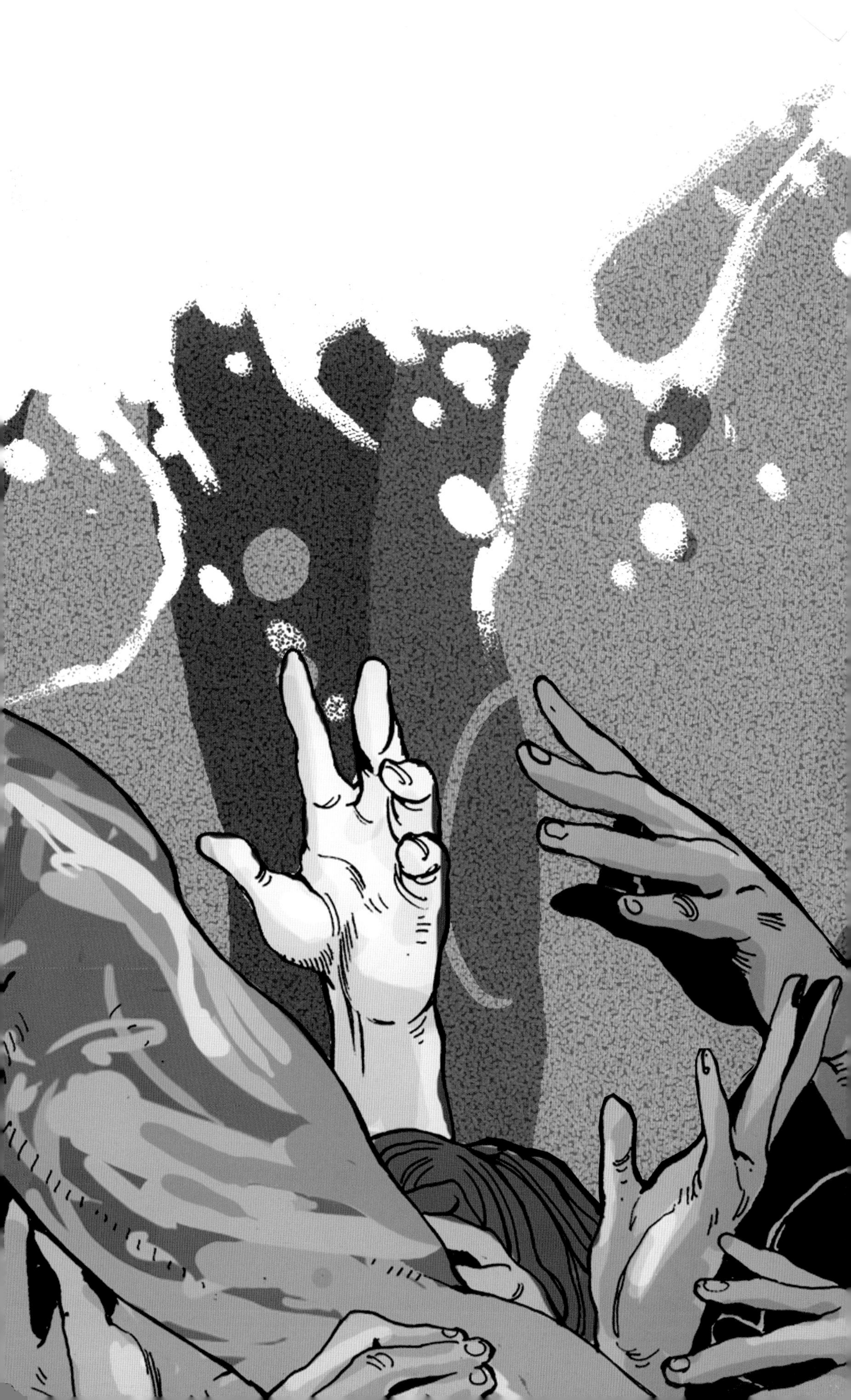

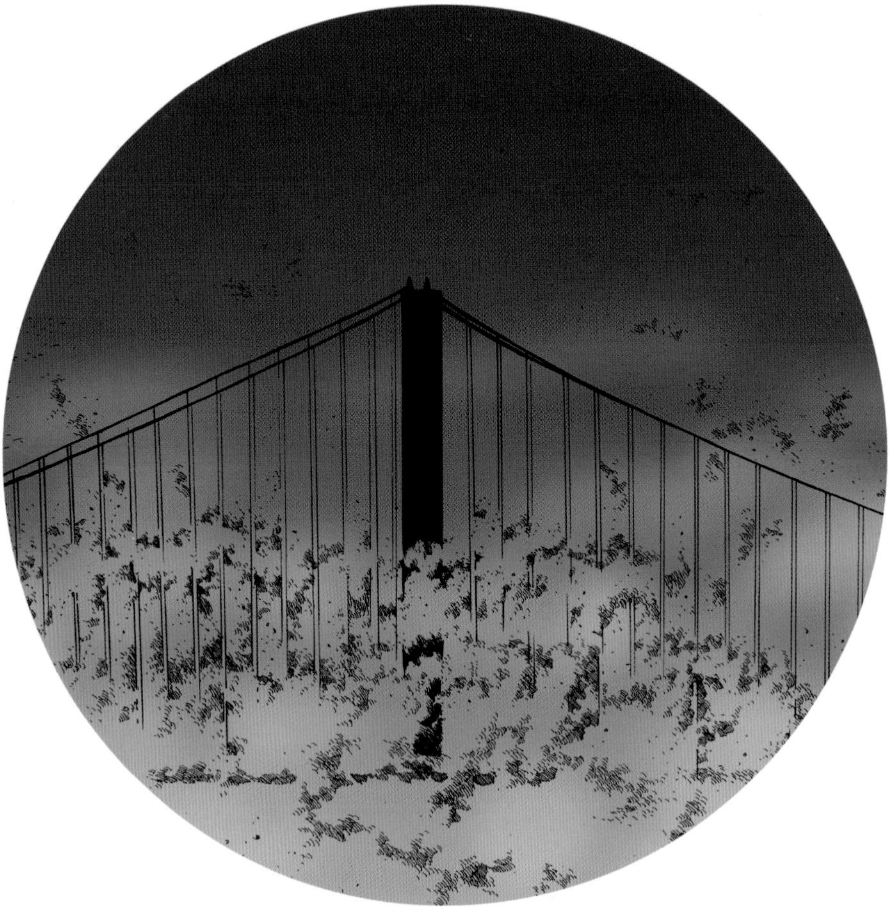

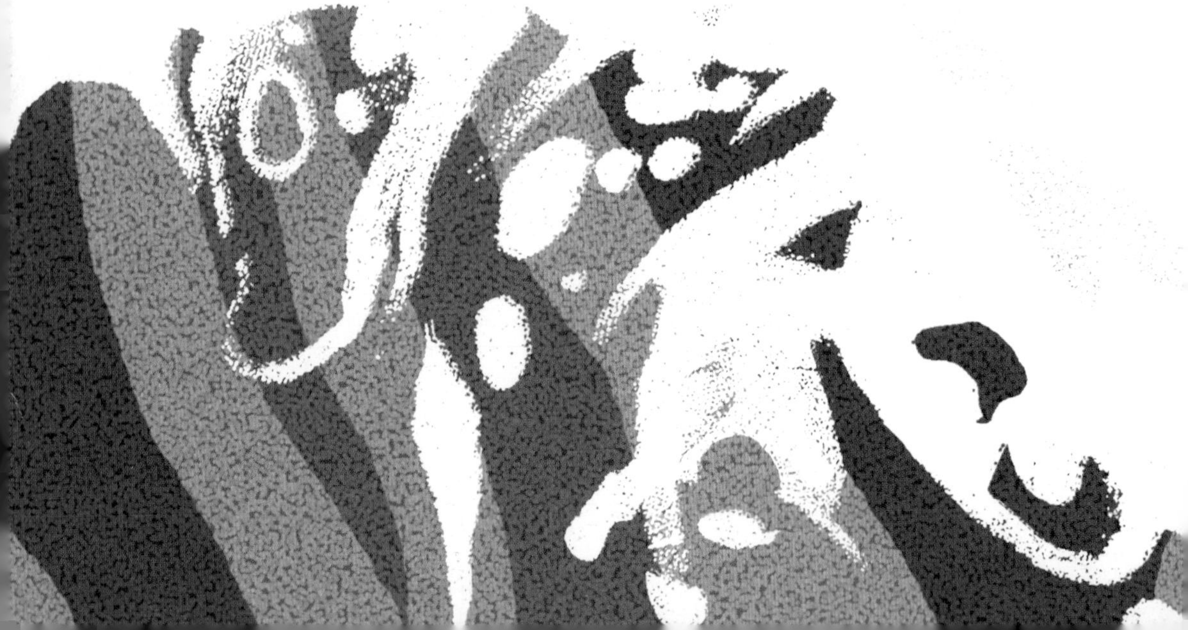

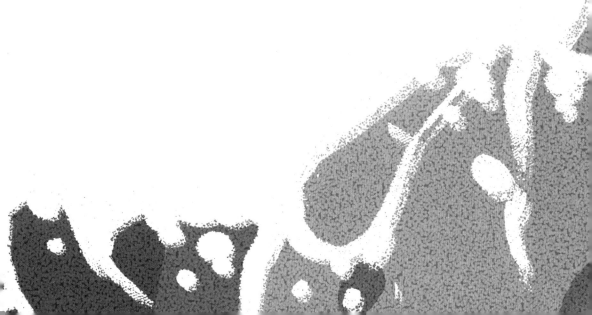

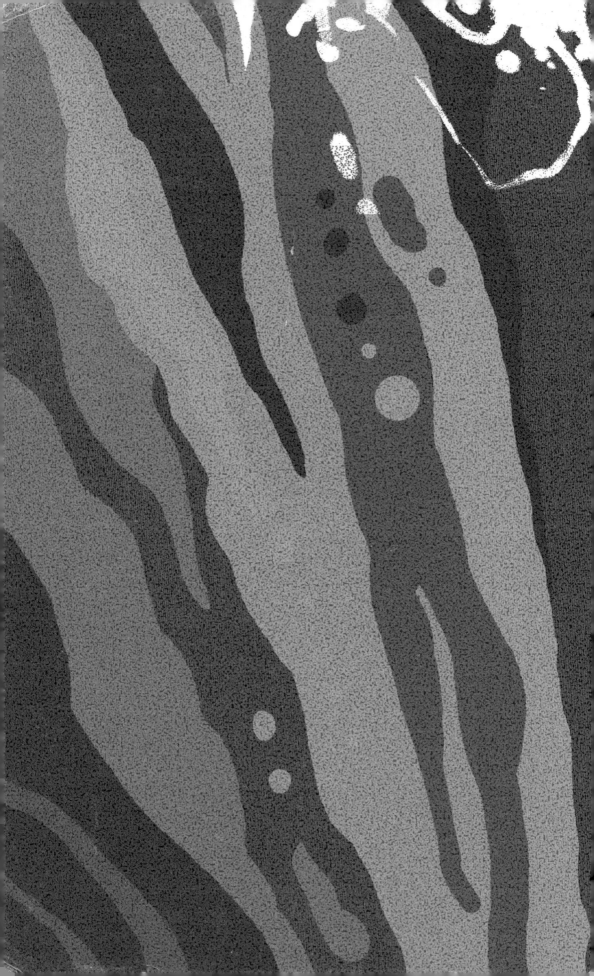